LIFE'S JOURNEY IN FAITH

Burma, From Riches to Rags

Saw Spencer Zan

authorHOUSE®

AuthorHouse™
1663 Liberty Drive, Suite 200
Bloomington, IN 47403
www.authorhouse.com
Phone: 1-800-839-8640

*This book is a work of non-fiction. Unless otherwise noted, the author
and the publisher make no explicit guarantees as to the accuracy of
the information contained in this book and in some cases, names of
people and places have been altered to protect their privacy.*

First published by AuthorHouse 9/25/2007

ISBN: 978-1-4343-1387-4 (sc)

*Printed in the United States of America
Bloomington, Indiana*

This book is printed on acid-free paper.

HARDLY ANYONE HAS HEARD OF the Karen people of Burma so allow me to introduce you to our Karen Family. We number about seven million and we are widely spread out in the southern plains of Burma and in the Karen State bordering on Thailand. I insist on the word 'family' because that is how we are, how we feel and behave. Our whole culture is family oriented. Every Karen child is given a name at birth and his or her name is personal and need have no connection with the names of its parents. In the case of a girl it will remain the same for life regardless of marriage which is an indication that men and women are equal.

On achieving adulthood they are addressed as Saw (Mr) and Naw (Mrs or Miss). However as one gets older one may be addressed as Uncle or Aunty, Grandmother, Grandfather, Teacher, Pastor, Doctor, Master etc. When the occasion arises and we are at a gathering of Karens, be it in one's home, village, town or even abroad, we immediately find ourselves surrounded by a family of grandparents, aunts, uncles, nieces and nephews, we feel immediately at home and happy to be there.

The Karen people are, by nature and culture peaceful, respectful and love to sing in groups or choirs. They are rarely aggressive and prefer to settle conflicts thorough arbitration by their elders for whom they have respect and whom they will obey. This characteristic is however very often mistaken for weakness, indolence and perhaps even a lack of intelligence. During centuries of the dominant rule of the Kings of Burma their docile appearance was often taken advantage of and they were abused as inferior and slaves.

Under the British colonial rule of law which started in the mid 19th century, the Karen people were able to develop and even flourished. The Christian missionaries brought them the Bible and helped them construct their own alphabet, start their own schools and university in Rangoon. They served the British crown in the civil services in the fields of law, medicine, education, local administration, forestry, police and military. True to character they remained loyal throughout their service both in peacetime and during the war against the Japanese invasion and occupation of Burma in 1941-45.

It was however anticipated by all the peoples of Burma, the Burmans, Shans, Karens, Kachins, Chins, Mons and Arakanese that they would eventually regain their independence each within their own autonomous states. The Karens having experienced massacres and atrocities from neighbouring Burmans during 1941 - 1945 and not wishing to return to the pre-colonial days of oppression, asked for the assurance from the British Government for the Karen State to be legally recognised. In recognition of their loyalty and assistance during the Burma Campaign 1941-45 the Karen request for their own State was promised to them.

The economic aftermath of World War II and the election of a Socialist government led by Mr Atlee in Great Britain hastened the dismantling of the British Empire with more concern for "How Soon" than "How To" carry it out. The promised granting and ratification of a Karen State was left undone. The loyal Karens were, handed over to the Burma Government without any protective assurances of their ethnic rights to justice. After independence the Karens had no alternative but to take up arms in self defence in January 1949. We were then labelled "rebels" and yes rightly we rebelled against injustice. The British Government sent arms to Burma to help put down the Karen insurrection. Our fight continues to this day for the survival of the Karen people against a deliberate, organized, cruel and calculated policy of oppression and ultimate elimination. Our beloved leader, Saw Ba U Gyi, killed in an ambush in 1950 had said "Surrender (of our identity) is out of the question."

As Saw Ba U Gyi's daughter by his first marriage to Renee Kemp, reading Spencer's life story has been particularly moving to me and has enabled me to get to know my extended family. Nita, Spence's sister, who married my father who was a barrister and leader fighting for justice for his people, gave him invaluable support and shared with him the hardships and anxieties until the end. She is lovingly known by all who knew herasMoNita.

"Life's Journey in Faith" is the story of a gentle Karen family. Like so many others they stand witness today of the tragedy of Burma. A land of abundance adorned with gaudy coloured costumes of diverse ethnic peoples contributing to its wealth, beauty and grace. Rich in soil and resources, protected by its mountains and forests, a jewel in the Indian Ocean. A paradise of plenty where no man needs to go hungry. Yet today; along the borders to the West with Bangladesh and India and to the East with Thailand there are strings of refugee camps sheltering hundreds of thousands of refugees driven from their homes either from ethnic cleansing or economic instability. They are not only homeless but also stateless without a future and unable to return home. Myanmar (the new name for Burma) has become an enormous social injustice against innocent men, women and children.

I would not like to leave the reader feeling the hopelessness of our Karen situation. The Karen was one of the first migraters to Burma. We have a long history of moving or being pushed on. History teaches us that there are always two sides to every situation. The good side and the bad side. We have learnt as a race that whilst the bad side is always having to give up what we had and move on, the good side has made us adaptable, getting our priorities right for the essentials of life and happiness and accepting that nothing is permanent. The 'family culture' which is our way of life keeps us united and we draw from it our strength and happiness. We believe that "to love life is to love God" and He is permanent.

Thelma Gyi Baerlein.

SPENCER ZAN'S MEMOIRS, " LIFE'S Journey in Faith" parallels the journey of Burma's evolution.; from an idyllic land of green fields and forests to a destitute state under military rule, where citizens are driven from their homes, some are hiding out in the jungles, and many others have become refugees in neighboring countries. In the time before this story, Burma was a land of plenty; no one ever went hungry. Now, Burma is among the poorest states in the world.

The Zans were and still are a distinguished Karen family. Ask any Karen if they know Spencer Zan, and the answer would most likely be in the affirmative. In pre-war Colonial Burma, the patriach, U Zan, was a high-level civil servant in the judicial system. All his children were active participants in the social, cultural and educational system of Burma. They were leaders in medical, educational and philanthropic organizations. They took it upon themselves to help those less fortunate – opening doors for children to higher levels of education, and helping them further their career opportunities. This way of life was also true of many leading families in Burma. This same sense of duty, of "giving back" existed among the Arakanese, Shan, Burman, Kachin, Chin, Mon and Karenni families that I personally knew.

All through the Second World War, the Zans were refugees like most families, going from place to place in search of safety. Sometimes they were together, and at other times, separated from each other due to circumstances. Yet, through all the personal tragedies and challenges, they maintained their faith and their values. They continued to reach out to those who were less fortunate than they were.

Following a brief period of calm, Burma became independent. General Aung San's vision for a multi-ethnic Burma, with equal rights for all the citizens, died with his assassination. Racism reared its head. Congenial neighbors became wary of each other. Suddenly, Karens became targeted as enemies. Karen leaders, including Spencer's father, U Zan, his brother-in-law, Dr. Marcus Paw, and many others, including my father, Saw Benson were jailed. In theory, they were under 'protective custody'. No charges were ever brought against them, but they languished in jail for many years, followed by more years of house arrest. Spencer himself was interned in a detention camp together with many Karen families for no other reason than being Karen.

What is most remarkable about Spencer's memoirs is that there is no trace of bitterness. Spencer and his beautiful wife Nu Nu still hold onto the same values that have sustained them. They have had to start over from the bottom, twice, since leaving their beloved Burma. As new arrivees in Thailand, they had nothing – just the clothes on their back. However, drawing on their faith, ability and tenacity, they were able to achieve some security, and were again in a position of helping others, including refugees from Burma. I too benefited from their help and guidance while they lived in Thailand. When they decided to immigrate to the United States, they had to start from scratch all over again. Yet today, decades later, they are still called upon to help those in need. Their faith, optimism and generosity are still very much part of who they are.

Spencer's memoirs are a very valuable record of the social and anthropological history of Burma. We see Burma as it was, through the unbiased eyes of someone who lived in a world that no longer exists. We get a glimpse of relationships between ethnic groups, within the Karen community, and within the family structure. Within the Zan family, although the father was head of the household he did not dictate. It was customary for him to consult with the whole family before making important decisions. The head of the household had the respect of his wife and children, but at the same time, he respected and asked for the opinion of his family members.

We are able to see through Spencer's eyes, without judgment, the upheaval and chaos that the country went through during the Second World War, including massacres of one group against another. At the close of the war, we follow the family back home to Rangoon, and see them settle back into their former lifestyle, only to be shaken apart again by the civil war a few years later.

Most of the young people who are now actively working towards regime change have never known any other Burma, other than one under military rule. They only know of a rule under which fear is the main motivator. They only know of a black market economy. "Life's Journey in Faith" lets us taste a world before this Orwellian existence that now prevails in Burma.

More than all else, what this amazing memoir has to offer, is a testament to the human spirit, and specifically, the spirit of Spencer Zan and his family. Their faith in their Creator, their faith in Goodness, and their Optimism carries them with dignity through their Journey of Life.

Louisa Benson Craig

We have gone forward, not traveling in a road cast up
and prepared, but walking through a miry place in which are
stones here and there, safe to step on, but so situated that one step
being taken time is necessary to see where to step next
(John Woolman)

...and we ask God to keep our feet; we do not ask to see the distant
scene. One step is enough for us.
(John Henry Newman)

We believe there is a wide country before us, though the horizon is
mist and shadow
(John Buchan)

ACKNOWLEDGEMENT

To Thelma Gyi Baerlein, Daughter of the late Saw Ba U Gyi, first President of Karen National Union, I am indebted for the fine Foreword she wrote for my book, giving the reader a brief account of who the Karens are, about their culture and their struggle for an autonomous state within the Union. I take great pride in being a part of her extended family. Also, many thanks to my dear friend Louisa Benson Craig, for the beautiful Preface. The Zan and Benson families have been friends since Louisa was only five or six years old, and the ties became even closer after my Dad became a business partner of Saw Benson. Our close ties continues to this day.

My gratitude to my good friend Reverend William Dunn for taking time to read my manuscript in spite of his heavy schedules, and for his encouragement and his opinion that I do not change anything in the manuscript but to leave as they are, my style of writing and my expression so familiar to many of my friends and acquaintances. I have to I agree with him because I believe that I am *talking* to you, the reader, sharing with you the story of my life through the pages of my memoir. I want you to *hear* my story, not *read* a boring treatise on my life. For that reason this manuscript is not edited.

Thank you, Edith Marante, author of *Burmese Looking Glass* and *Down the Red Hole*, and thank you, Benedict Rogers, author of *A Land Without Evil*, and thank you, Jennnifer Scheel Bushman, who co-authored with her mother Jean Artley Szymansky, the novel *Hard Sleeper*, for the strong and compelling 'blurps' you wrote for my book.

Also many thanks to my beautiful wife Nu Nu and my sons Lester and David who would go over the stories with me several times over the years, as we share our experiences in churches and Rotary Clubs as testimony of God's presence in our lives. Even our daughters in law, Irene and Ida joined Nu Nu to nag me into action to complete the book. To them I am forever grateful.

And last but not least, to all those who heard our story and asked me to put our experience in writing I say, 'Thank you', because without your encouragement this book would never have been published.

This book is dedicated
to
Our Grand Parents, U Aung Zan Myat
and Daw Hnin Zan
and my Parents
U Zan and Daw Thein Khin,
to
Nu Nu's Grand Parents
Rev U Ba Te and Daw Nu
And her Parents
Albert Ba Te and Daw Ngwe Hta
and
last but not least, to my dearest wife,
NU NU
who's constant urging to write the book
and complete it
has made possible the publication of
"Life's Journey in Faith"

LIFE IS A JOURNEY. IT is a journey with defining moments along the way, some which we plan and others come quite by surprise. This book is the story of my life, interwoven with events social and political, from my early days when life was all glory under British rule and through some three and a half years of World War II during which time Burma was under Japanese occupation. Then came the pride, the joy and jubilation of celebrating independence from over a century of British domination after the war was over. In spite of the political turmoil an insurgencies that plagued the country following independence, Burma was thriving economically and was largely regarded as one of the most advanced among the developing nations in Asia. The country was successfully experimenting it's first democracy under a national government. The Burmese people for the first time enjoyed as never before better lives with higher standard of living. Better life was for all, not just for the few privileged. International trade was expanding with many import and export firms owned or co-owned by nationals. The flourishing economy provided many job opportunities for it's citizens. Domestic trade was also booming with many local companies previously owned by foreigners now in the hands of nationals. Burma had a very high standard of literacy. It was, and still is, rich in natural resources. Burma was also known as the *Rice Bowl* of Asia, rice and teak being it's major export as were many other agricultural products and minerals that were still largely unexploited.

However, because of political in-fighting and inept handling of the government by Prime Minister U Nu, the army in 1962, under General Ne Win, deposed of the representative government, hauling to jail the President, the Prime Minister and his entire cabinet and unceremoniously trashed the constitution. Thus began a police state that practically took away freedom from the people. Dissidents were arrested and jailed without trial and soon the population began to live under a rule of terror.

Through it all many wonderful things happened in our lives as well as countless dreadful and alarming events. We experienced a life of joy, comfort and plenty as well as a life of need, anxiety, fear and danger. Through all these years we had seen the hand of the Lord leading us and protecting us, giving us wisdom, strength and direction, blessing us with His peace and comfort during our days of anguish and despair. This story covers a period in the history of Burma from my childhood days, through World War II, to the prosperous days after independence and later to the post independence years after which time Burma was tragically transformed from a country of plenty to one of the most impoverished nations in the world because of the gross mismanagement of the army and the widespread corruption that eroded the once thriving economy. Burma began it's downward spiral from *riches to rags* where it still remains today. The country is almost totally brain drained and the brains that still remained in the country dare not express their thoughts for fear of intimidation, harassment and even arrest. The ruling generals will not tolerate any criticism and are clinging on to power by imposing their ruthless and barbaric rules over the people.

The population of Burma consists of peoples from many ethnic backgrounds. All are Burmese, period. It is important therefore that no single race of this nation consider itself superior or inferior to another. No matter what ethnic race they are, they must be proud of their heritage, they must not have any complexes. They must not let politicians poison their minds. If politicians continue to instill prejudice in the minds of the populace to promote their own well being for personal and political gain, then there will never be peace in Burma even if the military is ousted and a civilian government under a democratic system is restored. I remember having read long ago a short article by Michael Aung Thwin in a newsletter, the *Burma Review,* that in Burmese politics no one wants to be Indian and that everyone wants to be Chief. I hope this is not true any more after what the country has been through. Politicians have to learn to accept any democratically elected leadership.

All peoples of Burma can live in harmony and co-exist in mutual respect. It is the politicians who drove a wedge of distrust and hatred between the majority race and the ethnic minorities. Politicians must create an atmosphere of harmony and understanding among the peoples. I hope that politicians, present and future, will have the sincerity, honesty and integrity to focus on what the nation really needs and deserves – peace, stability and progress. Those leaders in the field of science, engineering, education, health, business and religion should impart their knowledge and expertise to the younger generation who are the nation's future leaders, and nurture them to become responsible members of society and productive members the community. They must all be proud Burmese, proud of their country and their heritage. Each race must be allowed to retain it's own culture. The culture of all must be respected. Political, community and spiritual leaders must instill in the people a sense of responsibility and leadership so that they can contribute to the country's peace and stability. Only when people can coexist under peaceful condition will the country be able to progress.

It is the joint responsibility of all to restore the country to it's former status of a responsible member of the world community, a country of freedom and dignity, a country of honor and integrity. It is the nation's survival.

Spencer Zan

CONTENTS

FOREWORD.
Foreword by Thelrma Gyi Baerlein v

PREFACE
Preface by Naw Louisa Benson Craig.........................ix

ACKNOWLEDGEMENT xv

PROLOGUE... xix

CHAPTER 1
REFLECTION OF MY EARLY YEARS 1

CHAPTER 2
ON GROWING UP 15

CHAPTER 3
MOM AND DAD.. 27

CHAPTER 4
THE EVACUATION 33

CHAPTER 5
THE BOMBING OF MANDALAY................................. 45

CHAPTER 6
THE BATTLE FOR KATHA 53

CHAPTER 7
BACK HOME TO INSEIN 67

CHAPTER 8
EVACUATION AGAIN 83

CHAPTER 9
AIR RAIDS OVER RANGOON.................................... 95

CHAPTER 10
BACK HOME AGAIN 107

CHAPTER 11

SERVICE IN THE NAVY 117

CHAPTER 12
FROM NAVY TO PRISON 135

CHAPTER 13
RELEASED FROM DETENTION 155

CHAPTER 14
THE COUP 169

CHAPTER 15
ESCAPE TO FREEDOM 181

CHAPTER 16
SWISS FAMILY ROBINSON 195

CHAPTER 17
SHORT SOJOURN IN THE JUNGLE OF KWAI SOD 209

CHAPTER 18
BANGKOK BOUND 217

CHAPTER 19
HOUSE PARENTS AT BANGKOK STUDENT HOSTEL ..233

CHAPTER 20
OUR FINAL JOURNEY TO FREEDOM 253

EPILOGUE **269**

CHAPTER 1

REFLECTION OF MY EARLY YEARS

I REMEMBER RUNNING AROUND HUGE dark gray boulders on the hillside looking for my nanny who was carrying my baby sister Caroline and playing hide and seek with me. I must have been about three and a half or four years old at that time. I was born in 1923 in Pa-an, in the Karen State of Burma, in a white house on top of a hill. I can still remember that white stucco house with a full verandah in front. I cannot remember much of the rest of the house, but the verandah overlooking the Salween River beyond a football field remains vividly in my memory.

From this verandah Mom would welcome her five older children who were returning home each year from their boarding schools in Moulmein for the summer holidays. They returned in a double decked Irrawaddy Flotilla passenger steamer in first class cabins on the upper deck. The boat would be in full view from the house for a good half hour before it disappeared behind tall trees and a Buddhist monastery. While the boat was still in view Mom would let me stand on a chair so that I could see over the verandah. She had a white bed sheet hung over the verandah and waved the sheet while her brood responded from the steamer by waving their hanker chiefs. Sometimes Mom would use a mirror to reflect the sunlight at her kids and they would wave back. The oldest three of our siblings were Nita the eldest, Louise, and Audrey who were attending the American Baptist English Girl's High School in Moulmein and then Saunders and Dempsey who were attending St. Patrick Boy's High School, also in Moulmein. I'm sure they must all remember this house on the hill very well. My sister Louise wrote the following poem about the house on top of the hill.

1

THE HOUSE ON TOP OF THE HILL
Ah! I remember and remember so well
That knob-crested hill at the river's bend.
How it reared it's head as if to tell
That soon we'll be home with family and friends.
Chugging up the old Salween River,
The Flotilla boat bore a noisy load of youngsters,
Homeward bound when school year was over,
Filled with freedom, pure delight and laughter.
At the first glimpse of that blue knobbed hill
Hilarity broke forth mighty loud and shrill.
For there on the balcony mother with a large white sheet
Flying in the wind her young brood to greet.
Just a few minutes more and we'll all be there
With happy chatter and laughter filling the air.
Such was our childhood memory, thank God for the gift
When new pleasures remain our spirits to lift.
Oft in the silence and loneliness of latter years
Our mind relive with nostalgic tears,
Those family fun and laughter that linger still
Around that house on top of the hill.

Many years later while I was traveling by air to Moulmein, the plane stopped at Pa-an to pick up passengers and mail. When the plane took off again I could see that little white house on top of the hill. It brought a lump to my throat as I watched the house slowly disappearing behind the wing of the plane.

Burma was under British rule those days and Dad was a civil officer in the British administration. He was Sub Divisional Officer (S.D.O.) which was the title of a magistrate. I remember vividly when Dad was trying a criminal case on the lawn in front of the house instead of at the courthouse. Perhaps he was not feeling well that day and decided to have a court hearing at the house. There were lots of people, witnesses and relatives sitting and squatting on the lawn in front of the house. Dad was sitting at a table on which sat his type writer and a pile of papers. A peon standing behind his chair was fanning him with a huge palm leaf fan. Sometimes I would grab the fan from the peon and fan Dad myself. There were some policemen dressed in khaki uniform with long swords slung at their waists. Two or three prisoners with handcuffs squatted on the ground at their feet. Suddenly there was a commotion when several people jumped up and ran helter-skelter. We didn't know what was going on but a few seconds later I saw a policeman quickly draw his sword and strike at something on the ground. Then he raised his sword to show Dad the snake he had just killed.

Government officers were transferred from town to town every couple of years or so. Dad was now transferred to a town named Kyaikto. He was given a house with a tennis court. Dad had his friends over for tennis each afternoon. I remember being a ball boy picking up tennis balls at the games. At the end of the games there were cold sodas for everyone. Being a ball boy I was rewarded with a bottle of lemonade at the end of the games. Dad later was transferred back to Pa-an. This time he was given a government quarter, a huge rambling teak bungalow next to a Buddhist monastery. I made friends with all the young Buddhist novices and *phongyi kyaungthas*, (pupils attending monastery school). Dad allowed them to come and play football with me in our large front yard. Now I was attending the government elementary school in first standard. There were no public transportation those days and I had to walk the half mile or so to school each day. A servant would walk me to school, sometimes carrying me piggy back especially when there were puddles on the road after a rain. I remember playing with a little fawn we had as a pet on the front lawn. We also had a pair of peacocks which would chase me and the fawn around the compound in mock attack. Later the male peacock would spread it's tail like a huge fan to display it's magnificent and colorful feathers and dance before it's mate for several minutes and then both would fly back to the coop Dad had made for them under the staircase.

Dad was an ardent football fan and as the undisputed civil boss of Pa-an, he would enthusiastically root for Pa-an football team. One day the Pa-an team was to play against another team of a town across the river named Pa-ka. If separated, the two syllables 'Pa' (pronounced 'hpa') means frog and 'ka' means dance. Dad had Mom make a stuffed frog. He then tied the stuffed frog to a string like a leash. He took the frog to the football field with me following him. Dad had already arranged for a small musical troupe to be at the field where there were special seats for Dad and junior officials.

Before the match started Dad took the frog to the edge of the field and pulled on the string to make it jump up and dance. The musical troupe complete with gong, cymbal, clapper, *hne* (Burmese clarinet) and flute came up behind Dad and played a jingle made up for that occasion. He had a little stick which he used to strike the frog to make it dance, yelling, "Pa-ka, Pa-ka," meaning, "Dance, frog, dance". There were loud cheers from the Pa-an fans. The other team came only with a musical troupe. However, before half time was over someone on their team managed in the short time to fashion a stuffed frog that could spew water out of it's mouth. At half time, the Pa-ka's cheer leader brought his frog out to the field followed by his musical troupe and called out "Pa- an, Pa-an" as he stepped on the frog. Taken separately, Pa means 'frog' and 'an' means vomit. When he stepped on the frog, the frog spewed water out of it's mouth. As the crowd roared Dad got up from his chair, dragged his frog onto the field and started hitting it with his little stick as he yelled, "Pa-ka, Pa-ka". It was a lot of fun. The frog made by the Pa-ka team however didn't last long. To Dad's delight it came apart after just one jingle and brought loud cheers from the Pa-an fans. I never knew who won the game. It didn't matter. I was just having great fun jumping up and down, yelling and clapping my hands alongside Dad.

I remember the time I sent Dad on a wild goose chase with a posse of policemen. One day as I was playing with my *phongyi kyaungtha* friends in the field behind our house a man walked towards us and talked to the other kids. I watched the man as he was talking but did not pay attention to what he was saying. He had a dirty towel wrapped around his head. It looked like he had a scar on his forehead but it was partially covered by the towel. I thought he stuttered a bit as he asked some questions, apparently seeking directions. I saw some of the boys pointing towards the town in answer to his question. To me he looked like a beggar. After the man left we played for a couple hours more before I went home. When I got home I saw Dad in conference in the dining room with a group of men. Some wore police uniform and others were in regular civilian outfit. There were about eight people in all. I passed close to them to get a drink of water when I heard one man say, "If he has a scar on his forehead we can easily find him."
"He went towards town," I told them.
"Who are you talking about?" Dad asked me.
"The man with the scar on his forehead:," I answered.
"That's him," cried a police officer.
"Wait," Dad said, "tell us about this man."
"We were playing in the field behind the house. This man came and talked to us."

"What did he say?" someone asked.

"I don't know," I replied "I didn't listen."

"Can you show us which way he went?" Dad asked me.

I ran out of the house and they all followed me. I pointed toward town and said, "He went that way,"

"How long ago?" Dad asked.

"I don't know," I replied.

"One hour? Two hours? Ten minutes? How long?"

I didn't know and I simply shrugged my shoulders and said, "I don't know."

"Did you see the scar on his head?" Dad asked me.

"Yes, right here," I answered as I placed my hand on my forehead.

"He also stammered a bit," I added.

"That had to be him," a police officer said.

Dad ordered the police officer to send a squad of policemen to scout around the town to see if they could find the man and to get another squad to prepare to travel with him to go in search of the man with the scar on his forehead. Dad asked Mom to prepare his travel bag for a long trip. I didn't know why there was such an interest in this man with the scar on his forehead. After all he was just a beggar. But the British administration was hunting for a man named Saya San, a radical nationalist who started a rebellion against the British government with a small band of about a thousand rebels. He was last seen heading toward Pa-an or neighboring countryside. Dad received directive from the government to look out for him. Dad went in pursuit of the man he thought was Saya San who was reported to have a scar on his forehead and also stuttered. Dad returned several days later empty handed. He caught up with the man not far from the border with Siam (Thailand, today) but the man turned out to be not Saya San.

As a magistrate under the British system Dad had to pass sentencing on criminals convicted for crimes ranging from petty theft to murder. Often times many felons convicted for petty crimes prefer not to go to jail and the alternative sentencing during those days was flogging. Floggings were from three strokes to thirty strokes with a cane, depending on the severity of the crime and of course the physical condition of the felon. A civil doctor had to examine the felon and recommend the maximum strokes the person could physically endure. The flogging stand resembled a large easel. The felon had to step onto the frame spread eagle and his ankles and wrists were locked securely in special slots made for the purpose. His back was then bared as the peon - specially trained to administer the strokes – took position. The peon's name was Soe Maung. Our house was not far from the court house. Whenever a flogging was to take place, which was carried out in the open yard behind the court house, Soe Maung would come running to the house to take me to the court house and have me watch the flogging from the window of the store room. I would watch and cringe as the men screamed and yelled with every stroke. After every flogging a doctor would examine the felon and apply some kind of yellow solution to the buttocks. Some of them bled while others did not. While some yelled and screamed there were a few who didn't even make a sound. There were times when the doctor would stop the flogging before it was over when he thought the felon couldn't endure another stroke. After a while Dad found out that I was watching the floggings from the store room and disciplined Soe Maung for making me watch the flogging.

About two years later Dad was transferred to Thaton, a town much larger than Pa-an, with a British Deputy Commissioner as Chief administrator. There were no government quarters in Thaton. Dad had to rent a house, a beautiful two storied teak house with the ground floor used as servant quarters for the chauffeur and cook, and for storage and garage. There was a room for the maid upstairs next to the kitchen. On arrival at Thaton Dad bought a car, a British Overland Whippet, because the courthouse was too far to walk to. We had three dogs. Jenny was a large good natured hound but she was already quite old. Nero was half bull dog and half pariah and was very aggressive and had to be watched all the time. I don't remember how we acquired these two dogs. And then there was a beautiful hound Dad received from one of the town elders. It probably was a greyhound. Dad named the dog Crane because of the beautiful shiny gray color of the dog's coat. The house had a high fence around it with a well on one side of the compound. I joined the Government school in third standard and became friendly with a boy across the street from us by the name of Chit Thein who was also in the third standard in the same school but was in another class. We also had for the first time an American neighbor at the end of the street, a Seventh Day Adventist missionary family by the name of Wyman. The Wymans had four children, one of them was Frank, who was perhaps a year older than I was. Dad encouraged me to play with Frank although Frank was a little rough with me at times. But Dad wanted me to improve my English which he encouraged me to speak at home. All my older sisters and brothers were sent to English boarding Schools run by the

American Baptist and Catholic missions in Moulmein and they all spoke English as their first language and I had trouble keeping up with them because I was only attending an Anglo-vernacular school where the standard of English was not high.

Dad asked me one day to go to the Wymans to let them know that Mom and he would like to drop by for a visit. He told me that foreigners like to know ahead of time if someone was visiting to give them a chance to spruce up for the visit. It was not polite to drop by without notice, he told me. So off I went to the Wymans and knocked on their door. Mrs. Wyman opened the door.

"Hello, Spencer, how are you?" she asked.

"I'm fine, thank you," I answered in my limited English. "Mummy and Daddy will visit you. Daddy said get ready," I told her and ran back home. Later I went along with Mom and Dad as they walked over to the Wymans. A well dressed Mr. Wyman opened the door and as we were being seated by Mr. Wyman out marched Mrs. Wyman, followed by their four children in single file all dressed up as if they were going to church. Dad thought it was strange.

"Mr. Wyman, are you all going somewhere?" Dad asked.

"No, we are just waiting for your visit," Mr. Wyman replied. Dad looked at me.

"What did you tell them?" he asked me.

"I said, 'Mummy and Daddy will visit. Daddy said 'get ready,' that's all," I replied.

One afternoon, on a school holiday, I decided to walk to the court house so that I could take a ride home with Dad in his car. I took my neighbor Chit Thein along with me. Before we got to the court house we passed by a fair in a large field. We could not resist the music, the Ferris wheel and the rides. Both of us had a few change in our pockets so we decided we would have some fun before we continued our walk to the court house. We were really enjoying ourselves when we realized that it was already beginning to get dark. When we got to the court house we found it closed so we had to walk back home. By the time we got home it was almost dark. As I walked through the gate to the house I noticed several policemen looking into the well, flash lights in their hands and others walking around the yard with lanterns looking under bushes and trees. Mom caught sight of me and yelled, "He's back. He's back." And then she called out to me, "Come right back into the house, young man." As soon as I got to the top of the stairs she was all over me with a length of cane. I never had such a beating before nor after. I didn't cry. Of course I was also hiding a comic book which I bought at the fair inside my pants behind my back. Most of the blows fell on the comic book but Mom, in her rage coupled with relief that I was all right never noticed it. I never realized how worried they were until Dad told me that he had the police set up road blocks at all roads leading out of town because they thought I had been kidnapped.

Just a few weeks earlier, Dad had convicted a rather prominent businessman for bribery and corruption and sent him to a long prison term. I remembered that man visiting Dad at the house sometime back. I was playing downstairs when I heard Dad yelling at the man, asking him to leave the house at once. "Get out of here, you son of a bitch," he yelled at the man. The man ran down the stairs and walked over straight to me and gave me a bundle which I took. Lucky that Dad saw me take that bundle. He came running down the stairs, snatched the bundle from me and shoved it back into the man's shoulder bag, pushed the man hard and ordered him to 'get the hell out'. Then Dad scolded me for taking the bundle. He told me never to take anything from any one visiting the house or anywhere else. Dad told me that the bundle contained several thousands rupees. Mom and Dad thought that the man had me kidnapped to repay Dad for the stiff sentence Dad had passed.

It was while Dad was stationed at Thaton that the family would go along with him on his official tours during the summer holidays when we were able to enjoy some of the most exiting places in the region. I remember visiting famous caves like Bayingyi Gu and Hsat-tan Gu. I enjoyed most the two hot springs near those caves. There was a little shed on a landing at each hot spring, where we could change our clothes, with a makeshift bridge leading to the hot pools. The water was hot and smelled of rotten egg. To get into the pool we had to dip our feet first into the hot water and gradually lower ourselves until we were immersed up to the chest. There was a shallow side and a deeper side at each pool. I can remember that horse playing in the hot water got you very tired in a short while. However we didn't care. We splashed water at each other until Mom asked us to stay still and enjoy the hot spring.

There was another place that I remember very well. The place was called Ba-bwe Gon. There was a waterfall that did not drop vertically but flowed rather swiftly over forty feet of solid rock that sloped down at an angle of about thirty five degrees, and which was thinly covered with moss and was very slippery. Villagers would let us ride on their backs as they slid down the fall from the top into a pool below that was four or five feet deep. The water was clear and you could see the bottom. After they splashed into the pool at the bottom they would pick us up and take us up again to the top for another slide down the fall. It was here that my little sister Caroline, still too young and timid, enjoyed watching us slide down. She was standing at the top of the fall and all of a sudden slid down the fall all by herself standing up, then fell to a sitting position without hurting herself. She plunged into the pool below and was promptly picked up by Saunders. Mom cried out hysterically while Dad laughed and said Caroline was braver than us all because she could come down the fall all by herself.

Karen people are believed to make good and loyal friends and they can be depended on usually for their truthfulness. Of course there are always bad people in any community. Dad had a real honest murderer on his hand who was a Karen. This man's barn was burnt down by a Burman friend and neighbor after they had had a heated argument. The Karen was irate. He went home for his machete and went after his Burman neighbor and hacked him to death. Dad realized that the man reacted violently only because he was provoked. Dad felt sorry for him and did not want to give him a death sentence, and thought he could give him a life sentence instead. So at the trial he asked the man a leading question.
"You went to your neighbor's house with a machete to threaten him but had no intention to kill him. Was that right?"
"O, no, sir, I went to his house to kill him." Dad gave him the death sentence.

At another time a Buddhist man who committed murder was sentenced to be hanged. Dad always sent a pastor of his church to visit a condemned man in prison to try to talk to the prisoner about Jesus and try to convert the man. After several visits the man accepted Jesus and was baptized. On the day of execution, Dad went to the prison to witness the hanging. When a man was hanged the magistrate and a doctor had to be present. The converted man climbed up the scaffolding and when he got to the top he looked over the prison wall and saw a pagoda high up on a hill in the distance. The man immediately got down on his knees and worshipped the pagoda. Obviously the man was playing it safe with his dual faith.

I remember one day Jenny the old hound went into Mom and Dad's bed room and nudged Mom persistently with her snout. Mom didn't know what Jenny wanted. Finally Jenny left the bed room, and then turned round to look back at Mom as if waiting for Mom to follow her, which Mom did. The dog then went slowly down the steps and lay down at the bottom, turned to look up and gave Mom one sad look and died at Mom's feet. A few days later Nero the mutt got into a fight with a bull dog from Chit Thein's house across the street. Dad and Chit Thein's father tried to separate the two dogs without success. Both dogs somehow got a hold of each other's shoulder and fought violently. They were pushing, pulling and rolling in the dirt, snorting and growling angrily as Dad poured water over them to try to separate them. But neither dog would let go. The other owner beat both dogs with a thick stick to no avail. Both dogs were now bleeding from their shoulders. Yet they kept pulling and shaking as they rolled in the dirt. It must have gone on for at least ten minutes and by then both dogs were exhausted and stopped growling. Instead they were now only panting and snorting but they did not let go of their hold. After about another ten minutes both dogs let go momentarily giving a chance for Dad and the other owner to separate them. That was some dog fight I'll never forget.

Dad's next transfer was to Moulmein as Head Quarters Assistant (H.Q.A.) and Treasury Officer which was a promotion. There were no government quarters so he rented a large five bed room, two and a half story rambling house at 62 Dalhousie Street. My older siblings now could go to school from the house instead of staying in boarding schools. Nita and Louise had graduated from high school and were attending Judson College in Rangoon. Audrey was in her junior year in American Baptist English Girls' High School. Saunders was in eighth standard and Dempsey in sixth standard in St. Patrick Boys High School. I was in the fourth standard in Judson Boys High School. Caroline the youngest never went to any school regularly. But the American Baptist English Girl's School accepted her in second standard for private tuition. To take us to our different schools and for him to go to office Dad bought a new car, a Pontiac Straight Eight which had a super long bonnet. The chauffeur would drop us off at our different schools and return home to pick Dad up and drive him to his office. But Dad was in Moulmein only a little over a year when he was transferred to Akyab in the Arakan Division. Dad left the cook, the chauffeur and a maid to take care of our needs and gave Audrey the charge of the house. Mom and the other maid went along with Dad to Akyab.

Audrey ran the house well but she had problems with Saunders and Dempsey who couldn't get along and often got into fist fights. Of course Saunders being the older always got the better of Dempsey. Whenever Audrey was not around, the chauffeur or the cook, or sometimes even the maid, had to separate the two. I felt sorry for Dempsey because he was the loser always in a fight with his older brother. But he would never back down from Saunders. He told me, "I'm not afraid of him. One day I'll beat him."

One day I tried to knock off a small hive being built by flying ants on the wall outside the kitchen. I didn't have my shirt on as I poked at the hive with a bamboo pole. Suddenly the ants flew out of the hive and attacked me. I yelled and screamed as I ran into the back of the house and into the kitchen. The servants had to use dish cloths to kill the ants that were still on my back and neck. I received more than a dozen stings and developed a high fever and was in acute pain. Audrey had to take me to the hospital.

The following year Dad was transferred to Insein and instead of renting a house he stayed at Grandpa's house, on a hill Grandpa named Zion Hill. I attended the sixth standard at the Government School in Insein while Saunders and Dempsey attended the English Baptist High School in Rangoon some seven miles away, boarding at a friend's house. Audrey had graduated from high school and was now attending Judson College in Rangoon. The next year Dad was again transferred, this time to Mawlaik in Upper Chindwin. Caroline and I went along with Mom and Dad. I attended the seventh standard at the Government Middle School there. This was the school year that I especially enjoyed. I came from a school in the Rangoon area where there were better teachers with better teaching facilities and so I was usually ahead in my class. Soon after we settled down in Mawlaik Dad bought me a .22 caliber Winchester so that I could go hunting on my own. On weekends I used to bring home wild fowl, doves, squirrels or green pigeons. Once I shot an imperial pigeon, a huge bird, perched on top of tree at least a hundred feet tall. I became quite proficient with gun handling and was becoming a pretty good shot. Occasionally Dad would take me duck shooting or deer hunting with him. One day I brought down a duck in flight, my first experience with a shot gun. The recoil sent me reeling. As I picked myself up, the chauffeur who always came along on our hunting trips, shook his head and laughed at me as he went to retrieve the duck I brought down. I asked him later why he laughed at me when I brought the duck down.

"You never hit the duck," he told me, "The duck flew into your shots."

Mawlaik was also a military station with Sikh soldiers and British officers. We loved watching British officers and the Sikh soldiers play polo each weekend. I enjoyed watching the games, and often dreamed of playing the game myself one day. Dad had just bought me a bicycle and I thought I could get my classmates together and start a bicycle polo game. I managed to persuade my friends to get small tree branches that we would cut to make polo sticks out of. We finally got together three teams to play bicycle polo on our school football field using tennis balls. It became quite expensive when we had to change the spokes on the bikes every so often. But our games became quite popular and now we had a decent crowd to watch us play the game each evening after school. I called our team the "Whippets". Though I invented the game my team never won.

Once, while we were playing bicycle polo, all the kids jumped off their bikes and hit the ground and shouted at me to get down. I didn't know what was going on, but I hit the ground anyway. The next thing I knew there was a loud high pitched drone approaching the field then swiftly passed over us and faded beyond the opposite end of the field. When we all got up I asked what that was.
"Bees," answered one of the boys. "This happens every year about this time when the bees migrate from the hills to the south."

I was always easy going and good natured and didn't get angry easily nor did I get into arguments with others or get into fights. But I remember my first fight ever against an older and taller kid which lasted just a minute or less. This kid was a bully and all the kids were afraid of him. They would always stay out of his way. In class the bully sat right behind me. He had long legs and would kick me from the back when the teacher was at the blackboard and not looking. I would turn round and tell him to stop kicking me. The teacher caught me turning around and talking to that kid and warned me to stop talking. I was scared of this kid because I saw what he did to other kids so I didn't tell the teacher that he was kicking me from behind. The kid kept kicking me when the teacher was not looking. This went on for a while. The teacher finally asked me to stop talking with the kid behind me or he would send me to the head master. I didn't want to go to the head master to be punished so I told the teacher what really was happening. The kid denied my accusation but the teacher told both of us to behave or we would both be sent to the head master. During break between classes the bully came to me and said he'd fight me after school because I tried to get him into trouble. He was going to teach me a lesson for ratting on him. I was scared and could feel myself shaking. I didn't want to fight. I didn't know how to fight. Another kid who sat next to me in the front row came to me and told me not to be scared. He took me aside and told me that I could never beat this kid.

Then he said, "There is one way you can stop him from bullying you. Look, he's got long arms and long legs. You can never get close enough to hit him. Listen to me carefully. When he comes at you – and he always does that - just duck and close in with your hand straight out hitting him in the pit of the stomach right below the ribs." He showed me where that was. It was the solar plexus.
"But," he added, "do it with all your might. If you don't, he'll beat you up real bad. I'll help you if he did but you must first hit him in the stomach, *h a r d*," he emphasized. I could still feel myself shaking but I kept running in my mind how I would execute the tactic my friend had just advised I used until I was sure I had it pat in my mind. School was over and my friend escorted me to the back of the school building. I was surprised to see a whole bunch of kids there to see me beat up. My friend kept telling me, "Don't forget what I told you if you want him to stop bullying you."

I was still shaking when the bully came out of the school building and walked right over and got in front of the crowd. Then he called out to me, "Come on, Spencer. Do you want to fight or do you want to go home like a little dog with your tail between your legs?"
I braced myself and walked toward him. I could hear all the kids clapping and cheering my adversary. They were all waiting to see me beat up by the bully. Just then the bully came at me like a charging bull. I ducked as I threw my right hand straight out with all my might and lunged forward at the same time and landed my tight fist right in the pit of his stomach. But I lost my balance with that impact. I pulled myself up and turned round to see him on his knees clutching his stomach. At that point my fear was gone. I wanted to help him up because he was obviously hurting. But my friend came by my side and told the bully, "You leave my friend alone from now on or next time you will be fighting me instead." There was absolute silence as the bully got up and without saying a word walked away. No one cheered me. I guess they were still afraid of the bully. It was also here that I had my first experience in horse riding. My friend who rescued me from the bully had a couple of horses. We became good friends. Sometimes when I went hunting in the woods I would ask my

friend to come along with me. We both rode on horse back and I would let him use my Winchester because now Dad let me use his shot gun.

I passed my seventh standard that year and I couldn't go any higher in that school since it was not a high school. Now it was time for me to leave my parents for the first time and be away in a boarding school like my other siblings. I'd been so used to being with my parents all these years that it was hard to believe I'd be leaving them for several months at a time. Sometimes I cried in bed before I went to sleep. I was hoping Dad would be transferred to a place where there was a high school I could go to. Summer vacation brought my brothers and sisters back home. I remember the picnics we had in the woods out of town while Dad and Saunders would go deer hunting. Dempsey and I would go into the woods and go hunting dove, fowls and pigeons. Sometimes we'd go and watch polo games at the garrison on weekends. Occasionally our family would get invited by the garrison commander to dinner. Our summer vacations were always very enjoyable. Mom and Dad were great at giving us the best of times during the school holidays. They planned well ahead to take us to the most interesting and enjoyable places. But soon it was time to return to school.

It was different for me. I was not returning to school. I was going to a school, some seven hundred miles away from Mom and Dad to become a boarding student. Dad chose for me the Teacher's Training College High School in Rangoon. It was a teaching college where post graduate students went to get their Bachelor of Education degree. It was a school of excellent reputation and of very high standard. It was bad enough leaving Mom and Dad for several months till the next holidays, but I had to go and join this new school all by myself. Dad told me I had to learn to do things for myself. My siblings were all able to go about on their own and I should learn to do the same.

CHAPTER 2

ON GROWING UP

IT WAS ALL I COULD do to keep from crying as the steamer cast off and I waved Mom, Dad and Caroline good bye. Dempsey was going back to school at the same time with me. He was used to parting with Mom and Dad and was able to start reading right away the books and magazines he brought with him. I tried to read but I could not see the words. My eyes were filled with tears and everything I looked at was blurred. I felt a little better when we boarded the train at Mandalay on our final leg to Rangoon. By the time we got to Rangoon the next morning I was prepared for the new life ahead with no one telling me what to do. That fight I had with the bully in Mawlaik also gave me some self confidence. Dempsey asked me if I wanted him to accompany me to my boarding school. Dempsey and I always got along very well and we were very close. He was surprised when I turned him down. We took different taxis. He went back to English Baptist High School and I asked the taxi to take me to Teachers Training College.

When I arrived at the hostel at T.T.C. a couple of kids came out to greet me and helped me with my luggage and took me to the dorm. The dorms were for students in eighth and ninth standards. They were on two floors, each floor accommodating twenty students. There were two rows of ten beds with toilets and bathrooms at either end on each floor. I went to the warden's office and reported my arrival. The warden, U Kun, walked me through the dorm on the ground floor. He asked me if I had any preference. I told him that I'd like to stay on the ground floor if I could and would like to take a bed right in the middle. He told me that it was a wise choice because it was away from the bathrooms so it wouldn't be too noisy. He allotted me bed number six. I found out later that almost everyone liked to sing at the top of his voice once he got into the shower. I soon became one of those bathroom baritones myself.

Later I had to go and report to the principal. The principal, U Ba, shook my hand and asked me to sit down. I gave him a few papers I brought with me. U Ba said that he was happy that I chose to attend the T.T.C. and said I wouldn't regret it. He also told me that he expected me to be a model student and he was confident that I would not let the school down. I returned to the dorm and unpacked, putting my things into the locker and on my desk. Then after a shower I dressed up and put my jacket on and waited for the dinner bell to ring. In this school we were required to have our jackets on for dinner. A short while later the dinner bell rang and everyone lined up at the corridor waiting for the warden, the assistant warden and the two lady wardens to arrive. The lady wardens were in charge of a dorm in another wing housing twenty middle school students We entered the dining room after the wardens but did not sit until the wardens were seated. We all had our seats assigned and may not change our seats without permission from the warden. The dining room accommodated sixty which included kids from the middle school dorm. When the meal was over we stood up as the wardens left their seats. We waited until the wardens left the dining room before we left our seats. Study hour began at seven p.m. and lasted till nine p.m. But this first study hour was for orientation and the reading of rules and regulation by the warden. It lasted about an hour and a half. We had free time afterwards until lights out at ten o'clock. We sat on each other's beds and tried to get acquainted. As I went to bed that first night I realized that I was not at all home sick. I was happy because it was a new experience for me and it was also exciting. Sleep came early however as I must have been exhausted after three days of tedious travel.

The next morning we were directed to our classes to receive our book list and curriculums and class schedules. We were told that the next day we would have something like a placement test so that the teachers could place us in proper classes. We bought our text books, note books, pen, and pencils, as needed and went back to our dorm for free time till next morning. We did not need to put jackets on for lunch but we still observed the strict rules in entering and leaving the dining hall. After lunch I got together with a couple of new found friends and ventured into the city by bus to see a movie and after the movie stopped by at the Continental Cafe for ice cream and cake and returned to the hostel just in time for dinner. We were allowed to miss dinner on week ends but we were required to inform the cook by writing our name a register.

The next day we had our placement test which lasted almost the whole day. Two days later we were given the results of our placement tests and I was surprised that I would be attending the 9th standard instead of 8th standard for my social sciences – history, geography and English, while I would still be attending the 8th standard for Burmese and math, the subjects in which I was weak. I quickly wrote a letter to Mom and Dad about the good news and they were so happy with my grading that they raised my allowance from fifteen rupees to twenty rupees a month That was a lot of allowance for those days. The allowance would take care of four movies, a couple of meal at a restaurant, laundry, snacks etc and still leave me with a few rupees to carry over to the following month. On Friday and Saturday nights we were allowed to stay late until midnight. But there were times when we couldn't make it back to the hostel in time.

That happened to me once. I went to a late movie with a friend. The movie was not over until close to midnight when buses had stopped running. We had no choice but to walk the approximate three or four miles back to the hostel. My friend walked way ahead of me as we neared the school. Soon he disappeared into an almost complete darkness among the jungle of steles and tombstones of Kyandaw cemetery. It was a moonless night. My friend was taking the short cut to get back to the hostel as he must have done before. I tried not to lose sight of him in the semi darkness. I tried to take a few quick steps to catch up and noticed that my friend would then walk even faster. Soon I heard foot steps behind me and I further quickened my steps as I was scared of who or whatever was coming up behind me. For five or six minutes I was dodging graves, steles and stones in the dark to gain distance from whoever or whatever was coming up behind me. Was it some bad character trying to catch up with me to rob me or was it a resident ghost of the cemetery, I wondered. I was so scared I could hear my heart beating out of sheer fright. Finally I got to the edge of a well lit Prome Road where I found my friend waiting for me under the street light with a wide grin on his face. He admitted that he was scared which was why he was walking so fast. Then we looked back towards the cemetery and saw the person who was behind me.
"I was scared and was trying to catch up with you and you kept running away from me," he said to me. He was a student from a hostel at the

University College who also missed the bus as we did. We had to knock on the door of the hostel for several minutes before the durwan (night watchman) would open the door for us. Needless to say my friend and I were grounded by the warden the following week end for breaking the curfew.

Mom was hurt that I did not mention in my letters home that I missed her but Dad was proud that I was able to take care of myself. I wrote to Mom however, when I had a severe attack of malaria which lasted a couple of weeks. It was in the afternoon on a Saturday that I had my first chill which gradually increased until I was shivering uncontrollably. I began to run a high fever followed by a splitting headache. I wished Mom was there to take care of me. I remembered how Mom took care of me when I was sick with the cold. I would be coughing and sneezing with sore throat and chest congestion but she would not leave my bedside. She made sure that I was not disturbed while I slept. She would rub my chest with balm, and spoon fed me with hot chicken soup and nursed me back to health. She wouldn't let the servants come near me so they wouldn't get my cold and pass it on to other members of the household. She braved my cold, yet she never got it from me. I wished that Mom was now with me and for the first time I was homesick and cried. When the chill subsided my temperature came down somewhat but the splitting headache remained. I was taken to the University sanitarium that same evening.

The next morning my temperature was down to near normal. I wrote to Mom telling her how I loved her and missed her and how I appreciated her love for me. The chill returned precisely at the same time the next day and the next with the same high fever and throbbing headache. I was given strong doses of quinine from which I had side effects of loud dins in both ears. I was in the sanitarium for at least twelve days and did not get Mom's reply to my letter until I returned to the hostel. Mom wrote back to say that she thought about me every day and missed me. She knew that I was in good hands in the sanitarium because she prayed for me each day and knew that the Lord would take good care of me. She reminded me to read her favorite Psalms 121, "*I will lift up mine eyes unto the hills, from whence cometh my help.....*" which Mom had asked me to memorize. Until that time I had not fully memorized it. I cried quietly as I read the psalms and memorized the chapter that same day.

Dad always advised me to make friends with those students who were good in math so I could be helped with my home work in math. Actually in math I was only weak in algebra but was very good in geometry and not too bad in arithmetic. I wasn't worried because in the final results all three were aggregated so that I could always get better than decent passing grade, except that getting a zero in any one subject is not accepted and that was where I had a problem because, believe it or not, I never could get anything above zero in algebra! I just couldn't understand algebra. Dad's advice worked because it improved my algebra enough to make a passing grade. I managed to improve my Burmese by reading Burmese news papers and novels. That year I passed my eighth standard and would be going into the 9th standard, with a remark in the report card that I would be moved up to the 10th standard for my English, Geography and History. By now Audrey was a sophomore in college and Saunders was a freshman while Dempsey was a senior in high school.

For our next summer vacation we went home to Shwebo, an upper Burma town, where Dad was transferred as H.Q.A. It was very hot and dry in Shwebo but it did not deprive us of a lot of outdoor fun. Dad loved hunting and whenever he had to tour the district, or on week ends, he'd take us deer hunting. The heat didn't bother him. Dad had a rule. When we bagged a big game like a boar or a deer, the hunt was over. Tiger and bison were to be avoided even if we encountered one mainly because of the danger and also because of closed season most of the year. I remember our very first big game hunting in Shwebo. There were the four of us, Dad, Saunders, Dempsey and myself. The hunt lasted less than an hour when Saunders got a shot at a sambur. It was a huge animal as large as a horse, with a beautiful three pointed antler. I saw it daintily prancing with it's neck raised high above the bushes. I was waiting for a shot but my brother got the first shot that brought it down.

Another time we had a guide who was the headman of a village and was also a good hunter. A half hour after we entered the woods we saw a tiger swimming in a pond of lilies. It ignored us as we watched from behind the bushes and waited for it to move away. After about ten minutes it left the pond, shook off the water and walked away sedately in the opposite direction. The guide now asked us to take off our hats as we entered the thicker forest because he said, the spirits of the forest did not want people wearing western hats. We slung our hats behind our backs. Fortunately the forest was getting thick and we had no problem with the hot sun. After about a half hour of walk into the forest, the headman placed each one of us at different locations roughly twenty to thirty feet apart. He positioned me on a fallen tree which rested about five feet above ground. Dad was placed to my left about twenty feet away. Dad had asked the headman to have a dozen or so of his villagers to beat the forest for us to ensure that we bagged the notorious boar that was ravaging vegetable plots in neighboring villages. The headman said that the boar would be coming through at any one of the spots he placed us. He warned us not to speak to each other and to be absolutely quiet. Then he left us to move to his own position.

I had loaded my shotgun with a ball in both barrels. Before we left the house I had cleaned and oiled my gun. I was ready for the boar. I was almost shaking with excitement at the thought of a shot at a big wild boar. The headman warned me not to get on the ground but remain on the tree trunk. We waited for several minutes but nothing was happening. Then we heard a loud whistle responded by another, then another. Five minutes went by and then we heard the faint shouts and beating of trees trunks and tin cans coming from a distance in all directions before us. The sounds got louder and louder but were still at a distance. I looked at Dad in the far end on the left and he waved and pointed in the direction of the sounds signaling that I kept my eyes to the front.

Then I heard it. It had to be a huge animal. The hoofs thundered and shook the ground. I braced myself as I pointed the gun in the direction the sound was coming from. The sound became louder as the ground shook harder when I saw the huge head of the boar coming out of the bushes about seventy feet from me. I let it come closer as I tried to keep the bead on it's head right between the eyes. Then when the boar was at thirty feet I pulled the triggers, "Click- click." The boar thundered past below me under the fallen tree, turned toward where Dad was. Then two shots rang our, "Bang-bang" from Dad's gun. The boar went down on it's right shoulder then got up unsteadily and disappeared behind the brush. The headman came running back to us, shouting, "Don't follow it! Don't follow it." He then got us all together and asked me, "Why didn't you shoot?"
"I did, but the gun didn't go off. It misfired."
"This is a large forest," he said, "and the spirits are very powerful. They don't like people wearing western hats or even carrying them."
What really happened was, when I cleaned the gun I forgot to tighten the screws to the striker pins. The pins never struck the cartridges.
"It is dangerous to follow the animal," he said, "now that it has been wounded. I will follow, but you all stay far behind me."

We followed him at a safe distance until we saw him stop at a clearing. About a hundred feet in front of him lying on the grass was the boar facing him. The headman raised his gun and walked slowly forward. When he got to about fifty feet the boar rose unsteadily on all fours lowered it's head perhaps preparing to charge. The headman fired. The boar collapsed. It was hit right between the eyes. The boar laid on it's right side on the grass. By that time the villagers beating the forest caught up with us. They quickly cut bamboo poles and made ropes out of vines for slings to carry the boar back to the village. It took four men to carry the animal.

In Shwebo Dad had a rather unusual experience with murder cases that he had to try. Two or three times a month someone would be murdered, or mugged but often these cases were never solved. Dad had to take a 'dying deposition' each time someone was taken to the hospital for serious gun shot wounds or knife wounds. In almost all cases the victims refused to name their attackers. If the victim died, it is always expected that someone in his family would take a revenge on a member of the attacker's family. The vendetta would go on and on. I followed Dad a couple of times when he had to take dying deposition in the hospital.

Dad would ask questions like, "What is your name?" "Your age?" "Your address?" to make sure the person was in full possession of his faculties. To all these questions the man would give straight answers.

"Did you see your attacker?"

"Yes."

"Do you know him?"

"Yes"

"What is his name?"

Silence.

"Did you recognize the person who attacked you?"

"Yes."

"Who was he?"

Silence. Even police investigations usually turned up no suspect.

My older brother Saunders had a pet squirrel. He named it Bushie. Bushie slept in his pajama shirt pocket at night. At breakfast time we had to place a bowl of walnut on the floor otherwise it would knock over coffee cups and sugar bowl on the table. One day it disappeared for several daya. Perhaps it went back to the Ko-Ko trees for mating. Finally it came back with about four or five of it's harem in tow. The harem would only play and floric on the veranda while Bushie would come inside the house to be petted as it jumped from one of us to the other. Mom told us that after we all went back to school Bushie disappeared for good.

The next school year I was in the ninth standard (which was a junior year in high school). The highlights during that school year were my representing my school team in an inter school debating contest. We won the championship that year. I played for the school's football 'B' team in inter school tournaments but we never reach the semi finals. I got hurt and was in plaster for three months. I also competed in the interschool boxing competition and was T.K.O.ed early in the tournament. I enjoyed all these activities. In class I was just a slightly above average student.

By the time school was out for the summer holidays Dad had been transferred to Myitkyina, a town in Northern Burma on the Irrawaddy river, below the confluence of Mekha and Malika rivers in the Kachin District. We all came home separately except Louise who went to Scotland on a scholarship for her post graduate studies. Holiday was always fun. In the evenings we'd sing in harmony, popular songs of those days with accompaniment on our guitars and ukulele. A couple of times Dad would take us to the sanctuary where we could see the wild animals grazing in the meadow. Once we watched a pair of tigers basking in the sun on a fallen tree trunk yawning away lazily as we picnicked about only a hundred feet away under tall teak trees. Sometimes we would take a trip with Dad as he toured the villages along the Irrawaddy River in a government launch. The launch had powerful paddle wheels astern and moved very smoothly even against the current. Dad would stop at certain villages to hold meetings or try cases. We boys enjoyed those trips because we were able to go ashore and hunt to our heart's content always bringing back doves, teals and ducks for the cook to make delicious curries out of. I once shot a stork which had five live fish still in it's long throat.

I was now a senior in high school when we returned to school. As seniors we did not have to live in the dorm any more but were given individual rooms at the Men's Hostel and we dined together with the men and women of the college. I became more serious in my outlook for the future. Dad wanted me to study law in college and wanted me to join the civil service like he did. I was not sure that I wanted to do that but I knew that I had to try harder in my studies to be eligible for college. In those days, even if you passed the high school exam, it did not necessarily mean you could go to college if you only passed under the 'B' list. You had to pass under 'A' list to be eligible to attend college. Passing under 'B' list only qualified you to apply for jobs in clerical positions in government departments. For one who passed under 'B' list and wanted to go to college, it meant another year in high school, and making the 'A' list. In the past I had been lack luster in my studies and was satisfied with being just above average. But now I realized that I had to make sure I would graduate from high school and be able to go to college and not let my parents down. But this was a bad year for me as I missed classes for a whole month when I injured my hip playing football and had to be in the hospital with a cast on my hip for three weeks. A few months later I had an attack of malaria and had to be hospitalized for two weeks. After Christmas holidays I came down with typhoid fever and was in hospital again for three weeks. I was weak when I was discharged from the hospital and couldn't quite catch up with lessons I missed. Two weeks before final exam I found myself cramming into the late hours every night and sometimes into the early hours. By exam time I could hardly stand up. High school final exam is a government conducted exam and the results were published by the Rangoon Gazette. When the results were finally out I was elated to find my name under 'A' list. But in spite of cramming before the exam I didn't get a distinction in any of my favorite subjects.

It was in 1940 that I graduated from high school. That year tragedy struck our family. We were back with Mom and Dad in Myitkyina for the summer holidays. The entire family was with Dad on his usual tour of the villages on the river in the government launch, except Louise who was still in Scotland. We traveled down river stopping at different villages as Dad tried cases or held meetings. On the third day of the tour Dad took a break from work. An hour before lunch time Saunders announced that he would take a dip in the river. He walked upstream along the bank obviously intending to swim down with the current back to the launch. Audrey and Dempsey were also preparing to take a dip and had put on their swim suits. The current did not appear too strong around where the launch was moored. From the fore deck which was an open lounge, we watched Saunders get into the water about half a mile upstream. Saunders was a strong swimmer. He had won the cross lake badge when he swam across the Inya Lake in college, a distance of about a mile. We watched him as he swam down river. Then when he got to about fifty or sixty yards from the launch he raised his hand and yelled, "Dad! Help!" and then disappeared under the water. Dempsey tried to jump down form the boat but the crew pulled him back. As he struggled to free himself one crew member tied a rope around his waist and let him go. He jumped into the river but quickly got carried down stream by the current and had to be pulled back into the launch.

The serang (the boat captain) sounded the boat's siren and villagers came running to the launch to hear Mom call out to them, "Help! Help! My son has drowned in the river. Please help! Help!" Mother was hysteric. Dad had someone summon the resident doctor in case Saunders needed to be revived if found. Villagers immediately launched small crafts into the river and a search was conducted up and down the river. Saunders never came up again. After about forty five minutes Mom asked the doctor whether Saunders could be revived if he was found. The doctor told Mom that there was no chance he'd be alive.

Mom then turned to the crowd who were gathered on the bank and said, "God has taken our son away to heaven and he is now with the Lord." Mom was now calm and she continued to talk to the crowd about Christ's victory over death and death on earth being the beginning of eternal life in heaven and she continued preaching to the crowd. With Dad however, it was a different story. He wept. He wept because Saunders called out to him for help and he couldn't help. Dad didn't even know how to swim. His son called out to him for help and he couldn't do a thing to save his son's life. He got our family together in the lounge and he asked Mom to lead us in devotion to seek strength and comfort from the Lord. It was amazing how we were all strengthened from that short devotion. Every one of us stopped crying and we started to talk of different things like nothing tragic had happened to our family. The doctor suggested that Saunders had developed cramps as the water was very cold and that when he went under he must have grabbed and held on onto something which was why he never resurfaced.

In the evening Dad asked the serang to run the launch repeatedly over the area where Saunders went down in the hope that the turbulence would shake Saunder's body free from anything that he might have held onto. Boatmen were patrolling the river continuously. After dinner we were listening to a story Nita was telling us from the novel she had just finished reading. As we listened to the story we were also watching the boatmen patrolling in the river in the moonlight. At about nine one boatman shouted to the other boatmen for help. The body surfaced and he needed help to haul it into his boat. Saunders was found holding a small twig in his hand. The villagers prepared the body for the two day trip back to Myitkyina. The body was bound tight with strips of bamboo woven together and placed in a wooden coffin which was sealed tight with resin. We had an early start and traveled day and night against the current to arrive early in the afternoon the next day. Dad sent a message ahead about the tragedy and funeral arrangements were made for the funeral procession to take place straight from the launch to cemetery. Our family sang "Savior Thy dying Love" and "More love to Thee" at the funeral and none of us shed any tear. They were Saunders's favorite hymns. Friends at the funeral were amazed that none of us broke down as we sang the hymns.

CHAPTER 3

MOM AND DAD

MOM WAS BROUGHT UP UNDER strict Baptist tradition. Grandpa and Grandma were devout second generation Christians who took great pride in their own Home Mission with two pastors carrying out mission work in the hills of the Wa state in north eastern Burma. On their thirty six acres of land in Insein Grandma grew many varieties of fruit trees – mango, guava, jack-fruit and cashew besides rows of pine apple, asparagus and others vegetables. The estate was fenced completely by clusters of bamboo groves. The house was built of brick and teak on top of the hill Grandpa named Zion Hill which became the official postal address. It had five bed rooms and a large hall used as a dorm for younger grandchildren who were visiting. The sitting room was so large it looked more like a hall. Grandpa wanted all his children to have vacation at the same time during summer holidays for the schools so that he could have all his grand children together at one time. Grandpa had three daughters who together had fifteen children, and two sons who had seven children between them, altogether a total of twenty two grand children. When the younger grand children arrived at Grandpa's house for the holidays they routinely rushed to their favorite mango and cashew trees to stake their ownership for the entire summer.

Grandpa always had three family devotions a day, seven days a week, after breakfast, lunch and dinner. There was no exception. No one was allowed to pluck flowers or fruits, go to the movies, read novels or buy anything on a Sunday. In spite of those restrictions we all loved to be at Grandpa's during summer holidays. Grandpa had a gong that he would sound at half past seven in the morning, half past one in the afternoon and half past seven in the evening to summon everyone to come to the sitting room for devotion. All male members of the family

had to wear jackets for the devotions. His devotion lasted one hour and by the time the devotion was over in the evening, the young ones had to be carried to bed as they were all fast asleep on the floor. There was no wake up bell in the morning but everyone had to get up early to be at the breakfast table by six o'clock. If someone was still in bed Grandpa would go into the bedroom and pull the person off the bed by the leg. Grandpa refused to say grace until everyone was seated at the table. The long teak table accommodated eighteen adults and the young ones had two low round tables, eight to a table. The meals could be as noisy as we wanted but manners had to be observed. Grandpa was deaf and we had to speak loud so he could hear us. But then, if we happened to speak too loud, he would snap, "Don't you yell at me." He also had an uncanny ability to know it when we said something about him and ask, "What are you saying about me?" Grandpa had an upright Steinway in the living room and our favorite pastime after the evening service was to sing in full harmony the popular songs of the time. While one of the girls played the piano we boys would accompany with our guitars and ukulele, mandolin and violin. The only thing I didn't like it at Grandpa house was Grandpa asking us to walk on his back and legs for hours at a time. When we thought he was asleep we would try to get off. But then he would shake hig legs and tell us to get back on." One day my cousin Bobby and I were walking on Grandpa back. We were getting tired. After a while Bobby gave me a wink and shouted, "Grandma, I'm walking on Grandpa". Grandpa woke up and asked, "What are you shouting for?" and Bobby answered, "Grandma is calling me, Grandpa."
"Go, go quick to your Grandma," he told Bobby. "She must want something." Bobby walked away with a smisrk on his face. Actually Grandma never called and I was left alone walking on Grandpa.

Mom was the disciplinarian of our family. She would scold, chastise, spank or punish. In spite of the fact that we had enough servants to do the work needed we were all required to share in the upkeep of the house while we were home from school for the holidays. "Unless you know how to do house chores yourselves, you won't know how to manage the servants," Mom used to tell us. But Mom was never a slave driver with the servants. In fact she was kind to the servants and allowed some to return to their villages to visit their families while we were home for the summer holidays. She would even buy tem clothes or other necessities to take home for their families. Mom had a large roster with our names and our different responsibilities written on it which she placed on a wall near the kitchen. Wherever Dad was posted, Mom would look for a Women's circle in a church and become an active member of that church. She loved to organize Christmas programs such as Christmas plays, carol singing and recitals for children. She would buy Christmas presents for underprivileged children of the church, nothing that was expensive but something that a child would appreciate, like dolls for girls and rubber football for boys besides goodies and snacks like peanuts, candies and fruits and a Christmas dinner for the poorer families of the church. I've never heard of people humming in their sleep. Mom would hum a complete hymn in her sleep. Mom hummed a different hymn almost every night. She hummed whole verses and sometimes even the choruses. It was eerie to wake up in the middle of the night and hear Mom humming. But she never knew she did.

Dad on the other hand was the son of a poor farm share cropper who was a Baptist but had no education at all. Dad was the youngest of five children. None of his siblings went to school but his father decided that he would send his youngest child to school in Rangoon. Because there were no good schools around Pyaw Bwegon, Dad's village, which was some forty miles from Rangoon, they had to walk two hours to reach Pegu where they took a train to Rangoon. Upon arrival in Rangoon, Dad was taken by his father to Pegu Karen High School, an American Baptist school, and registered him as a boarding student in the first standard at age seven.

Dad's father was so poor he could provide Dad with only one change of clothes. Dad told us of his ordeal resulting from his lack of change of clothes. One night he wet the pants he slept in and in the morning quickly folded it and hid it under the mattress so the lady supervisor wouldn't see it. In the afternoon when the supervisor came into the dorm she at once noticed the stench. She asked if anyone had wet his bed at night. When his turn came Dad answered, "No," and tried his best to look innocent. The supervisor walked up and down the dorm until she knew exactly where the strong smell of stale urine was coming from.

"Zan," the supervisor asked, "did you wet your bed last night?"

Still trying his best to look innocent Dad replied, "No."

The supervisor lifted one corner of the mattress on Dad's bed and a strong stench filled the dorm.

"Is that your pants, Zan," the supervisor asked.

Dad said he burst into tears.

"That is my only other pant," he sobbed.

When the supervisor took him into her office Dad thought that he was going to be punished. But the supervisor opened a closet and took out a bag and brought out some clothes and asked him to try them on. He came away with three extra changes of clothes. Dad used to tell us stories of his childhood days every summer when we returned home for the holidays. We made Dad sing and dance for us just like he used to sing and dance in his school concert. He would hop around and sing, "I am a little rabbit...." Or recite 'Hickory Dickory Dock., the Mouse ran up the Clock." and danced and hopped round the dining table as we all sang and hopped along with him. He was a real sport. He graduated from high school from that same school and went on to Judson College and graduated from there and sat for the Burma Civil Service Exam and became an officer of the Burma Civil Service.

Dad's siblings were all farmers, growing rice on lands they lost to the Chetya (Indian money lender/land owner). They had very hard lives and frequently owed the Chetya more money than they made selling their crops. Dad started work as a Township Officer and was quickly promoted to Sub-Divisional Officer. After his father died Dad was determined to help his siblings out. He bought lands back from the Chetya that his siblings were farming piece by piece until all the land lost to the Chetya was recovered.

Dad used to take us to a lake on the farm where he would ask the farm hands to dive for large shrimps. Dad named the lake *Kyar-gan-gyi*, meaning 'great lake of lotus.' Those shrimps had huge heads and the tails were almost as large as lobster tails. The farm hands would then throw live shrimps into burning embers, retrieve them and give us the freshly roasted shrimp to eat. They were juicy and delicious. Dad would arrange for us to have hay rides on bullock carts. Hay was piled high on the cart and we would be sitting on the hay as the bullocks raced over cart tracts on the farm. Sometimes we would sit on separate carts and have cart race and Dad would reward the winners with choice portion of food at dinner time. We were treated like royalties by villagers of Pyaw Bwegon, as well as by our relatives in the village. They held concerts for us and we also participated in their programs by singing or taking part in their plays. Dad's Christian upbringing at home and at a Baptist school and a Baptist college made him a responsible father who cared about our spiritual well being. He made it a habit for all of us to have devotions every evening when we were together. When we were by ourselves, he taught us to have a personal communication with God each morning and night. Mom and Dad always told us to be humble and not to be arrogant and boastful because, they said, every one was our equal.

I went to Judson College in 1940. Before I went away to attend college Dad warned me that there would be lots of temptations, including a temptation to stay away from church or to forget to read the bible each day. Mom and Dad did not have to worry about me deviating from my religious and moral upbringing. Judson College Church choir was led by Mrs. Rickard who had a beautiful voice. The church choir and music was so good I couldn't stay away from church services each Sunday and eventually I joined the choir. I also got together with three other students from my class to form our own vocal quartet singing both religious hymns and popular secular songs. We sang for prayer services and other special occasions like birthday parties that we were invited to. Dempsey had a Kalamazoo guitar and I took over Saunder's old Gibson. In the evenings after dinner several groups of students with their instruments would sit out on the lawn in front of Benton Hall, the Women's Hostel, and serenade the ladies until the bell rang for dinner. The girls were allowed to come out to meet with the boys until dinner bell.

My first college year ended with a two weeks University Training Corp (U.T.C.) camp at the British Army base in Maymyo in Upper Burma. Dempsey was a corporal in the U.T.C., which was an army training unit for those students who wanted to receive small arms training. It was more of a past time activity for students although there were some who seriously aspired to sooner or later join the armed services. Senior instructors were professional army officers and the N.C.O.s were mostly senior students who rose in ranks over the years. Many who graduated from the U.T.C. later joined the army and became Army of Burma Reserve Officers (A.B.R.O.).

CHAPTER 4

THE EVACUATION

As Christmas 1941 approached I looked forward to the holidays to return home to our parents in Prome where Dad was Head Quarters Assistant and Treasury Officer. However, the holidays came earlier than usual when the Dean of Judson College announced during the morning assembly on December 9 that college was closing immediately to allow students to return home to be with their families because of the possibility of war coming to Burma. The announcement came two days after we heard over the radio that Pearl Harbor was attacked by the Japanese Imperial Air Force inflicting heavy damage to the American fleet.

After lunch my brother Dempsey got hold of me outside the dining hall and asked me what I intended to do. I told him that I would like to stick around at the hostel for a couple more days before going home. He replied that it was all right with him and said he would wait for me at Grandpa's place in Insein. Dempsey was a home person while I liked to hang around with my friends. Now I knew that I may not be seeing some of my friends again for a long time if war did come to Burma. So I remained at the hostel after Dempsey left for Grandpa's house. The next day I saw some friends off at the train station and others at the jetty and said my farewells to them.

I left the hostel two days later to join Dempsey in Insein. Grandpa's house sat on top of Zion Hill overlooking the air strip at Mingaladon Airdrome, as the air port was called then. Planes flew past over the rooftop in landing or at take off each day. The air field was especially busy now with Royal Air Force planes in flight training. As I entered the house I could hear Grandpa singing at the top of his voice, "Glory, Glory Hallelujah."

That was his favorite hymn when he took a bath. Grandma asked if I had dinner already. I said I hadn't.

"Didn't your friends feed you?" she asked.

"No, I saw a few of my friends off at the station and we had no time to eat," I replied. "Don't you have any food for me, Grandma?" I asked.

"I'm only teasing you," she quickly replied, "You know we always have plenty of food in this house."

At that time Grandpa came out of his bedroom and boomed, "What took you so long to get here? Your brother was here two days ago."

"I was seeing friends off, Grandpa," I shouted into his ears.

"Don't you shout at me," he barked. "Can't your friends take care of themselves?"

That evening, after dinner and devotion, Dempsey and I sat down and re-read a letter we received from Dad that afternoon. Dad wanted us to return to Prome soon. He said it was important that we came home. He also wanted to have the girls back home as soon as possible. Louise had returned from Scotland and was now teaching together with Nita at American Baptist Mission Karen High School in Moulmein in the south. Audrey the youngest of the three older girls was teaching in A.B.M. High School in Henzada. Dad wanted us to come home because there were things he wanted us to know which he did not want to tell us in the letter.

"Are you ready to leave tomorrow?" Dempsey asked.

"Sure. I'm ready any time," I replied.

We took the train back to Prome the next day and arrived home in the afternoon. Dad was at his desk. Dad maintained an office at home since he occasionally brought work home with him.

"What's the matter Dad?" Dempsey asked. "Things look bad?"

"No. I just thought that at a time like this the family should all be together," he said and continued, "I also wrote to the girls to come home as soon as they possibly can."

"There is rumor circulating in Rangoon that the Japanese will invade Burma," Dempsey said. "Dad, do you think they will?"

"That could be true," Dad answered. "Who knows? But this is confidential," Dad said. "Japanese soldiers are reportedly seen near Mergui and Tavoy. That's why I wanted you boys back here in case the girls have problems coming home."

"Do you want us to go and get them, Dad?" Dempsey asked.

"No, that is not necessary at this time. I sent them a letter. Let's wait to hear from them."

"Read these instructions," Dad told us," He pulled out a manual from a large envelope. "I need help with these messages in code."
"Sure," I replied. Dempsey and I read the instructions and tried to decode the ciphers. It was interesting. Each day had a different code. It was a little complicating at first but after some practice we managed to decode a message from the British Commissioner in which he asked Dad to prepare for possible evacuation and destruction of the treasury and government documents in the event war came to Burma. There were no details except for Dad to await further directives. In another message there were information about Japanese infiltration in some areas of northern Malay and unconfirmed reports of sightings of Japanese soldiers in the southern tip of Burma.

A few days later Dad received a letter from Nita saying they would be back early for Christmas. There was no letter from Audrey so Dad sent her a telegram to come home as soon as possible. Nita and Louise arrived ten days before Christmas. Their train was two hours late. They said the train stopped a couple of times between stations and picked up some British and Indian soldiers in three or four empty carriages reserved for them. They said most passengers on the train seemed to be families, mostly from the south, evacuating to the north in anticipation of a Japanese invasion. There was still no news from Audrey. So Dad sent her another telegram telling her that Dempsey and I would be picking her up in a couple of days. Two days later Dempsey and I left to bring back Audrey from Henzada. It wasn't a long drive to Tharrawaddy across the river from Henzada. Dempsey took the ferry and after about three hours came back with Audrey in tow. We got back home a little before dinner time. Mom had the cook prepare an elaborate dinner because for the first time in almost a year the family was together, all eight of us. It was a noisy meal. Everyone was asking a question or answering one. The dinner took a whole hour. As the servants were clearing the table Dad announced that he would like to hold a meeting in the drawing room.
"What meeting?" Nita asked.
"I thought we'd discuss about where we are going to evacuate to," Dad answered.
"Daddy," Audrey said, "we're having a good time trying to catch up with everything. Let's do that tomorrow, Daddy."
"No, we'll do that now'" Dad told her. "Let the servants clear the table. We'll go into the drawing room."
When everyone was seated Dad began, "Listen. This is important. We don't know if the Japanese will overrun Burma, but I know that the government

is directing all civil servants to be prepared for a possible evacuation. There are unconfirmed reports in the news that Japanese soldiers are seen in parts of southern Burma. We do not know for sure but government reports seem to confirm these rumors. I am concerned because I have a big family to take care of. I am asking Dempsey and Spencer to go to Insein and fetch your grand parents. That will make our family even larger. I will have to look after my family's safety and at the same time I have my duty as a civil officer and head of Civil Defense recently formed by the Commissioner. It will be too much of a burden for me to do both. So I am planning to send the family, meaning the women folks, and the grand parents, away to a safer place in the north somewhere, you decide where. That's why we're meeting now, so that I can carry out my responsibilities without having to worry about the family. Now the question is where do you think is a safe place to go to?"

Everybody looked around to see who was going to make the first suggestion.

"We can go to Bhamo," I said, "many of my friends live in Bhamo."

"But we don't have anybody we know there," Louise said. "And I'm talking about family friends."

"Mawlaik is a good place," Audrey suggested. "Dad was stationed there a few years ago so we are bound to have some people we knew there"

"How does Myitkyina sound?" Dempsey asked.

"No, that's too far north." Nita said.

"We should go to some place we are familiar with," Louise said, "a place where we know some people or have some relatives."

"Yes, Myitkyina is too far," Mom said, "Uncle Albert is in Mandalay. Don't you think we should go there? Your Uncle Albert will be delighted to have us." Uncle Albert was the husband of Mom's younger sister, Aunty Hta. He was the Deputy Director of Agriculture Department.

"I think that is a good choice," Dad said. "But what do the rest of you think?" he asked.

"Mandalay sounds great," Dempsey said.

"What about everybody else?" Dad asked. "Raise your hands if you think we should go to Mandalay."

All hands went up.

"Well, I guess that settles it. Mandalay is where we'll go to," Dad said.

"When do we go, Daddy?" Louise asked.

"Soon after New Year sometime," Dad replied. "We'll have to get your grand parents first. We'll watch the situation and decide very soon."

Mom asked Dad to say a prayer. After prayer we all retired to our bed rooms.

There was news report that Rangoon was bombed. Trains were packed to capacity with evacuees leaving the cities in the south for safer destinations in the north. There were persistent rumors that the Japanese were already in the southern tip of Burma. Government news on the radio however denied the rumors. Although we expected Christmas to be dismal and empty of holiday spirit, our Christmas turned out to be quite an enjoyable one despite the prevailing war fever. We exchanged gifts, and sang carols. Mom invited several friends who were still in town and had the cook prepare a lavish dinner for the guests. The only thing missing was the fact that Grandpa and Grandma were not with us. Mom had written them that Dempsey would pick them up before Christmas but Grandpa said he wanted to spend Christmas with his two sons and their children. There was a general air of suspense and people everywhere were now worried about what would happen next. Conversations were always about impending Japanese invasion, and possible commitment of atrocities by the Japanese soldiers. Somehow everyone seemed afraid of the Japanese possibly from tales of the atrocities they committed in China. Soon after Christmas Mom dismissed all the servants to allow them to return to their families.

The day after New Year Dempsey and I went to pick up Grandpa and Grandma. Mom had written them ahead so when we arrived at the house they were all packed and ready. Mom had told them to pack just a suit case each, nothing more. But Grandpa had a suit case and a large trunk. Grandpa had a heated argument with Dempsey who insisted that he left the trunk. Grandpa had packed into the trunk his hats, shoes, clocks, gifts and souvenirs he had collected over the years and his ceremonial Police Officer's uniform including his police helmet and a long ceremonial silver sword he was awarded by the Britich government for outstanding service. Grandpa was a retired Police Inspector. He refused to leave the trunk and continued to argue with Dempsey until Grandma cut in, "You say you have no use for worldly things, and don't need them. You say that God comes first in your life. What are these things that you refuse to part with? Have they become your gods? Why don't you stay back with them? I'll go to my daughter and let God take care of me."

Without a word Grandpa opened the trunk again and took a long look at the contents and smiled. Then he said, "You are right my dear. Lord forgive me." and slowly closed the trunk. He picked up his suit case, straightened up and looked at Dempsey with a wide grin and said, "So, what are we waiting for? Let's go."

"Not so fast Grandpa," Dempsey told him, "there's no train till tomorrow."

The Airdrome was now very busy with R. A. F. planes taking off and landing at all hours either on flights training or taking off and landing after reconnaissance flights. The Flying Tigers, or the A.V.G. (American Volunteer Group) as we knew them then, were also now operating out of this airfield. The next morning, just before we were about to leave for the train station we heard the sound of an airplane flying very low with the engine coughing and backfiring loudly. Dempsey and I were outside the house at that time. The next moment we saw the plane, a Blenheim bomber, approach the airfield and loosing altitude rapidly and missing the roof of the house by only about fifty feet and nose dived into the rice field just outside of our bamboo fence. There was no explosion but the crash sounded like a huge tree crashing to the ground. Dempsey and I rushed to the crash site just beyond the bamboo grove on the edge of the field. The mangled nose of the plane rested against a tree, with the fuselage and tail grotesquely pointing skyward then settling slowly to the ground.

There was no fire except a wisp of black smoke that rose from the plane into the thin dry air. As we neared the plane we saw an airman crawling out of the wreckage and continued crawling towards the bamboo grove. Dempsey ran ahead towards the man to help but the man waved him off yelling, "Get away. Get away." Then an ambulance and a covered army truck pulled up about a hundred feet from the crash. Soldiers poured out of the vehicles and ran towards the wrecked plane. A couple of soldiers came over to us and shooed us off. We retreated into our own compound and watched the rescue being carried out from the hill top. When the rescuers extricated a man from the wreckage Dempsey suddenly remembered that we had a train to catch. We ran back to the house only to realize that we had missed our train. The next afternoon we were back in Prome. Mom and the girls were all very happy to see Grandpa and Grandma.

Civil administration was still functioning and Dad still ran his office in addition to his duty as Treasury Officer and was still trying cases at the court house as Head Quarters Assistant. Ciphers were coming in everyday and Dad became very concerned for the family because the information seemed to indicate the inability or the unwillingness of the British troops to check the Japanese advance. In mid February Dad hired a bus to take the family to Mandalay as planned. Dempsey and I remained with Dad. A few days after the family left for Mandalay Rangoon was bombed twice. That got Dad worried a bit because our house was situated halfway up the hill behind the town of Prome and it was very conspicuous from the air. Also there were anti aircraft guns near our house and on the hill. Dad didn't relish the idea of being a target for trigger happy Japanese pilots.

So a week later Dad had us move into the military barracks in spite of Dempsey's protest that the barracks would be a more inviting target for the Japanese planes. The Garrison commander, Col. Lionel Po, son of a well respected Karen leader Sir San C. Po, was a friend of Dad's. He invited us to move into his quarters. He had sent his family to Bassein a few weeks earlier and there were two bedrooms we could use. This arrangement was convenient for Dad because as he received coded messages from the Commissioner, he could compare his information with those the colonel received from his army head quarters thereby getting a better picture of the situation. As Civil Defense Chief Dad had to consult with the military anyway and so Colonel Po's quarters now became a convenient Civil Defense office for Dad.

The day before we moved to the army barracks I walked around the house from room to room looking at all the familiar things that we would be leaving behind for looters and vandals. When the rest of the family left earlier, all they took with them were just enough clothing for themselves, and a very few personal belongings. Expensive *longyis* (sarong) and *aingyis* (blouses) were neatly folded in the drawers. Even the beds were made. Family portraits and class pictures still stood on the dressers or hung on the walls. Then I walked into the dining room to take a look at Mom and Dad's portrait painted by an English artist from London hanging on the wall. Both Mom and Dad looked down at me through the bubble glass of their ornate picture frame with a touch of a smile, just for me it seemed. Below on the side table the silver gong was hanging from a pair of shining bison horns set on a beautifully carved teak mount. There was the polished teak table and chairs sitting idly waiting for the familiar diners who would never return to grace them. I opened the cupboard and there were expensive china dinnerware, dishes and cut glasses and beautiful vases which Mon had used many times to entertain foreign guests like British officials amd American missionaries. Then I walked into the drawing room. Dempsey forgot to turn off the radio and the GE radio's magic eye was still blinking at me. I turned it off. I looked over at the corner of the room where Dad's type writer sat sedately on his office desk and at the teak and cane settee and chairs on a Persian rug covering the concrete floor. They looked like a fine drawing room suite on display in a furniture shop. I could already see looters fighting over these polished fine furnitrure.

"Dad, aren't you taking those portraits and the silver gong with you?" I asked Dad as he was walking by.

"Are you out of your mind?" Dad replied. "We are evacuating, running away. We can only take what we need to survive, clothing and a few personal things. Son, these are material things. We can always get these things back later, and much more."

Now that we no longer had a driver I drove Dad every day to the courthouse. Dempsey didn't like going to the court and would rather spend his time in town with a college friend of his, whose family was still in town. Two weeks after we moved in the barracks were bombed. Fortunately all the soldiers were away so there were no military casualties although a few buildings were damaged. The colonel's quarter was not hit. Dad and I were at the court house at that time and Dempsey was with his friend in town. Some buildings in the town were hit and there were few casualties but no deaths. The air raid siren never sounded. I was watching a trial proceeding in a murder case when the first bomb exploded. I heard the high pitch drone of planes but never thought they were Japanese planes. Everybody ran out in panic and haded for the trenches when the bombs exploded, except Dad and me. We pulled two chairs into a corner and sat down and prayed together. Dad started to talk about the possibility of evacuating the city sooner than he had planned. Only now the air raid siren sounded but the bombs were already exploding. It was a small air raid and it was over in less than five minutes. The all clear sounded a half hour later. When everyone returned to the court room, Dad announced that the courthouse was closed for the day so everyone could go home to check on their families. When we got back to the barracks, Dempsey was already there admiring the blue convertible he had just brought back. He was at his friend's house during the bombing. The friend's family was leaving town the next day but they could not take all their three cars with them so they offered Dempsey their Graham Page.

One day in late March Dad left court early to return to the barrack because he needed to consult with Colonel Po. The colonel was home so they sat down together for a couple hours in serious discussion. It turned out that Dad had the latest instruction from the commissioner. He was ordered to immediately destroy all government documents and records, treasury notes and money and, working with the army, blow up all petrol storage and bridges in the district. He was then to dismiss the entire staff and hand over the administration to the military authority. The next day Colonel Po had his soldiers load all the documents and records from the treasury vault together with treasury notes and bags of coins and trucked them to the jetty where they were loaded onto a barge. The army then loaded explosives into the barge and had it towed midstream. The barge was then blown up and immediately sank midstream. The entire procedure was witnessed by the Colonel, Dad and the Deputy Superintendent of Police. The Colonel decided that Dad could now evacuate and join the family without destroying the petrol storage and bridges because the army still needed those facilities. Dad had notices placed at the Court House and at other public places that the town was now under military administration.

The next day Dempsey and I spent all day looking for dry goods and canned food to take with us but we had a hard time finding what we needed because most stores that still remained open did not have much of anything left. Other stores outside town had been looted. But we managed to buy a couple of dozen cans of sardines and corned beef which local people seldom used for regular meals, and we also bought some potatoes and cooking oil. We loaded those into the Graham Page. Then the air raid siren sounded and we had to get into the shelter. After about fifteen minutes bombs exploded all over the town, some close to the barracks and some on the hill. We didn't even hear the planes till after the bombs exploded. Japanese bombers flew very high and their drones were high pitched. Part of the town was on fire but fortunately it was only a rice mill and a few houses around it that were ablaze. After about another hour the all clear sounded. Again there were few casualties because by now most residents had left town. The soldiers were busy keeping looters away from homes that were still occupied and shops that were still opened. Gun shots were heard throughout the night. And also for the first time we could hear regular shelling in the distant. The colonel assured us that we were not to worry because troops were out there to check any movement by the Japanese and there were no report of any presence of Japanese troop anywhere in the immediate area. His duty done, Dad decided to leave the next morning. But we herd planes approaching about nine in the morning and in a few seconds the air raid alarm sounded. A few more minutes later we heard bombs exploding but this time only in the distance.

We didn't get to leave Prome until noon after we had had our lunch. I drove the Pontiac and Dempsey followed in his Graham Page. Between the three of us we had three fire arms. Dad had a .405 elephant rifle, I had a shot gun and Dempsey had a .22 Winchester. We were told that two bridges were down near Chauk and Yenangyaung and that we would be crossing sand streams at those places and that there were already several stalled vehicles in the sand streams and we were to be very careful. Dempsey and I agreed that we would wait for each other before we cross the sand streams and that only one car would cross at a time. Our progress was slow as there were army vehicles moving in both directions and there were potholes we had to look out for. We had never driven on this stretch of highway before. There were no maps and no street signs. We must have driven for at least five hours when we reached a spot where there was a makeshift barrier on the road. Was this where the bridge was down where we were to cross the first sand stream, I wondered. I looked back but saw no sign of the Graham Page.

Dad suggested that I turn back. After we drove back a couple of miles we spotted the Graham Page but no sign of Dempsey. Dad asked me to turnaround and pull alongside. As I pulled alongside I noticed that Dempsey was sitting on the running board on the blind side holding his Winchester at the ready and facing a crowd of about twenty men or so about forty feet away. As I pulled up Dempsey quickly got into the passenger seat beside me and sighed, "The fan belt broke. I was scared the men would jump me. I thought you'd never come back."
Dad then called out to the group of men in Burmese, "Help yourselves to whatever is in the car."
"Dad," I said, "What about the sardines and corned beef in the Graham Page. Aren't we keeping them?"
"Yes, I forgot," Dad replied. "Well, let the rascals have them all."

I drove back to the place where the road barrier was and saw a track leading off the road. I followed it until I got to what looked like a stream but it was absolutely dry. Then we saw a group of about ten men walking towards us from the opposite side of the stream bed. I was going to drive across but Dad told me not to. He waited for the men to get close, then called out to them, "Can you men push us across the sand stream?"
"That's what we've been doing all morning for other cars" one of them replied.
"We just got a car across. It will cost you twenty rupees," said another.

"Put your gear in low and move very slowly and don't stop," instructed a man who looked like the leader.

"Let me drive," Dempsey told me. I got out of the car and went round to the passenger side as Dempsey moved over to the driver's seat.

"You can drive slowly now," said the man.

Dempsey drove very slowly in low gear as the men pushed. Every time the rear wheel dug into the sand the men lifted the car out of the sand. The stream was only about thirty to forty feet wide and we made it across in no time. Dad gave the leader twenty rupees and they walked away as Dempsey drove off. After an hour or so we came to a place where the bridge had obviously been destroyed by a bomb. There was no road barrier this time but we could see the twisted bridge. There was a track leading off the main road and Dempsey drove slowly along the track. There was a car ahead of us with four or five passengers. The driver was on the ground studying the wide sand stream. There were at least ten, perhaps more vehicles - army trucks, jeeps, private cars and a bus - all stuck and abandoned in the sand. The driver of the other car told Dempsey that he was going ahead and told Dempsey to follow him but to avoid the exact same track that he made so that the wheels would not sink into the sand. "Drive in first and drive very slowly," he cautioned as he went back to his car. This stream was wide - about 150 to 200 feet at least. The driver of the other car obviously knew what he was doing. He studied the stream with it's debris and he drove in as straight a line as he could between the wrecks and made it safely to the other side. We were still about 100 feet behind him and wondered if we could make it the rest of the way. The other driver got out of his car and quickly ran back towards us and started to guide Dempsey the final 80 feet or so. Dempsey made it across, then thanked the man and drove off.

We were now approaching Yenanchaung the oil town of Burma with it's backdrop of oil derricks against the skyline. Soon we got to a busy part of the town with tea shops and restaurants most of which however were closed. It was beginning to get dark and we needed to stop for the night. Dad knew a friend but he did not have his address so he asked Dempsey to pull over near a group of men talking by the road side. He got off the car to talk to the men. He got no help there. He went on to ask others at a nearby a tea shop. Dad came back to the car with a young man following him. He got back into the car and asked the young man to get in. The young man directed Dempsey to his house several blocks away. The house belonged to the young man's uncle, Gibson, the friend Dad was looking for. Dad told his friend later in the evening devotion that he was silently praying all the way knowing we'd have to stop for the night somewhere and asked God to lead him to his friend's house.

Several days earlier Gibson had sent his women folks to Bhamo in Upper Burma in the Kachin State in the north. His nephew, the young man who brought us to the house, prepared dinner for us. We had a good rest and slept well after a rather tedious eight or nine hours' drive. We were told that the next day the oil wells would be blown up. When we left at around 9 a.m. the next morning the derricks were still standing. We arrived at Mandalay sometime after noon and since we knew the city well Dempsey drove straight to the Agricultural Department and to Uncle Albert house. When we got to the house we found it locked. We walked around the house but saw no one. Then out of nowhere a man came out. It was the care taker for the staff houses on the campus. He said Uncle Albert had left a note inside the house. He opened the door for us, picked up the note from the table and gave it to Dad. .

"Dear Ko Zan," (Brother Zan) the note read, *"We have to move while it's still easy for us to do so because I have fifteen people to take care of. It will be next to impossible if we have to wait any longer. You and your two sons will have little difficulty. The only choice we have now is Katha and you'll know how to get there."*

CHAPTER 5

THE BOMBING OF MANDALAY

IT WAS APRIL, 1942, AND the sun was hot. Good Friday was just a few days away. Dad wanted to stay around a while looking for the best way to get to Katha. While he and Dempsey were looking for a passage to take us to Katha I was visiting friends. Then on Good Friday, while Dad and Dempsey decided to take a rest and stay home I decided to visit Uncle Earnest, a cousin of Mom, who was a foreman at the railway yard. I took Uncle Albert's old bike and went to the railway quarters where Uncle Earnest lived. But when I got to the house, Kyin Yone, Uncle Earnest's wife, was not home. But there were guests in the house. It was a family trying to evacuate to Bahmo. The guest, Mrs. Kywe, whom I knew, was waiting for passage for her family of eight. She told me that she lost her husband some time ago and was struggling to raise her family of six children. The older girls were already in their teens and they were getting ready to go into the city for Good Friday shopping spree.

Just as they were leaving the house I heard the familiar drones of Japanese bombers. I looked up the sky and saw the unmistakable formation of Japanese bombers gleaming bright in the sum and I shouted to every one to get into the trench. I grabbed hold of Mrs. Kywe and dragged her and her younger sons into the trench. But the girls did not believe me and kept on walking. Then came loud rattles and shrill whistles as the bombs raced to their targets. In only a few more seconds there were ear splitting explosions all around us. Hundreds of bombs must have been dropped. Fortunately by the time the first bombs dropped the girls just managed to reach the trench unscathed but crying hysterically and praying aloud as I helped them into the trench. The explosioins around us and around the city lasted several minutes. Then all was quiet except the sounds of people crying and yelling outside.Then Mrs. Kywe cried out, "My baby, my baby. She's still in the house."

I got out of the trench and jumped over Uncle Albert's twisted bike and almost landed on a bloodied body next to it. I ran up the house which was already ablaze and found the nanny with the year old baby crouched in the far corner of the bedroom. I dragged them out and pulled them into the trench. As I jumped in after them into the trench I noticed that there were several bodies lying a few feet from the trench. I could hear people crying and yelling.

"My money bag is in the sitting room," Mrs. Kywe cried out to me. "Please get my money bag. It's hanging on the wall in the sitting room."

Out of the trench I went again and up the house and looked into the sitting room. Part of the sitting room was already on fire. I saw the bag hanging on the wall in the opposite corner from the fire but it was too hot to go in. I looked around and saw a bamboo pole by the verandah. I grabbed it and tried to reach the bag with it. The bag was hanging on a nail and it took me a while before I could maneuver the bag off the nail and onto the bamboo pole. Then I raised the bamboo pole and shook it to let the bag slide down into my hand. I took a quick look into the bedroom which was also burning now and saw a suitcase which I quickly picked up and took with me into the trench.

The bombing seemed to have stopped and I stood up to take a quick look. There was utter mayhem with people running, shouting, crying and screaming. It was total chaos. Inside the trench the girls were still crying and praying aloud. I told them to expect another wave of bombing and to pray to God not to let our trench get hit. They prayed aloud crying at the same time. The second wave did come and this time it was much worse, with a lot more explosions which seemed to be concentrated at the railway yard which was just across the main road from where we were. There were so many people out in the open running in every direction searching and calling out for their children or loved ones that I knew the casualty would be very heavy. I can remember the next bomb that dropped. The explosion was very loud, like a very loud clap of thunder, only much louder. It was so close and the jolt so violent that we thought the trench was hit. We ran our hands over our bodies to see if there was blood. After a short while I stood up and took a look again outside the trench. The scene was unbelievable. There were bodies all over on the ground before me, the dead and the wounded. Scores of men and women were crying and running in panic in every direction, screaming and calling out names.

Then I saw it. We had to get out of here. It's tail was sticking grotesquely out of the ground at an angle, less than ten feet from our trench. It could go off at any time. It was either a time bomb or a dud.

"Listen to me, every one," I yelled into the trench. The house fifteen feet away, was now burning furiously and the bomb only ten feet or so from the trench could explode at any moment. We would all be buried alive if it exploded. We couldn't take any chances.

"Listen carefully," I yelled again into the trench. "Every body follow me. Hold on tight to each other and do not let go. Do not get separated. Just follow me." I had no idea where I was taking them but I silently prayed, "God, take us out of here to a safe place." I didn't bother to pick up the suit case I had brought into the trench. Our lives were more important. We were literally stepping over wounded men and women and dead bodies after we made our way out of the trench. It was also difficult for us to keep together because every so often someone would be running right through our group and for a moment we would get separated. As soon as we could get back together we had to count our numbers, which was nine, or call out names to make sure every one was accounted for. Men and women were running in every direction, crying, screaming and yelling in search of a child or other loved ones as we moved through a mass of people in panic. We must have walked in this manner for about half a mile. There was a sea of frightened crying people all around us all walking or running away from the place that had just been bombed. I held Mrs. Kywe's hand tight as we moved with the crowd. I could feel that she was getting tired and began to slow down and maybe about ready to pass out. Just at that moment I saw a *zayat* by the main road. It was a resting place donated by someone for travelers to rest or take shelter from the sun and rain. No one was looking for a place to take a rest at this time so the *zayat* was empty. I led my group to the *zayat* and told them that I would be back and that under no circumstance must they leave the *zayat* as it would otherwise be absolutely impossible for me to find them. I took a quick look behind me and saw that the city was burning in several places. The railway yard, a half mile down the road across the main road was in flames. I immediately thought of Uncle Ernest who would be at work and said a quick prayer for him and I also prayed for his wife, Kyin Yone. Then I started to run towards the College which by now was just about a mile away.

When I got home I saw Dempsey at the porch waiting for me.

"Are you all right, Penn?" he shouted.

"Yes I'm all right. But I have to go back and pick up a family. Mrs. Kywe and her family are at the *zayat,* the one just before you get to the railway yard. Get the car."

"You stay back. I'll go get them. Tell me again where they are."

I told him and he ran to the car and took off to look for the Kywes.

Dad was just coming out of the house as I got in.

"Where were you? Are you alright?" he asked me.

I told him I was at Uncle Ernest's house.

"Did you see Kyin Yone?" he asked.

"No, she was not home. She was visiting somewhere in the city," I replied. "But U Kywe's wife and family were at the house. I took them out of the house because the house was hit and is on fire right now."

"Did you see your Uncle Ernest?"

"No Dad, he must be at work at the railway yard."

"Where were the bombings, do you know?"

"The railway yard got bombed heavily, Dad. Bombs exploded all around us. Uncle Earnest's house was burning when we left the house."

"You said U Kywe's family was there. Where are they now?

"I left them at a *zayat* and Dempsey has gone to pick them up."

Dad retreated into the bed room to pray for Uncle Earnest and Kyin Yone. I walked quietly into the room and sat beside him on the bed and he started to pray aloud so I could hear. He also prayed that we would be able to make the trip to Katha to join the rest of the family.

As we walked out to the porch we saw Dempsey turning into the driveway with a load of eight passengers. Dempsey unloaded his passengers and was now on a mission. He asked me to go with him to look for Uncle Ernest and Kyin Yone. So we left for the city once more. As we approached the city we could see the devastation as far as the eye could see. Fire was burning all over the city. Dead bodies and the wounded were everywhere. The sheds and buildings in the railway yard was burning furiously spewing thick black smoke and orange flame a hundred feet into the sky. Uncle Earnest's house was now only a pile of burning ember. I didn't see the tail of the bomb any more. It must have exploded. It was almost impossible to go on with bodies lying in the streets and the wounded struggling along the roads to try to get home or get to the hospitals. Hundreds of others ran up and down the streets calling out names of their children or spouses, their faces contorted by fear and anger. There were other vehicles trying to get through the streets dodging debris and maneuvering between dead bodies. We just couldn't believe the carnage we were looking at.

"It's no use," Dempsey said. "We will never know where to find them. You stay here. I'll go to the yard to see if I can find out anything." He got out of the car and I slid into the driver's side and waited for him as he went to search for Uncle Earnest. During that time I observed so much anger, despair, and grief on the faces of people, many bloodied, crying or moaning, walking past the car. Some even stopped to ask whether I'd seen their sister or mother describing what they looked like or what they were wearing. A few looked up to the skiy and swore at the Japanese. It was heart breaking. Dempsey came back after a half hour.

"I know where his workshop is but it's in flame. I walked all round the buildings, and the fire is too hot." he said. "There are dead bodies all over the yard. Men are picking up the bodies and placing them into a truck. I looked at the dead bodies but none of them looked like Uncle Earnest. Let's go back." His face was black with soot.

When we got back to the house we found Mrs. Kywe and her two older daughters busy cooking out of whatever they could lay their hands on in the kitchen. The poor family lost everything except the clothes they were wearing and of course the bag of money I retrieved. Thank the Lord that I managed to recover her money bag from the burning house. I wish I had picked up the suitcase as we left the trench.

We had just started to have dinner when we heard someone crying aloud on the porch. It was Kyin Yone. She told us between sobs that Uncle Earnest was killed in the bombing. She had her seven year old son Jesse with her. The boy kept saying, "Mummy, please don't cry." It was heart breaking to hear the boy pleading with the mother not to cry. Mrs. Kywe went to comfort Kyin Yone as best she could as she herself was also crying. Dad called everybody together and he had a short devotion. He read from Psalm 23 and said a prayer for all concerned and especially for Kyin Yone. Later we huddled around the dining table again to finish our dinner then we retired for the night. We let Mrs Kywe and Kyin Yone and Jesse sleep in one bed room and Dad and the two of us slept in the other bed room. The rest slept on the hard floor in the living room. The crying went on all night and by morning when we were all awake Kyin Yone was soundly asleep.

Dad and Dempsey left early for the general hospital morgue to find out if Uncle Earnest's body would be there and to claim it for burial. Fortunately the hospital was spared and Uncle Earnest's body was there in the morgue. They managed to buy a coffin. It took them a while to find a priest to conduct the burial ceremony. Finally they found a Karen pastor who lived near the railway yard. The pastor's house escaped the bombing but it completely burned down in the ensuing fire during the night. He was planning to leave Mandalay on the day of the bombing and move into a village outside the city. He managed to save a few possessions but lost everything else he had. Thank God his family was safe. After the burial Dad and Dempsey came back to the house and we discussed our next move. We decided to get the next available transport to get to Katha. Dad told the care taker that the Kywe family and Kyin Yone would remain at the house for a few days until they could leave. He left some money with the care taker for food for the Kywe family, Kyin Yone and for the care taker himself.

We loaded our luggage into the car and drove to the jetty the next morning to try to catch a steamer for Katha and we found one. But it was a private steamer belonging to a match company and it had a fully loaded barge tied alongside. The steamer was already full of passengers to capacity. All passengers were evacuating to Katha. From there some would make their way overland across the Chin Hills and to India. We went on board. Dad talked to the Captain who said he had been waiting three days for order from his company but had heard nothing. Dad was still a civil officer and as such had authority to commandeer a vehicle or steamer for official use in an emergency. So Dad showed the Captain his credential and said the steamer was now commandeered. All the six first class cabins were vacant. So we unloaded our suit cases from the car and took them up to the steamer. The care taker came along with us to the jetty. Dad gave him the key to the car and asked him to take the car back to Uncle Albert's house and told him he could use it. But the care taker did not know how to drive. He told Dad that he would just leave the car where it was and return to the campus. An hour later we were steaming up the Irrawaddy river on our way to join the family in Katha.

We would be traveling upstream all the way. The fully loaded double decked steamer with a barge tied to it's side naturally made very slow progress. Dad arranged with the captain for the crew's cook to serve us meals because we could not bring any food with us. So we had meals served us three times a day. On the second day at about noon time there was a lot of commotion. Women were screaming, kids were crying and men were shouting on the decks, crouching and taking cover. Then we heard the plane. We ran back into our cabins and took cover. For several minutes nothing happened. Then Dempsey looked out and saw the plane turn back. He watched to see the plane return and make a second pass over the steamer and then it flew away. We did not know whether it was a Japanese plane or a friendly plane. We brought books and magazines along so throughout the next two days we did a lot of reading. The rest of the trip was uneventful and unexciting. There was nothing to do but read and re-read the books we brought with us.

CHAPTER 6

THE BATTLE FOR KATHA

WE ARRIVED AT KATHA AT about ten in the morning of the third day. We waited for all the passengers to get off the steamer before we disembarked. The town seemed deserted. There were no coolies and passengers were carrying their own bags and luggage. Some just sat on their luggage apparently not knowing where to go. We had three suitcases and three guns between the three of us but Dad was never one for carrying anything except a gun. He was so used to others carrying things for him that Dempsey and I had to take turn carrying an extra suit case. Like some of the other passengers we didn't know where to go either, so we piled our suit cases across the street from the jetty and sat on them in the hot sun.

We could see that Dad was silently praying. A while later a man approached us and asked Dad where we wanted to go. Dad told him he wanted to go to the government quarters. The man offered to take us there. He picked up Dad's suitcase and took the 405 from Dad and slung it over his shoulder. We followed the man for about a half mile and then we saw the government buildings looming before us half a mile away. When we reached the houses we could see that they were all unoccupied. We stopped at the first house and put our suit cases down on the porch. Dad and the man walked around the back of the houses to see if any care taker was around. In the servant quarters of the third house they saw a woman washing clothes at the tap. The woman told Dad that her husband was the care taker but he was away. Then she asked Dad if he was looking for a family with lots of women and an elderly couple. When Dad told her that he was, she got up and headed to the second house, opened the door and went inside. There was a letter left by Uncle Albert giving direction to Zayitchaung, a village where he and the family had gone to. Dad asked the man who brought us if he knew where the place was. The man said he did. As we followed him he told Dad that the town of Katha was almost completely deserted and houses and shops were being looted at that very moment. All government officials including the police had left town and thugs were running wild in the market square. He said he himself came into town to loot but it turned him off when he saw the actual looting and looters fighting among themselves over the loot. He was walking away to return to his village when he saw us at the jetty. He told Dad that we were going into a good village. There were many Christians there, he told Dad, and they would take good care of us.

"There is the village, Zayitchaung," he pointed towards a bamboo grove and tall trees. The first building we came to was the village Baptist church built on stilts. Behind the church was an unfinished house also on stilts but it had no walls.

"They're here, they're hear," Audrey screamed and came running to give Dad a big hug. Then the whole clan appeared from everywhere with everyone screaming and asking questions. "Just in time for lunch," shouted Mom from her cooking pit. "We're cooking wild boar meat for lunch," and she came over to meet us. It was a noisy reunion. The house that Uncle Albert built could not be completed because materials were no more available since the only lumber yard in town had burned down. The roof was up but there were no walls. However it was enough to shelter the family from sun and rain. Cooking was done out doors with a pit dug for fire and stones were used to set pots on. Dad thanked the man who brought us and gave him some money.

"Clang, clang, clang, clang." Grandpa was beating on an empty cooking pot. Grandma didn't allow him to bring his gong. So he had to use the pot to gather the clan for devotion. It was noon and time for devotion. Everyone was quiet now. We all knew what was coming.

"Time, to praise the Lord. Everyone, come into the house. We must thank the Lord for taking care of us. The end of the world is near. We must be prepared. Christ will be returning any time now. Let us prepare ourselves to meet the Lord when He comes," Grandpa shouted at the top of his voice. Having said that, he retreated into the open house, and went for his bible. We marched up the house and sat cross legged on the floor in semi circle. There were no partitions, only a wide open floor. The younger ones passed the hymnals around and Grandpa began the devotion. After devotion we came down for lunch. There were no tables or chairs. We just held our aluminum plates and walked around as we ate and talked. There was a lot of catching up to do for everybody. We were so noisy that some neighbors came round to see what was going on. Then there were introductions and more talk as neighbors asked us if we knew of their relatives and friends in parts of the country where we came through. There was little we could share but we got to know the neighbors. There was a doctor, Dr. San Khin, who was the Chief Medical Doctor of Katha General Hospital. He became a good friend of Uncle Albert and the two had gone hunting together in the nearby forest and they had bagged deer and other small games. A few days earlier they got a good sized wild boar whose meat Mom was cooking now.

Zayitchaung was a small village outside of Katha consisting of mostly Karen Christians. Uncle Albert was allowed to build a house next to the church. While Dad moved into the house with the rest of the family, Dempsey and I opted to make the ground floor of the church our living quarters. We managed to collect some scrap wood and built ourselves a cot each. Dad and Uncle Albert went hunting almost everyday mostly feather games like wild fowl and pheasant which provide us with decent meals every day. Dr. San Khin joined them on weekends. While hunting, Dad and Uncle Albert ventured far beyond the nearby forest and walked into another village, named Bawma, where they became friends with the village chief. It was a large village of ethnic Chinese Shan (Shan-Tayoke). The village with over fifty homes was some four miles north of Zayitchaung. By now Dad and Uncle Albert knew their way in and out and around the forest between the two villages like their own backyard.

About ten days or so after our arrival at Zayitchaung we noticed that groups of refugees, eight to twelve or more to a group, were walking behind the village and into the wood. We found out by talking to some of them later that they were trekking to India. Most of these refugees were Anglo Indian or Anglo Burmese. They were afraid of imprisonment or mistreatment by the Japanese because of their British link. There was a perpetual stream of refugees everyday and where they came from we never knew. One day as Dempsey and I were watching, there was a commotion among a group that was approaching. Men and women were yelling and a child was screaming. When all calmed down and the group moved on we saw a two year old baby with blond hair sitting on the roadside crying his heart out. In front of him on the ground was a tin plate with some rice and a small cup of water. We watched for a while to see if someone would come back and pick the child up. No one did. The group disappeared into the wood behind the village. Should we take the baby home, I wondered aloud. Dempsey said to wait because some one else might pick him up. He thought the kid was a little brat and the family was better off trekking to India without the burden of a stubborn kid on their hands. Each day the volume of refugees grew. It was like a perpetual march of two or three abreast, all of them carrying only light items. How many of them would reach India and how many would perish on the way was anybody's guess. Before they even reached the Chin Hills, a very high mountain range, they still had to cross the Chindwin river. We walked home silently. As we neared home there was a series of explosions in the direction of the jetty. Only then we heard the unmistakable high pitched roar of Japanese bombers. There was nothing more to bomb and still the Japanese were dropping bombs.

When we got home we found no one. "Where's everybody?" Dempsey shouted.
"Get in the trench quick," Nita yelled at us from inside the trench. Dad and Uncle Albert were out hunting so there were only the women, Uncle Albert's four kids and Grandpa and Grandma in the trench.
"The planes have gone. Come out of the trench," Dempsey called back. This was the girls' first experience with an air raid. They refused to come out of the trench. We walked over to the trench and sat down at the entrance and told them they could come out now. Grandpa was the first to come out against Grandma's protest. Then slowly the rest came out one by one. They all seemed shaken, except Grandpa who started singing, at the top of his voice, "Glory, glory Hallelujah" as he climbed up the stairs and walked into the house.

Every day after that we would all leave for the forest early in the morning because Dad said he did not trust the Japanese who were capable of doing anything to create panic among the population. He said Japanese planes could strafe the village or even drop bombs. We each carried with us some supplies for cooking and also materials we needed to while away our time like playing cards, books and games. Dad and Uncle Albert took us to a part of the forest two miles away where there was a dried up narrow stream with very high banks where we could take cover if it became necessary. After the girls cooked and we had had our meals, we would play cards, read or sleep under the trees. We would come back to the village about three in the afternoon and have dinner around six. It was like a picnic and it was fun. We looked forward to it everyday because it was a pleasant diversion.

One day a couple of weeks later, after we got back from the forest around four in the afternoon we could hear the planes. There was nothing more to bomb in Katha. Perhaps the planes were just on a reconnaissance flight, we thought. But the next moment we heard bombs falling as they screamed toward their targets. Everyone ran into the trench. The explosions were in the direction of the town. But then we heard a couple explosions in the direction of the waterfront near the hospital. When it was all over Dempsey and I came out of the trench and saw smoke and flame rising high into the afternoon skies over the town. From the church we could see the general hospital which was less than half mile away near the bank of the river. Smoke was rising on the water front beyond the hospital. A half hour later the rest of the family came out of the trench. After dinner Dempsey and I started towards town just to look around and see where the bombs dropped. But when we got near the hospital we saw scores of people making their way to the hospital. Some were being helped or carried while others, bloodied and maimed, tried to crawl toward the hospital. Many, unable to make progress, just remained by the roadside asking us for help to get them to the hospital. We decided to go the hospital instead. We saw people dead or unconscious on the hospital steps and along the corridor. There was blood all over the floor. We had to watch where we were stepping. Someone grabbed my leg. He was lying on the floor in the corridor. "Please give me a cigarette," he begged, "I need to have a smoke before I die." Another was pleading with us to go and tell his mother that her son was dying. Still another asked for water.

"We need help. Come on in," a nurse cried out to us. We walked in and saw Dr. San Khin in a ward working over a woman who had a long piece of shrapnel lodged in her thigh.

"Go help," I told Dempsey because I knew I couldn't take it. There was a big gash on the woman's thigh with a piece of metal protruding. I quickly turned away as Dempsey went to give a hand. Just then another nurse came and pulled me away to a cot where an Indian woman was lying. The woman was crying in pain. One quick look and I saw that the lower part of her left arm was almost severed from the upper arm at the elbow. "Hold on to her upper arm," ordered the nurse. I did and looked away. I had no gloves. There was a scream from Dempsey's patient. While I was still trying to adjust my grip, Dr San Khin came over and examined my patient's arm. He yelled out something to the nurse. She came back with some instrument that looked like a small saw. Dr. San Khin started working on the woman's arm as she screamed. I turned away so I couldn't see him cut the arm off. Then the nurse applied some yellow liquid to the stub and put a lot of gauze and a tight bandage on the stub. I had a hard time trying to keep the woman's arm still so the nurse could bandage. After much screaming the woman passed out. Obviously there were no anesthetics to numb the pain. The stub kept moving up and down and rotating although the woman was totally unconscious. Dempsey was now at another cot with Dr. San Khin and another nurse. A nurse called me to go with her to a storage room to get something. When we got near the room at the end of the long corridor we saw that the wall of the adjacent room and part of the wall of the storage room was on fire.

"Tell the doctor I have gone home," she yelled, "and tell him to leave right away. The place will blow up in another ten minutes"

"But you can't leave your patients," I yelled at her.

"You have to leave too. The store room will blow up soon. Go tell the doctor and get out!" she yelled, then ran down the steps and disappeared around the corner.

I raced back to the wards and saw Dr. San Khin busily working on another patient with Dempsey and a nurse. I told the doctor that the other nurse had left and that the storage room and the room next to it were on fire.

"O my God," he cried out aloud.

Then with a wave of his hand he yelled at us and the nurse, "Get out of here, all of you. Get out of here quick."

"What about you?" the nurse asked

"I'll be all right. You go. All of you go. Get out now," he yelled.

We left. The nurse was crying as she walked away with us. She was quickly joined by two other nurses. They all lived in the same village where we were staying.

"I'm not crying because I'm afraid," the nurse told us as she sobbed, "I cry for the poor patients. They will all be burned alive and there is nothing we can do. We just received a large shipment of spirits for the army's medical unit in several drums and they're in the storage room. And one army officer left two large drums of petrol in spite of our protests."

She then ran back all the way to the village followed by her two friends. Our hands were bloodied, so were our clothes. We threw away our clothes and had a good bath when we got home. But even before we finished our bath we heard Audrey yelling, "The hospital is on fire." We quickly ran out and saw the hospital engulfed in flames. A half hour later a man slowly walked by with his head bent low, his hunched shoulders shaking in spasms. Dr. San Khin had to leave his patients to die after all the hard work he had done to save their lives. Dempsey walked over and placed a hand on the doctor's shoulder and walked him back to his house.

The next day was Sunday. Mom suggested that we stayed put that day to observe the Sabbath and not go to the forest. Dad agreed. The entire village was now deserted and we, and perhaps one or two other families, were the only ones left. The pastor had canceled church meetings until later when things returned to normal. We had no idea where all the villagers went. We were preparing to have church service all by ourselves when a dozen Chinese soldiers came and ordered us to leave right away. They looked crude and were very aggressive.
"Go now. Go now," shouted one who looked like an officer.
Mom smiled and walked up to the officer and tried to tell him that we were going to worship in the church and would leave after worship.
"No, No. You go now," he yelled at Mom.
"You got gun?" he asked.
I hid my shot gun and Dad's rifle up in the church. Not wanting to get into trouble with the Chinese I signaled to a soldier to follow me up the stairs. I showed him the guns and a couple of army socks full of .303 ammunition. He looked very pleased and took the guns. He didn't bother to search the church. Dad tried to tell the officer as best he could that we wanted to take provisions with us. He seemed to understand and allowed us time to get our stuffs together. The girls had everything prepared every night for our trip to the forest the next day so it didn't take us long to get our things together. So off we marched out carrying our own stuffs as usual. We did not see a soul as we walked through the village. Dempsey and I walked with Grandma and Grandpa because they needed help over stones and uneven ground. Naturally they were very slow and soon we lost sight of those ahead of us. Grandma seemed to be a lot weaker as she insisted on taking a short rest every few minutes. Soon she was taking longer rests. She had a hard time getting up each time. We encouraged her to take as long as she needed to get rested before she continued to walk.
"If you can't walk any more, I'll stay with you," Grandpa told Grandma. "God is with us. He will take care of us."

At that moment we saw a family of three coming from the direction of the village. They were one of two families who stayed back. They were Karen, a father, a mother, and a teen aged daughter. They stopped to talk with us and told us that Chinese soldiers ordered them out and did not allow them to take away anything with them. As they were leaving the soldiers ransacked their house and shot and killed their pigs and dogs. They were still relating their story when another family, a woman and three boys, came running toward us, all crying hysterically. They had also been ordered by the Chinese soldiers to leave without taking anything with them but the husband tried to take a package with him. The soldiers checked the package and found a gun in it. They shot him dead on the spot. The woman was sobbing uncontrollably. She told us between sobs that she had to leave her husband's body because she did not want the soldiers to hurt her three young boys as they were the only things she had left. Grandpa prayed for them. Dempsey and I were silent.

"I cannot continue anymore," Grandma told us. "I'll just stay here with your Grandpa"

"You can't do that, Grandma," Dempsey told her, "we don't know what's going to happen now. We've got to catch up with the family."

"We'll have to join the family and stay together, Grandma," I said.

"We'll wait till you get rested, Grandma," Dempsey told her. "Take your time. We'll wait for you."

"No, no. I know I cannot walk another step," Grandma replied. "You two go ahead and I'll stay here with your Grandpa."

"What's wrong, Grandma? You walked every morning into the forest with us before," Dempsey told her.

"I know," she replied, "I just can't do it now and I just don't know why."

"Dempsey," Grandpa said, "go and look around for a place we can rest comfortably," Grandpa told Dempsey.

"Yes, Grandpa," Dempsey said and went off.

The man who came out from the village followed him. Meantime Grandma was consoling the woman who lost her husband telling her to take strength in the Lord, that she still had her three boys to take care of and to remain strong for them. Twenty minutes later Dempsey and the man came back. They found a shallow ditch between two bamboo groves with a bed of bamboo leaves and lots of shade. We led Grandma and Grandpa slowly to the spot and noticed that the new families followed us too. The man told Dempsey that he would remain with our grand parents and take care of them since he knew we had to join the rest of our family further up the forest. The woman who lost her husband also asked to stay with them.

"God bless you. God bless you. Come back and check on us later," Grandpa told us.

When we got to our hideout the girls had finished cooking and everybody already had had their lunch. Uncle Albert and Aunty Hta were playing cards. Uncle Albert's children were talking among themselves and laughing. It was just another day of picnic. Since everybody had eaten Dempsey collected leftovers, while I got some crackers from our supplies and some water and we rushed back to where we had left our grand parents. Dempsey and I did not get a chance to eat at all. It was just as well because now our grand parents had a sizable family with them and they could share the food with them. When we got back to our own hide out the girls had finished cleaning up. Some of us had started to read or play cards or just relaxed.

Then all hell broke loose as machine gun fire reverberated throughout the forest, burst after burst after burst. Everyone rushed into the gully for cover leaving everything behind. The firing was not random. Whoever they were, they appeared to know where their adversary was because their firing was directed at a target that responded in kind. The exchange of fire continued with more intensity during the next couple of hours. We were right in the middle of the two fighting forces and the gully was certainly a God given shelter. A couple of hours later mortar fires were now added to the exchanges with both sides lobbing shells at each other's position. We were all praying hard throughout the exchange that the shell wouldn't fall short and hit our gully. The breaking of a twig or crushing of a dried leaf would immediately invite machine gun fire in our direction. We had to keep very still and not make any kind of sound.

The sun began to set and naturally in the thick forest it got dark early. As we looked up in the darkening daylight we could see tracers as bullets raced back and forth. Sometimes shots hit tree trunks or rocks and ricocheted with ear splitting twang that echoed throughout the forest. Our gully seemed to be the dividing line between the two forces. The firing became consistent and intense as it turned totally dark. Uncle Albert's year old daughter, June, cried for water and we tried to hush her. But then we noticed that every time she started to cry the firing around us stopped. Later, whenever gun fire came close someone would pinch the child to make her cry so the firing would stop. At times we could hear thumping of heavy boots just above us, and conversations going on in a language we did not understand. We tried to stay as quiet as we could, suppressing our coughs and sneezes and only talking in whispers. No one was able to sleep all night. After midnight the exchanges became even more intense. Mortar fires were like a round every couple of minutes for the next two hours or so. We were hoping that there would be no hand to hand fight. After about two hours the firing became more sporadic and seemed to move further and further away to the south. By now it was about three in the morning and we were all tired and fell asleep.

"Wake up, wake up," a voice called out in Burmese. "The Japanese masters are here. You can come out of your hiding place."

We looked up to see several men in uniform staring down at us. A few of them were obviously Burmese.

"Burma has now been liberated by our Japanese masters. You have nothing to fear from the English now. Come out of there and you may go wherever you wish. The Japanese masters are your protectors now. Come out."

We climbed out of the gully. The Japanese officer shook hands with Dad and Uncle Albert and with a wave of their hands left us.

"Where do we go now?" Mom asked.

"I don't know." Dad answered. "What do you think, Albert, if we go on to Bawma instead of going back to Zayitchaung?"

"Good idea," Uncle Albert answered. "The headman can take care of our folks."

"It's only about a mile and a half from here," Dad said.

Then Dad turned to Dempsey and said," Go check on your grand parents and see if they are alright. See if you can take them to Bawma, or make some arrangement for them to join us."

"Yes, Dad," Dempsey answered and went off to look for Grandpa and Grandma.

We trudged behind Dad and Uncle Albert toward Bawma. Each of us managed to collect bits and pieces of our belongings and within an hour reached Bawma and were warmly welcomed by the village headman. He moved his family somewhere else and let our family have the whole house. Except for the headman's house, which stood about three feet above ground, all other houses were built on stilts about seven feet above ground. As we arrived we saw that all houses had refugees under them, mostly families of Karen soldiers who left their wives and children to trek to India along with British and Indian troops. Some soldiers deserted and remained to take care of their families and families of their buddies. We also saw some villagers from Zayitchaung. Later in the afternoon we saw Dempsey entering the village ever so slowly with Grandpa and Grandma. There was also a man and a woman and their teen aged daughter who were helping them. But the woman with three sons was not with them. I ran over and helped escort Grandma and Grandpa into the house. They were totally exhausted.

The headman's house couldn't accommodate our entire family. So Dempsey and I had to look for our own place to stay. Dempsey managed to find a crawl space under the floor of the headman's house. He arranged some boards over the mud floor and had less than three feet of clearance to the floor above. It gave him a floor space of about three feet by six feet and he was very happy with it. I was not so lucky. I went to the next house but the ground under that house was practically full of refugees, men women and children. But I saw a spot right in the middle and asked if anyone had that spot. No one knew. I walked over to the other houses all of which had refugees occupying every available space. I managed to get a ground sheet from an ex soldier and went back to the first house and placed it at the empty spot to stake my place for the night. I sat at my newly acquired spot for a while to let everyone know that I was taking that space for the night. I made sure everyone knew I owned that spot. Then I got up and walked over to the headman's house to let the family know where I was staying. The headman's wife cooked for our family and after dinner Dempsey and I walked around to see if we could find anybody we knew among the refugees. We came across two young soldiers and a corporal who said they were from Moulmein. They retreated with the British but decided to desert when they were told that they had to march to India. They would rather return to their villages to see if their families were all right. Since they were from Moulmein Dempsey asked them whether they attended the American Baptist Karen High School there. All of them did and they were students of our older sisters Nita and Louise. So we took them to the headman's house to meet the family. Nita and Louise were very happy to see their old students. While talking to these three young men Dad learned that there was a sergeant among those refugees whose father he knew. One of the boys left to look for the sergeant. After a short while the young man came back with Sergeant Maw Doh who stood to a stiff attention and gave Dad a salute.

"It's good to see you Maw Doh. How are your parents?" Dad asked.

"Well, the last time I saw them they were all right."

"Are they still at the same place or have they gone away anywhere?"

"They didn't evacuate. The British never made a stand there and there was no need for them to evacuate. I saw them briefly as we were retreating. They were all right."

"Maw Doh, I need more men in our group. Can you young men stick around with us in case we need manpower?"

"Sure, Pha Ti. (Pha Ti is uncle in Karen) We are away from our own family so we need a family too."

Now we have four men added to our big family.

As it got dark I returned to my spot under the stilted house next door and found my place still intact. I was proud of my people the Karens. They were honest, friendly and respectful. No one took over my place and I still had a place to sleep that night. My young sister Caroline brought me some dessert. I was tired. So after I ate my food I quickly fell asleep in spite of children crying around me and the constant noise of people talking and laughing. I woke up in the middle of the night. Water was dripping on my chest. I sat up and water was now dripping on my head. No, it was not water. It was warm and smelled of urine. Yes, it was urine. Someone was passing urine upstairs in the house through the crack in the floors straight down on me. No wonder my empty spot was not taken by anybody while I was away. They'd been here under this house a few days and they knew someone or a kid upstairs used the crack in the floor to relieve himself or herself at night. And they didn't tell me. I looked around to yell at somebody, but everyone was sound asleep. I slowly got up, picked up my ground sheet and walked out into the open and headed straight to the village well. I took off my clothes and poured a couple of buckets of water over me. Put my pants back on and washed my shirt and went to Dempsey and told him to move over.

"What's up?" he asked.

I told him. He laughed and moved over for me.

Next morning after breakfast at the headman's house, I walked around the village from house to house looking for a decent place for myself without luck and returned to the headman's house. As I approached the house this time I noticed a shed behind the house with just the roof on four posts and a center post. There were dried and fresh dung all over the dirt floor. I went closer. There was no animal under the shed. There was a board propped up against the loft in the shed. Across the board at intervals of twenty inches or so were slats nailed into the board to provide foothold to climb up to the loft. I went up to the loft and looked around. It was used for storage. There was a hoe, a pick, a couple of shovels, a broom, a couple of wicker baskets and some ropes lying on some loose boards. I tried to shift the boards. They were not nailed down. I rearranged the boards so that I could place the shovels and picks at one end leaving an empty space of about four feet by six feet. But would I like a place above some animal dung? Of course I wouldn't know till I tried. So I decided I would spend that night in the shed to see for myself. That afternoon it was hot and muggy but there was a warm breeze blowing. Surprisingly there was only a very faint odor from the dung and I was sure I could live with that. That night I took up a couple of books and a candle to read but my matches were soggy and didn't light. So I used the books as pillows and soon fell asleep. I must have slept for a few hours but woke up with a start when the shed swayed violently. It was now already dark and I was preparing to jump down. Then I realized that it was an animal rubbing it's neck against the center post. I peered down in the dark saw that it was a huge black buffalo. I went back to sleep.

At about ten the next morning there was a great commotion. Village women were running out of their homes pulling refugee women along with them and ran into the woods. The headman told our family women to do likewise because Japanese soldiers were seen approaching the village. They might take some women back to their barracks as they were known to have done in China. It took only about fifteen minutes for all the women of the village to disappear. The Japanese soldiers did come. There were about ten of them. They wanted to buy chicken from the village. All the men got out of their houses and rounded up their chicken and put them in bamboo baskets. They collected about maybe twenty chickens and gave them to the Japanese. The Japanese officer paid for the chicken in brand new crisp kyats notes, currency issued by the Japanese to replace the rupees used during the British rule. The Japanese left and soon all the women came back to their homes.

That same afternoon while I was talking to Dempsey, we saw young men jumping out of their houses and running to the woods. Dempsey and I did the same but we didn't know what it was all about. I was wondering what we men would be running away from. Dempsey and I climbed up a tree each and peered through the branches. The village was quiet. I wondered where the rest of the men were hiding. After a little while we heard a lot of voices. About fifty men wearing shabby uniforms were entering the village. Obviously they belonged to the Burmese Independent Army, (BIA). We could hear them speak in Burmese. They were very loud. Then they started firing the guns into the air. They were demanding money, as contribution, for their effort in driving the British out and bringing the Japanese masters in for an independent Burma. They were in and out of each house and it was obvious this fund drive was not organized. Many residents later told the headman that their homes were entered more than one time by different groups and when they told them that they just contributed earlier to another group some of the residents were slapped, or were threatened. One man was so scared that he gave all his money to the first group that came and had none left for another group that entered his home later to demanded contribution. He was hit by a rifle butt and when his wife pleaded with the soldiers, she was kicked in the stomach. But when the BIA soldiers came to the headman's house, they did not ask for any contribution. We later learned that we were running away to hide from the BIA which was known to forcefully recruit young men into the new national army under the Japanese. Many refugees moved back to Katha or to the vicinity of Katha after those incidents. It was better, they said, to stay closer to the Japanese where they could be protected than in the countryside where they were open to abuse by their own soldiers.

CHAPTER 7

BACK HOME TO INSEIN

DAD CALLED FOR A MEETING of the family, the four young soldiers who promised to be with us and the village headman. Dad wanted to know what we all wanted to do, stay put for a while or return to Insein. We all wanted to go back to Grandpa's house in Insein, but Dad did not want to work under the Japanese. If he was back in Insein the Japanese army could conscript him to serve under the Japanese civil service. The headman suggested that Dad and Uncle Albert build houses deep in the woods behind Bawma away from sight of the BIA. The soldiers said they would undertake to build the houses from raw materials in the wood. It sounded good to all because some of us were still wary of the Japanese army. We wanted more time to get to know the Japanese better so we could interact with them without getting into trouble. We were also wary of the BIAs after we heard unconfirmed news that some Karen villages and churches in southern Burma were burned down by the BIA who also massacred many Karens in Tennasserim and in the Deltas. It was disturbing news. The BIA was supposedly led by some of the 'Thirty Comrades'. But the fact was this new national army was recruited from riff raffs along the way by the Japanese army and the thirty comrades as they marched into Burma. They were not led by trained officers and were loosely organized. The purpose of creating the BIA was to help chase the British out of Burma. However the British army which included Karen soldiers retreated just ahead of the Japanese as they marched into Burma. Karen soldiers were used by the British to quell national uprisings in the early days and perhaps BIA soldiers were ordered by petty political upstarts to hunt down and kill Karens in revenge. Maybe it was for that reason that Karen villages and churches were burned down by the BIA. Villagers were massacred along the way, in Mergui, Tavoy, Papun and then in the Deltas as the BIA advanced north with

Japanese troops. Many prominent Karen leaders and their families were among those slaughtered. The Karen retaliated just as fiercely and the death toll on both sides of this communal clash was in the thousands before law and order was finally restored by Japanese Colonel Suzuki and BIA's General Auung San. I later learned that a few of my friends were among those executed by the BIA.

Dempsey and I joined the four soldiers cutting down timber from the woods. The woman folks cleared the ground, made roof and wall shingles out of teak leaves, swept the grounds and cooked meals for the men. It took us five days to build three barracks. One barrack was for our family, excluding Dempsey and myself, the second barrack was for Uncle Albert's family and our grand parents and the third barrack was for storage and kitchen and for all the men. We had never imagined a life like that, living in the jungle in makeshift barracks and not knowing what kind of future we would be facing. But looking back now, I don't remember anyone complaining. In fact we seemed to enjoy this new experience in the wilderness. Our only worry was Grandpa. He insisted on having devotions three times a day seven days a week and he wanted to sound his 'gong', and sing at the top of his voice. We were trying to hide from the BIA and did not want to attract attention. He was very angry when we told him not to sing so loud or sound his 'gong'.
"Are you more afraid of those BIA than you are of God Almighty?" he would challenge us.

A couple of weeks after we moved into the hideout in the wood, Mom, and Uncle Albert's children were gathering vegetables and berries in the wood and along the jungle path. Then we heard a thunderous sound of hoofs as horsemen rode down the path. There were about forty BIA soldiers on horseback. They stopped when they saw Mom, and the children.
"Come along with us," the leader ordered and drove Mom and the children slowly in front of them. We could see from the edge of our hide out as they led Mom and the children into the village. When they entered the village they fired several volleys into the air and then as they got off their horses announced that they were there to collect donation. Mom walked into the headman's house, the children following her. She calmly went into the kitchen and went through the motion of preparing a meal. Sergeant Maw Doh called us men for a quick conference. "This is a raid," he told us. "They are robbing the village. We've got to get them when they come out. Get your guns," he ordered. He indicated trees, and

rocks behind which we could take cover to ambush the B.I.A. soldiers as they rode back.

"Get your guns, quick." he ordered.

We ran to where we had hidden our guns. Dempsey and I were given a service rifle each by some soldiers who went back into Katha with their families. We checked our rifles, magazines and made sure everything was working. I took up a position behind a large teak tree with a thick bush just in front of it. Perfect I thought. Here was my chance of getting a BIA soldier. My hands were shaking in excitement and I wondered if I could even shoot straight. Meanwhile, Uncle Albert wrapped a dirty towel on his head and pretended to be one of the villagers and calmly walked into the village and went straight to the headman's house. He took some money with him to 'donate' if demanded. He never caught any attention. The men were entering one house after another, this time in an organized manner. They were not threatening and they were not abusive. Then an officer entered the headman's house and requested donation and as the headman was going to get into the bedroom to get his money, Uncle Albert told the officer, "I am the son. Here is our donation to our great cause."

The officer thanked him and left. Uncle Albert then quickly came back to our camp and saw that we were preparing for an ambush. He asked Maw Doh to call it off.

"We cannot possibly get them all and the survivors will go back and report to their unit. They'll then come and search for us and then we'll have hell to pay. Think of the women, the children and the old folks. Call it off."

We agreed, but at the same time disappointed that we wouldn't be getting back at the B.I.A. for what they had done to the Karens in Lower Burma. Looking back now, I am glad we did not ambush the BIA.

The next morning Dad, Uncle Albert and the headman went into Katha to report the incident to the Japanese authorities. They were gone all day and when they returned in the late afternoon they told us that the Japanese would be sending carts for the women and the old folks to return to Katha. Dad realized that he had no choice but to return to Grandpa's house in Insein. But he still did not want to work for the Japanese. He called Dempsey and me aside and had a serious talk with us.

"You boys know I don't want to work under the Japanese," he told us. "I met the Japanese commander the other day when we went to report on the BIA raid of Bawma. The Japanese seem to be very decent people.

They were polite and paid us a lot of respect. One of them spoke fluent English. I didn't recognize the rank. He could be a colonel. He wanted us to return to where we last served under the British government so that we can help the Japanese administration in the civil service. I think that is a fair expectation. Your Uncle Albert is going back to Mandalay. I told the Japanese officer I would like to go to Insein instead of Prome where I last worked for the British. He said it was all right. So we are going back to Insien. The Japanese army is commandeering a riverboat for us to make the trip. The reason I want to talk to you two boys is this. I've watched the two of you from the time we evacuated from Prome to the present. Both of you are still in your teens but the way you conducted yourselves proved to me that you are both matured and capable of taking care of the family during the Japanese occupation without my help." He paused to see our reaction, then continued, "Now, my question is, can the two of you take care of the family without my help, and if so, will you?"

As there was no response from us, he continued, "I want you to think about it for sometime. If your answer is no, I'll understand. You are both too young for that responsibility."

"I don't know, Dad," I replied.

Dempsey kicked me in the shin.

"Sure Dad, we can do it," Dempsey assured Dad.

"Yes, Dad, we can do it," I echoed.

"Sleep on it," Dad said and he hugged us.

I really didn't know then what Dad wanted of us. Was he sick and couldn't work any more?

"Is Dad sick?" I asked Dempsey later.

"Are you stupid?" Dempsey retorted. I was angry. Dempsey never spoke to me like that. He never called me stupid. Without warning I took a swing at him. He blocked and said, "Sorry."

"You know Dad is trying to make responsible men out of us and wanted to see if we are ready to accept the responsibility."

"Sorry," I replied. "I just lost my temper. You called me stupid."

"I didn't. I just asked if you were stupid."

"It's the same thing," I said, still angry.

"I'm sorry, okay? " he said. "You think you can help take care of the family?" Dempsey asked.

"Sure I can," I replied.

"Then why didn't you say so when he asked us that question?"

"I don't know," I answered. "But I know we can do it."

Dempsey stood up and shook my hand.

The next morning the carts arrived. We loaded the women and the old folks onto the carts and led them back to Zayitchaung. Now Grandpa was free to sing at the top of his voice and he did. As soon as we got back to the village, he had all of us assembled to have a family Thanksgiving devotion. Grandma was feeling a lot stronger after a long rest in our jungle camp in the forest. The town of Katha returned to life as markets and shops reopened and people came back to their houses. Dempsey wanted to know the Japanese better. He said if the Japanese were going to be here for any length of time, we had to know them well so we could get along better with them and stay out of trouble. Dempsey's theory was right because the Japanese appreciated friendly and law abiding people and had no use for unruly and lawless behavior. We discovered that they would treat a decent person with decency and respect but cruelly punish those who break the law. Looters or thieves who were caught were taken to the market square, bound to a lamp post with a placard about their necks which would read, "I am a thief." Or "I am a looter" etc. They were kept out in the market square all day in the hot sun and returned to jail at night.

While we were still waiting for the Japanese Garrison commander to get us a boat to return to Insein Dempsey tried to make friends with some Japanese soldiers and got invited to dinner on occasion, sometimes taking me with him. The Japanese loved to sing and have their 'saki' before and after their meals and on occasion would have girls they brought with them serve them food and 'saki' and sing and dance for them.. I was shocked the first time Dempsey took me to such a dinner at a Japanese mess. To get to the mess hall we had to pass a covered well where Japanese girls were taking their bath all in the nude. And worse, as we passed them, they'd gesture to us to join them or they would sing zesty Japanese songs as they waved at us. Dempsey waved back and walked past them without looking at them and I quickly followed him. The girls yelled, screamed and laughed at us. After we passed them Dempsey told me that they were girls brought by the Japanese army from Manchuria and China to entertain the soldiers. We found out that once you get to know them, the Japanese were very friendly and polite. Yet we also witnessed the Japanese in their worse moods and behavior when they were angry. We heard stories later about people who had problems with the Japanese and about their horrifying experiences at their hands of Japanese soldiers. We were fortunate that those Japanese officers and soldiers whom we came into contact with were decent and friendly and valued our friendship. Once they had accepted you as a friend you could expect to have their respect also.

With the help of the Japanese Garrison Commander Dad finally found a huge river boat to return to Insein, a trip of five nights down the Irrawaddy River and the Hlaing River to Insein. The boat was a real beauty. It was at least forty or maybe forty five feet long with a beam of eight or ten feet. It had a twenty foot long cabin at the quarter deck with a bamboo thatched roof. At the stern was a high chair for the helmsman and forward of the cabin was the cargo hatch. It had one mast on the fore deck for the mainsail.

After breakfast we boarded the boat for our trip home. There was another family of four who were also returning to Insein. The husband was also a civil officer. It was a sunny morning with a cloudless sky. Grandpa and Grandma were anxious to return to see if their house was still standing. Most of us stayed on deck to watch the scene as we sailed past one village after another and waved at the children and women bathing in the river. As we were approaching a large village after a couple of hours, Nita asked the helmsman who was the owner and captain of the boat, to stop so she could buy meat and vegetables to cook lunch. The captain then eased the boat closer to the river bank and maneuvered the boat just beyond a small bamboo pier where women were washing clothes as children, some completely naked, swam or splashed in the water. As the captain brought the boat alongside the bank his deck hand jumped ashore to tie the stern of the boat to a tree stump then came back on board to let down a gang plank. The captain then asked the deck hand to accompany Nita and Audrey and take them to the market place. Meantime venders came from the village to sell snacks and fruits. Mom bought some fruits from one vender. Then the other venders wanted Mom to buy from them too. So Mom bought from each vender a variety of snacks and fruits which would last us the entire trip. After about forty five minutes Nita and Audrey returned with two small baskets of vegetables and meat. The deck hand was behind them carrying a basket containing five or six chicken. We were on our way down river again. There was no breeze at all and the sail was never unfurled. The captain then told the deck hand to do the cooking. However the girls ended up cooking by themselves because of the small area in the galley which was below the rear end of the cabin. We had a spread of delectable dishes as we squatted around the table at lunch time – chicken curry, fish curry, vegetable soup and salad.

After the meal the captain ordered Dempsey and me to wash the dishes, which we did by drawing water from the river. Then he asked us to wash down the deck where Nita, Audrey and the deck hand had left mud stained foot prints. River traffic was almost non existent so the captain took the boat to the middle of the wide river where the current was the strongest. He then signaled to Dempsey to take the helm and showed him how to handle it. Actually there was no need to steer but to keep the boat steady as it drifted down with the current. The captain then went down to the crew's quarter which was below the cabin to have his lunch. He came up to check occasionally to make sure the boat was on course. After a while we saw a motor craft approaching our boat. It had a Japanese flag on it's short flag staff and a soldier was waving. Dempsey called down to the captain to come up. By then the motor boat was maneuvering to come alongside. A Japanese soldier jumped into the boat and secured the craft to let his officer board the boat. The officer came on board and demanded in sketchy Burmese to see all the passengers. Dad came out of the cabin first and bowed Japanese style and offered his hand. They shook hands. The officer asked again that all passengers came out from the cabin. Dad called out to the family inside and one by one they came out but before everyone was out the Japanese soldier looked into the cabin and said something to the officer in Japanese. The officer looked into the cabin and bowed several times towards Grandpa and Grandma. Then he smiled and said something to the soldier who promptly jumped back into his craft. At that time Dad handed a letter to the officer, a letter written by the Garrison commander in Katha. The officer read the letter and returned it to Dad with a smile and said, "Ahmyagyi kaundai" which was Burmese for "Very good". The soldier came back with a small box which the officer took. He then went into the cabin and handed the box to Grandpa. The box contained Japanese cookies called 'mochee', which was sticky rice bun stuffed with sweetened mashed black bean. The Japanese are well known for their respect for the elderly and we were fortunate to have come across some of the better brought up Japanese officers and men during the war. The Japanese officer then shook Dad's hand and the soldier bowed as they left our boat. Dempsey was still at the helm. The captain asked him to hand over the helm to me which Dempsey reluctantly did.

From the high seat of the helmsman the entire scenery was totally different. It was extremely beautiful. I could see a distant village set beyond the lush green rice field in the foreground. Tall coconut palm trees and flame of the forest trees with their bright red leaves and flaming red flowers in and around the village plus the back drop of a blue hill with a white pagoda delicately sitting on top made a spectacular picture no artist could duplicate. Such scenes we saw all the way down the Irrawaddy river. As the sun began to set the scene changed to beautiful auras of colorful cloud formations as hills and trees cast long shadows across the spectrum to display the spectacular beauty of God's creations. Those were some of the moments in my life that I felt very close my creator. I was interrupted in my reverie when the captain asked the deck hand to take over from me so that I could join the family for dinner. We had leftovers for dinner because so much had been prepared for lunch. A light breeze began to blow and the captain ordered the deckhand to unfurl the mainsail as he once again took over the helm. We spent a quiet first night sailing down the river. The only sounds we heard were water lapping against the hulls of the boat and the steady flapping of the sail in the light breeze.

Dawn arrived and we noticed that the river traffic was beginning to become busy with crafts of all descriptions moving in both directions transporting passengers and wares. As we neared Mandalay later in the morning we saw bigger crafts like we were in or even large barges. They were carrying full loads of rice or other goods such as earthen wares, or aluminum wares like pots and pans, woven products and silkware on their way to brokerage houses along the Irrawaddy River front in Mandalay or further downriver to other towns. There were also a few bamboo rafts and rafts of teak logs floating down river on their way to Rangoon or timber mills along the river. There was only a light breeze and the sail flapped above on the main mast when another Japanese craft approached our boat but made no attempt to come alongside. From a distance a soldier, obviously a B.I.A. soldier, speaking in Burmese, called out to ask the captain what he was transporting.
"I am taking government officials and their families back to Insein," he called back.
"Are you carrying any cargo?" the soldier asked. .
"No, only passengers," the captain replied.
"Do you have any arms of any sort?" continued the soldier.
"I don't have any and my passengers don't either," he replied.
Then the soldier waved our boat on. We had a few more checks the rest of our way.

As we approached Mandalay river traffic became heavy. We could see the busy riverfront as we slowly cruised down river with boats plying passengers in all directions, while larger boats were loading or unloading at the landings. There were steamers moored to the piers. We could hear voices of people talking and shouting from the boats and warehouses. Some boats were carrying passengers who seemed to be on their way to a festival or a wedding. Women were gaily attired in their colorful *longyis* under the shade of their blue, green and yellow parasols. Another boat was carrying a musical troupe whose music we could hear above the noise of the sail flapping and sounds from the busy river front. At least war was over for now and life seemed to return to normal with people going about their usual business. We spent three more nights on the boat. The scenery down river was breath taking. It was so beautiful and surreal unlike an artist's canvas. Scenes of dozens of pagodas and stupas stretched as far as the eyes could see on both sides of the Irrawaddy. Some pagodas were delicately poised on top of hills while others were in the fields and villages among coconut palm trees and flame of the forest trees with their brilliant flowers blooming in force. At night the stars shone brilliantly with a thin cresent moon on the horizon. Three more nights and we were docked at Insein but we arrived too late in the night and had to sleep on the boat that night. After a hurried breakfast the next morning we left the boat to return to Grandpa's house on Zion Hill.

Grandpa had left his house in the care of his younger brother Harry and the Indian gardener Muthi. The house was in shambles with some windows broken and some furniture missing. Grandpa was furious. "Harry," he yelled. Harry came out of the house surprised that we had arrived back home earlier than he had expected.
"Gangs of young men ransacked the house," he told Grandpa. "They threatened to kill us when we tried to stop them. They even beat up the gardener."

Harry, Grandpa's brother, never went to school. He had a daughter whom we lovingly called Auntie Rosie, who had only some elementary education. But her husband Henry Hughes, was an Englishman. He was Chief Civil Engineer of Public Works Department. When we vacationed at Grandpa's house during school holidays, Auntie Rosie would send her uniformed chauffer to pick us up in her sleek black sedan and take us back to her house on a hill overlooking Royal Lake. The Hughes had two daughters. Betty was an adopted daughter about the same age as Louise. The younger daughter, Hilda, was about my age. Then there was a niece, May Taylor, also about the same age as me living with them. After lunch, Auntie Rosie would usually take Betty and our sisters to town. Where they went we never knew. They never came back until late at night. Dempsey and I would spend time with Hilda and May. We either played tennis or roller skated.

They had two tennis courts. One court had a crack in the center. We used that court for our skating rink. The other court was well maintained for tennis. Even when Auntie Rosie was away, their butler would always have dinner prepared for us. In the evening after dinner Dempsey and I would dance with May and Hilda on the well polished floor to the oldie tunes like '*The Old Black Magic*', '*When the Poppies bloom again*', or waltz to such tunes like "*Your're the one Rose that's left in my Heart, Dear*', and "*If I should fall in love with you*", until Auntie Rosie and the girls returned. They usually brought back icecream and cakes which we would have before we went to bed. Auntie Rosie spoke broken English. She never got angry when we teased her about her pronunciation or grammar. She would even laugh along with us. One day Uncle Hughes got angry with her and scolded her for something she forgot to do. He kept scolding her until she sould not take it any more. "Henry, stop it," she yelled at Uncle Hughes. "If you don't stop I will jump the window!" Uncle Hughes couldn't stop laughing. He winked at us, walked over to her, hugged her and said, "I'm sorry, Rosie, darling." Aunty Rosie's father Harry had a weird hobby. He tried his hand on alchemy, and he imbedded into his arms lead, copper and stones as charms to bring him luck. It had not worked for him as far as we knew. Sometimes he made amulets and other charms and sold them in the market.

We proceeded to clean up the house, sweeping, dusting and throwing away broken chairs and debris. There was the Steinway piano still standing in one corner of the sitting room but it had been vandalized. The covers were off exposing broken strings, loose felt hammers and straps. Grandpa had the gardener get some friends to help take away the piano and trash it. As they were carrying it away I told them to store it in the detached garage. I went to the garage daily to look at the piano to see if I could try to restore it. I was pretty sure I could do the job. Since there was nothing else much to do I started to put the pieces back together. Fortunately no one had vandalized the garage and the tools were still intact. I joined the broken strings back by knotting the two ends together using two pliers. I bought some good glue, and went to a foundry to have a socket made to fit the tuning pins. Finally I had all the loose felt hammers glued back and the straps adjusted. But the piano was totally out of tune. It took me several days to tune and retune the reattached strings because as the knots tightened the strings became slack again after a while.

Finally when all the knots held and the piano tuned it was ready to play. I had never played a piano. I practiced playing the rhythm with my left hand and the harmony with my right hand. It took me a few weeks of practice to play a poor semblance of *Blue Hawaii* and *We'll meet again,* the first two songs I taught myself to play. When I thought I was playing pretty well I had the gardener and his friends take the piano back into the house. As the men were struggling up the stairs with the piano Nita screamed, "What's going on there?"

Then Audrey yelled, "Quiet there, we're trying to sleep."

After the men placed the piano where it used to stand I pulled up a chair while the girls were still screaming from the bed rooms, "Stop making that noise." But before I even finished playing the introduction to *Blue Hawaii* all he girls came running out of the bedroom, pushed me off the chair and took over the piano. I mentioned this little episode because some time later during the war I was able to make a living tuning and repairing pianos in the city to help support the family.

Grandpa was now happy because he could have hymns accompanied by the piano during devotions three times a day and he could sing at the top of his voice. He was now back in his elements, praise the Lord. A few nights after we got back the air field was bombed. The next day Dempsey and I with the help of Muthi dug a large air raid shelter to accommodate the entire family on the side of the house under a couple of mango trees. The ground was hard and it took us all day to dig the dirt out. We returned the next day to place cover over it and lined the floor of the trench with woven bamboo mats. We then placed foliage on top and at the entrance as camouflage.

Early each morning Dempsey went to the riverside to look at wares brought in by boats from the countryside to sell at brokerage houses along the river. Some boat owners did not want to remain for days or sometimes even weeks to get their wares sold to brokerages houses. In cases like that it was possible to buy off the wares from these boats at greatly reduced prices, rent a small space at the pier and resell the wares back later to a broker or any buyer that came along for a smaller profit. There never was a loss and though profit was small it certainly was better than not earning anything. The money earned each day had to be carried back in a tote bag because of inflation. Thousands of single kyat notes could be earned each day which did not mean much in terms of value. Soon singles were no more accepted by merchants. Dempsey used to bring back money in a tote bag full of single kyats, wrapped in fifties, hundreds and thousand bundles. One day when he came back with a very small tote bag Dad asked him, "Business bad today?"

"No, it was even better today," Dempsey answered.

"But you brought back a small bag today," Dad told him.

"They're all in hundred and thousand notes, Dad," Dempsey told him. "Merchants are not accepting singles and tens any more. Not even twenties."

Whenever big transactions, like sale of a home or purchase of big lots of goods were made, people had to lug money in sacks. Dempsey always asked me to stay with the family in case a man was needed for an emergency while he went out and tried to look for bargains to make money for the family.

One day Uncle Albert arrived from Mandalay and told Dad that he had to go to Myaungmya, a town in the Deltas, where the BIA massacred many Karens. He wanted to check on his brother, Richard and his family. He left for Myaungmya the next day. Dad thought that he should also check on his family village, Pyaw Bwegon, to see if his relatives were all right. He took Dempsey with him and left for the village. Dad came back after a short stay with news that the village was intact and the relatives were not harmed. Dad's village, Pyaw Bwegon, was only a mile away from a large, predominantly Burman village which was always on the lookout to help smaller Karen villages around the area. Uncle Albert however came back after several days with news that the entire family of his brother Richard was killed. The youngest child Christine, who was with a nanny at that time was missing.The nanny somehow escaped but Uncle Albert could not get any information about Chris. A few of my friends, both Karen and Burman, also died trying to defend their families in this communal riot. The BIA held men in a stockade and beheaded twenty each day until Japanese Colonel Suzuki and BIA's General Auang San came to stop the massacre. These tragedies were hard to accept knowing that the victims on both sides, Karen as well as Burman, had done nothing to their attackers to deserve to die horrible deaths.

There was a time when some Japanese officers from the Kem Pe Tai, secret police, asked Dempsey and me to follow them to their head quarters near the Insein market. We didn't know why they wanted us to go along with them. I thought that they were going to detain us or arrest us. But Dempsey thought that they were going to ask us to join the Japanese army. When we got to their office we heard screams coming from an inner room. Then the inner room door opened slightly and someone inside called out in Japanese. The KPT officer who brought us told us to follow him to the inner room. We saw a man on a table sitting upright, his back against a board. His hands were secured to rings on the board. His feet were stretched out and secured to two rings on the table. A Japanese soldier was sitting on a chair near by holding what looked like a rolling pin. As we entered, the man on the chair stood up and placed the rolling pin on the shins of the man on the table. The man yelled even before pressure was put on the shins. The Japanese then pushed down with his weight and rolled the pin along the shin. The man screamed and threw his head back in agony. The officer then took us to another room where a man was lying on a table. There was a rubber hose about three quarter of an inch diameter, with some sort of an attachment on the table. The man was lying still but he was not unconscious. There was a soldier standing beside the table. After the Japanese officer said something to him the soldier picked up the hose and placed the hose attachment into the man's mouth. The man struggled. Then I noticed that the man's hands were secured to the table. The soldier kept on talking to the officer and later took off the hose from the man's mouth. He was probably explaining to the officer how the hose was used to torture the man. The officer took us back to the front room, and asked in staggered English, "You want to police? Okay? No?"

So he wanted us to join the Japanese police force. Dempsey raised both hands, slowly shook his head and said, "No."

The officer smiled and said, "Okay, you go."

We left and hurried home. The officer never came back.

One day Dempsey and I went down to the bamboo grove behind the house to get some fresh bamboo shoots for lunch. After collecting enough shoots we started to get back to the kitchen where our three older sisters were preparing lunch. Both Dempsey and I had wooden clogs on, but with the clogs you could not climb up hill as your feet would slip off the smooth surface of the clogs. We took off our clogs and started up the hill when I stepped on a broken twig with long sharp thorns. The thorns on this twig were more than an inch long. The thorn broke off a quarter inch inside my foot and it was so painful. Dempsey helped me up the slope back into the kitchen.

"What happened?" Nita asked.

"He stepped on a thorn. It's still in his foot," Dempsey told Nita..

"Why didn't you have your clogs on?" Nita yelled at me.

"You can't climb up the hill with your clogs on, Nita," Dempsey yelled back.

I was grimacing in pain. Audrey was standing beside Nita.

"It's your fault," Nita continued. "If you had the clogs it wouldn't happen," she yelled into my face.

I had a machete in my right hand. I raised it high and threw it crashing down on the cement floor sending it flying across the opposite end of the kitchen.

Right then Audrey slapped Nita in the face.

"Don't you understand he couldn't have the clog on. He is hurting and you are yelling at him."

Louise then asked Dempsey to go and get the doctor in Nanthagon.

Dempsey helped me into the house and up into the sitting room and immediately ran off to get Doctor Deb. The thorn hurt so much each time I moved a muscle that I had to scream and roll on the sitting room floor. Everyone came round to see me but no one could help me. After screaming for one hour on the floor I was told that Dempsey had returned back with the doctor.

"Spencer, I do not have any anesthetic to work with. You must try to bear the pain. Good boy, okay? It would only take a minute."

"Doc, just get the dam thorn out," I grunted. "Get on with it."

Dempsey had me lie face down on the floor and pulled a chair over so I could hold onto it's legs. He then sat on my back to keep me still as the doctor made the incision.

"Ahhhh! Ahhhh!," I screamed. "go ahead. Just get the damn thing out."

"It won't take long, boy" said the doctor.

"Take as long as you need. Just get the damn thing out," I screamed.

It seemed like hours. But in less than a minute Dr. Deb pulled the missile out of my foot. The pain of the incision remained, but what a relief.

Nita came over and hugged me. "I'm sorry, Spence." She was the only one in the family who called me Spence.

Other Japanese officers or soldiers visited our house every few days. Some stayed a couple of hours just to learn English from one of us as we also learned Japanese from them. A couple of weeks later, some senior Japanese officers visited our house one evening and got into very friendly general conversation with our family. They were from the Japanese Imperial Air Force and were billeted near the air field. The senior officer wanted to know if we could teach some of their men English. They mentioned that they liked the house. "Very nice," they often said about the house. We began to believe that they were possibly looking over the house with a view of eventually getting it for their living quarters further away from the air field which was bombed every now and again. We kept teaching a few of them basic English and at the same time we realized that we were beginning to understand and speak the Japanese language fairly well. We didn't take any money for the lessons while the Japanese in appreciation would bring us almost daily a variety of Japanese cookies or sometimes food they just bought from the market. Since we had developed a good relation with the Japanese we did not have to worry about security at all. However the frequent bombings by Allied planes worried especially the women folks. Every time the city of Rangoon, about seven miles away, was bombed, the air field also was bombed. Harry, Grandpa's brother, had a dog named Bonima. She was like a sort of air raid warning for us. When an air raid siren sounded and we would all get into the shelter, Bonima would sit sedately at the entrance of the shelter unperturbed. Those were the times when there would be no bombing or when the bombings would be some distant away. But when Bonima ran into the trench before anyone else, trembling and whimpering, that was the time when the bombings would be real close. So we learned never to get into the shelter when an air raid sounded until we saw Bonima make a run for it. At first the girls did not trust Bonima's intuition. They would always run for the trench at the mere sound of the siren or even when it was just a rumble that was felt from the bombing somewhere in the city several miles away. However they eventually accepted that somehow Bonima's knew when the bombs were going to be close. When we had to move again we wanted to take Bonima with us but Harry, Grandpa's brother, refused to let us have the dog.

CHAPTER 8

EVACUATION AGAIN

ONE NIGHT AFTER THE AIR raid siren sounded we walked to the shelter. But there was no sound of bombers flying above and no sound of anti aircraft guns. It was a clear night and the only things we could see were beams of search lights crisscrossing the sky searching for any invading bomber. Bonima sat quietly at the entrance of the shelter with all of us waiting and chatting near her except our parents and grandparents who almost always went into the shelter anyway. It was a good half hour before the first bombs dropped in far away Rangoon. Still Bonima didn't budge. We felt the slight rumble as the bombs dropped miles away. A couple of minutes later the dog jumped up and ran into the trench and all the girls followed. In less than a few minutes later there were loud explosions in the direction of the air field that shook the ground.

Dempsey and I sat at the entrance of the trench to watch in spite of protests from Mom and Dad. Anti aircraft guns were now firing and the sky was peppered with black puffs from exploding AA shells but we could see no air crafts. Finally a huge bomber came into view caught in the beam of several searchlights. Japanese fighters were swarming all around it and then it got hit. Smoke trailed behind it as it began to lose altitude and then we saw burning debris falling from the plane as it lost height and disappeared into the night. Dempsey was giving a running commentary of the whole scene that unfolded before us while the girls were praying aloud for the Allied airmen who were shot down. A few minutes later there was another series of loud explosions that shook the ground as search lights continued to crisscross the sky. Suddenly one beam caught a bomber at rather low altitude and all other searchlights quickly converged on it. There was no escape for this bomber. Obviously it was the one that just released the bombs and now it looked like it was flying above the runway and away from it after it had unloaded the bombs. It was hit. The tail end was blown off and the open fuselage was spitting out furious orange flames as the bomber rapidly lost height and flew past us beyond the bamboo groves missing the house by just a hundred feet of so. Where it crashed we never found out. The girls were crying and praying for the Allied airmen who were shot down. That was it, for them and for Mom. They wanted to move out of the area right away. So after the all clear sounded and we got back into the house Grandpa got us together and prayed that the Lord would find us a place to move to, away from the danger of bombs.

The very next day a colonel from the Japanese air force visited us. He thanked us for teaching his men some English. This was his first visit. He walked around the sitting room, looked out of the windows and kept saying, "Nice house, nice house." Now we knew why he was visiting. He finally told Dad that he wanted to take over the house on a lease for an officer's quarters. Dad consulted Grandpa who happily agreed. Grandpa believed that God sent the colonel in answer to our prayers the night before so that we could move out. We absolutely agreed with him. Sometimes God does answer our prayers directly and without delay. The colonel told Dad that he would talk over details with him in a few days. Dad had heard that some of the people he knew had moved to a town called Twante about sixteen miles to the west of Rangoon on a canal by that name. The Twante Canal was a vital link between Rangoon and the Delta districts to the west. Dad took a quick trip with Dempsey and came back two days later with news that we could evacuate to Twante. There were already a large number of evacuees from Rangoon and the suburbs who were now living in Twante. An old friend of Dad had an estate and was willing to let Dad build a house (actually a bamboo hut) on the property. Dad sent Dempsey and me a few days later to go to Twante and build the house. When we got there we inspected the lot given us and decided that we could build a pretty large hut to comfortably accommodate the entire family. We both had had good experience building a number of huts out of scratch with the Karen soldiers in Katha.

We bought bamboos, thatch roofs and woven weed walls. We completed the hut in under a week with some help from a couple of kids we hired. In fact it was a huge hut built in three separate levels, for the kitchen on the lowest level, then the landing in the mid level with the sleeping quarters in the top level. Mom and Dad, the girls and Grand parents would occupy the top level, seven feet above ground, while Dempsey and I would sleep on the second level which was also a landing, where we would receive guests or have our meals, four feet above ground and the kitchen was on the low level three feet above ground. It was a pretty good looking hut – not just a shack. We went home and proudly reported back to Dad. We were told that Grandpa and Grandma would not be living with us in Twante after all because they wanted to be with their older daughter, Moms older sister, Aunty Gyi, who had lost her husband only a few months earlier. It also happened that Aunty Gyi's husband had just rented someone's house in Twante but died before they could move. When our family moved to Twante Dempsey went along to stay with them while Dad and I stayed back in Insein.

AuntyGyi's husband was also a civil officer. I really dodn't know his family background, but his older sister, a dowager, ran her house like a royal court. You walk up the steps onto the well polished floor of the living room which extended into a long hall. Her chair, an intricately woven piece of fine cane furniture, sat on a carpet between the sitting room and the hall. Standing behind the chair was a maid, combing her long, thick black hair. There was a chair on the other side of her chair for a visitor. She did not like anyone talking to her while standing. We loved her. She was very hospitable and very generous. When we visited, she would dig into her handbag and call out, "Gilbert, take Penn Penn and the boys to a movie."

Gilbert, her younger son of about twenty five, was a very handsome and tall young man with a beautiful atheletic body. Those day people did not line up to buy tickets. You just had to get to the ticket window the best way you could pushing your way through the thick and unruly crowd. Sometiimes there were fights. You could get pick-pocketed too.You could also buy tickets from scalpers at a higher price. There was no problem for Gilbert. He just moved into the crowd pushing those in front of him out of his way till he could push his hand through the window. In no time he was out with tickets in his hand. At one time I saw a young Anglo Burmese girl at the window waiting before it was opened. When the window opened the young lady bought her ticket but she could not get out. The crowds pushed and surged to the window. I saw her rise in the air and then disappear and later rise again as the crowd pushed. She kept screaming as she rose and disappeared a couple of times until she could finally extricate herself from the surging crowd. Then there was Eldred, the dowager's elder son. He drank a lot. When the mother asked him to take us boys to movies, he'd grab the money and take us to the movie house. After he had bought the tickets, he took us in. The usher led us into the darkened hallway up to the very first row up front where we had to strain our necks and look high up at the screen. We got the cheapest seats with the extra money going to Eldred for his whisky. We had to call the dowager *Jee Daw* or *Amay Jee (*Big Aunt or Big Mother). There was a lot of food at her house at any time of the day and anyone visiting was served a hot meal no matter what time of the day or night. I enjoyed visiting *Jee Daw* many times when I was in high school and college.

A group of Japanese officers finally arrived a few days later with a drawn up lease for the house. They wanted to lease the house for one year and would put the entire money down with option to renew the lease on a yearly basis. Dad thought that it would be a burden to come and collect the payment every year because of frequent air raids and the inconvenience of traveling in his old age. But the colonel said that they were authorized to renew the lease only on a yearly basis and if Dad wanted the lease to be on a two year basis they would have to refer the matter back to their superiors. So Dad agreed to wait. We waited a week before we heard from them again. Meantime my English students still came to me to take lessons two or three times a week during the day. Harry, Grandpa's brother, cooked for us since neither Dad nor I knew how to cook. One day after a heavy rain we could hear frogs croaking all around. There had been no bombing for several days now and just out of curiosity I walked into the shelter to take a look. There I found several frogs sitting on dry ground at the far end of the shelter. Four of them were huge. I went back into the house and got a bag and came back to the shelter and put the four large frogs into the bag and gave it to Harry who knew what to do with the frogs. Since then, we had frog curry every once in a while without me having to go to the market to buy meat. When I didn't have any student to teach I practiced playing on the piano while Dad would go and visit friends in Nanthagon, a village just a short walk away.

I was sitting on the steps in front of the house with Dad one night after an air raid siren sounded, waiting for Bonima to make a move for the shelter. It was so dark you could hardly see anything in front of you. We heard foot steps and a dark figure appeared. The figure came right to the steps and I recognized that it was a Japanese soldier. He grabbed my arm and pulled me away and said, "Biruma, take me my house." *(Burmese, take me to my house)* I knew then that the soldier had lost his way and

86

was trying to get back to his billet wherever that was. He was dragging me along in the dark. We could now hear planes flying above. They were not heavy bombers and they were flying low.

"Okay, okay," I told him. He eased his grip on my arm but did not let go. I knew my grounds well and intended to take him as far as the main road from where he would be able to find his way home. Suddenly bombs exploded somewhere nearby and rocked the ground. I dropped on the ground and in so doing pulled the soldier down with me. As he was lying next to me in the dark I realized that he was reeking of liquor. After a few moments I stood up and said, "One, two, three, run," as I pulled him along in the dark and ran toward the main road with him still holding on to me. Just then there was another shrill whistle as more bombs headed to their target. I hit the ground pulling him down with me. Now he had let my arm go. I wanted to get rid of him because I didn't know where he would take me if I went along with him. So when we got up this time I told him again, "One, two, three, run," and he ran, but this time without me. I spun round instead and hid behind a mango tree and stood still. It was pitch dark.

"Biruma! Biruma!" (Burmese, Burmese) he kept calling for me in the dark. He was on our private lane. "Biruma! Biruma!" he kept shouting. If he kept walking he'd soon reach the main road and eventually find his way home.

"Biruma! Biruma!" he continued calling. By now I knew he was almost at the main road and from there he would be able to find his way home.

The Japanese officers finally returned. This time they had a Japanese woman with them.

"Good morning. How are you?" said the woman to Dad in perfect American accent.

"Good morning. You speak perfect English," Dad responded.

"I'm from Hawaii and also went to study in New York," she said and continued, "Now we have everything for you just as you wanted. Two year lease for the house and two year full payment now and an option to renew the lease every two years. How is that?"

"Excellent," Dad replied, "and thank you so much."

"You are welcome," she responded.

The lease was typed in Japanese. The woman picked up the papers and translated it for Dad. There was a bundle of paper currency on the table. She touched the bundle with her hand and said, "This is all yours. All you have to do to have it is sign the papers. We are also giving you a rough translation of the lease in English."

"Thank you very much," Dad told her and he turned to the other officers and bowed. They bowed in return.

Then a Japanese officer rose to place the papers in front of Dad to sign. After Dad had signed several copies the colonel asked Dad, "When you leave house?"

"I can leave tomorrow," Dad replied.

"No need. Stay two three days okay," he told Dad.

"No, I'll leave tomorrow," Dad replied. "I want to see my wife and family," Dad told him.

An officer sitting next to Dad who was my English student slapped Dad's back and said, "Oh, you miss wife very much."

"You are doing very well," I told him, "You speak good English now."

"O, because you very good teechaa," he responded.

That evening they brought food and cookies and wine to celebrate and there were singing and dancing by Japanese girls they brought to entertain us. The party lasted till past midnight. Dad and I left the next day for Twante. Finally for the first time, Dad saw for himself the house that his sons built. He was very pleased with it.

Our house sat at the bottom of a small hillock at the end of the estate and the only water supply was from a community well some hundred and twenty yards away. It was an open well with water level at seven to ten feet depending on the time of the season. Two logs were placed across the well about two feet apart. We had to stand on the logs, a foot on each log, to draw water using a two gallon bucket tied to a rope and drop the bucket into the well and pulled it up. We emptied the bucket into two four gallon kerosene tins. The tin was loosely attached to one end of a bamboo yoke which we balanced on our shoulders to carry the water home. It took us a while to be able to perform that task – awkwardly at first until we became so proficient that we hired ourselves out to homes which did not have any man to do the job. It was very tiresome and taxing but we regarded it as exercise and enjoyed watching our muscles develop every single day in the full view mirror Dempsey picked up in the market. For the house we each did at least six to eight such trips to fill up some thirty gallon jars for bathing and for cooking. For drinking water we had jars placed under bamboo gutters along the eaves to collect fresh water from the rains.

Dempsey and I also bought a prized rooster and several hens. We built a chicken coop of about sixteen by eight feet with shelves for the hen to lay eggs. We had to make the walls and the doors very strong because at night civic cats or even dogs would come and try to get at the fowls in the shed. We also had a few ducks. The ducks occupied the mud floor in the coop. We had to clean the floor every morning after collecting duck eggs on the mud floor and chicken eggs from the shelves. We then fed the ducks and the fowls. We had a little pond in front of our house which kept our ducks from moving into other properties. Each morning we could wade into the pond and pick up a few more duck eggs at the bottom. Ducks are not good at hatching their eggs. So we let some hen sit over duck eggs. When they were hatched it was amusing watching the little ducklings rush into the pond to swim while the mother hen marched up and down in panic along the edge of the pond clucking frantically ordering her 'chicks' to return to solid ground. We also bred pigs with a sty set way back of the house. Dempsey and I found out that pigs made very loving pets. They also understood commands almost like dogs do. Our chores were heavy beginning very early each morning, with feeding the animals and cleaning the coop and sty, besides replenishing our water supply and fetching water for other homes. Our sisters appreciated our hard work and each morning gave us large servings of well balanced and nutritious breakfast. By the time we were done with all our chores it was past noon and time for lunch. When we had to be away for sometime we hired other kids to do the chores for us.

Japanese soldiers wore only loin cloth on hot days. A string was tied around the waist to hold the loin cloth with the ends hanging down the front and the back. Since we didn't have too much change of clothes and the days being hot Dempsey and I adopted the Japanese way of staying cool. We ignored the stares from neighbors until they got used to us. We made wooden clogs for our footwear to walk on hard ground during summer and cut up old tires in the shape of slippers and put straps on them for muddy grounds during the raining season. We even made peak caps, or baseball caps, to wear in the hot sun, and we made underwear which we had on sometimes, despite the stares.

One day a Japanese major come to our house for a visit and introduced himself as the garrison commander. His name was Heijima. He spoke sketchy English and wanted to know if we could teach him some more English. It seemed to be the Japanese way to get to know the citizens better and thereby feel the pulse of the general population in regard to their attitudes toward Japanese occupation. We agreed to do so and he became our constant visitor. At about the same time Dad had undertaken to adopt two young daughters of a nephew who had recently lost his wife. The girls, May Paw and Pauline, were eight and six years old. When Heijima saw the two girls he burst into tears and drew out from his pocket a photograph of his wife and two daughters also about the same ages as May Paw and Pauline. Mom immediately held his hand and said a prayer for him. Sometimes Mom would read the bible to him. We took turns teaching Heijima English and he would often ask the two sisters to sing for him. Pauline, at only six, could accompany her sister by singing alto. Heijima loved to hear them sing and soon he became a part of our family. With every visit he would bring us cookies and cakes and would stay till dinner or sometimes would join us at dinner. The advantage of Heijima being a friend of the family was that Japanese soldiers were very respectful to us and for that matter it was also true of local law enforcement personnel. Dad was recognized by the Japanese as well as the community as one of the local community elders. In any case we had a very quiet and law abiding community in the town of Twante and as far as we knew the Japanese had very little problem keeping law and order in that town.

Dempsey wanted to dig a larger trench for air raid shelter at a different location from the one he had dug before. We selected a spot but had a problem deciding whether to have a Z shaped trench or an L shaped one. Dad was watching us from his bed room window. The discussion on the advantages and disadvantages of each type of trench ultimately led to a heated argument until I lost my cool and lashed out at Dempsey. He blocked and threw a punch back at me. I ducked. I put up my guard and was about to hit Dempsey again when we heard Dad call out to the girls,

"Come quick girls, come quick. We have a boxing match here."

We both looked up and smiled sheepishly at Dad as the girls gathered at the window and yelled, "Come on boys, get on with the fight. We're making bets here."

We finally agreed that the trench would be L shaped since Twante was not such an important target for the bombers after all. Rangoon was a constant target for the bombers. We could hear very faintly the explosion of bombs in Rangoon and a few seconds later feel a slight rumble. On a clear day we could see the bombers making their way to Rangoon. We had a grand stand view of the raids and loved to watch dog fights as Japanese Zeros swooped, and circled in the distant sky and dived to empty their magazines on the escorting Spitfires or Hurricanes. We saw fighter planes from both sides shot down as bombers sedately continued their flights over Rangoon to drop their deadly loads. On a clear and sunny day we could even see bombs falling like strings of sparkles racing down to their targets below. Puffs of dark smoke from exploding anti aircraft shells dotted the sky and on rare occasions the anti aircraft guns hit their targets. The crippled bomber would then turn and fly away westward trailing black smoke behind probably to crash into the sea close by some allied aircraft carriers anchored in the gulf.

Dempsey and I also were involved in local Christian youth group visiting villages and distributing medicines and used clothes. The group called themselves the Christian Endeavor. On one such occasion we had to travel by boat to a village a couple of hours away. Since the CE could not get a boat big enough to accommodate the twenty or so of it's members, we went in small groups, plying our own rented boats. Dempsey and I rented a dugout and went by ourselves. Neither of us had any experience rowing in a river with strong tide and strong wind that caused waves to crest to over a foot in the open stretches of water. For more than three hours we struggled against the tide, and the dugout rolled and yawed over one foot waves in the wind and rain but we finally made it to the village which was actually less than two hours away in fine weather. That village would be our base for the next seven days.

The next day Dempsey and I were to deliver some medicines to a sick elderly man in another village. Although we were advised not to make the trip that day because of the continued strong wind Dempsey and I, nevertheless, with two girls in tow, set out to our dugout. It was still blowing hard as we pushed the craft into the water. We had the girls get into the dugout. Then we tried to push the boat out without success as the wind kept pushing it back to the bank. Finally we managed to get the boat to head the wind and kept it steady. We jumped in and started to row but the wind took over again. As the boat rolled the girl sitting in front of Dempsey jumped off in panic. Dempsey dived after her and dragged her back to shore. The boat rolled once more and the other girl jumped off and disappeared under water. Why I dived after her I had no idea. I was not even a mediocre swimmer. I was just a beginner at swimming. Still, I was there ten feet at the bottom. I could barely see the girl in the murky water. I grabbed her by the waist and kicked. Thank God that she didn't struggle. When we came up to the surface I did the side stroke but didn't seem to get anywhere as the waves were beating against us from all sides. Dempsey saw my plight and dived in and dragged us to the shore. Immediately the four of us went to the group leader and told him about our close call and asked him to join us in praising God in prayer for His life saving grace.

I used to have an attack of malaria each year at about this time of the year since I was in high school which would last for twelve to fourteen days with uncontrollable shivering and high fever leaving me with a splitting head ache. Three days after that incident in the river I had an attack of chill and was shivering violently. I felt so cold yet my body was getting hot and I began to have a head ache which I knew would get worse. Dempsey placed blankets over me and sat on me and tried to keep me warm and from shivering. It took an hour for the chill to subside as the temperature went up followed by a terrible head ache. The owner of the hut where we were staying walked in just then. Dempsey told him that I was having a bout of the chill from malaria. He laughed and without saying a word left the house. He came back after about half an hour, two live eels in one hand. He told me that he would get rid of my malaria for good. I prayed to God that he would. He cooked a curry of eel with lots and lots of ground black pepper which he asked me to eat after my temperature went down. It was very delicious but so hot with black pepper that my whole face flushed and my ears and cheek became so numb that there was no feeling left in them. I slept like a log that night and woke up fresh in the morning. Believe it or not from that day on until today I have not had any attack of malaria. I thank God each year about the same time that I used to have the attack, that the attack did not recur. For medical doctors reading this, it will be worth to take note and try it on their malaria patients. This medication is delicious.

At another time Dempsey and I were traveling with a large group from the CE to attend a wedding at a distant village. There were lots of young girls and women in the group and few men. Most of us were refugees from Rangoon. Our group leader told us that he wanted to travel at night so that we could sneak pass a gang of robbers at a village called Ma Letto, that stopped travelers to collect money or rob them. He warned the women folk, most of whom were evacuees from Rangoon, not to wear jewelry or expensive clothes. We left after nine at night and quietly passed Ma Letto village on the opposite bank at midnight and arrived safely at our destination early in the morning undetected. We congratulated ourselves in making a safe trip past the notorious village. However during reception after the wedding a messenger from Ma Letto village came and told our group leader that the robbers at Ma Letto would be waiting for us on our way back. The gang leader was very angry that we did not to stop at their village to pay the dues like everybody else. Before we left the village after the wedding our group had a special prayer for a safe encounter with the gang. This time the group leader decided to travel in daylight and to stop at the village. What ever money we were carrying we were prepared to hand over to the gang.

As we approached the village, our leader told us to be quiet and not to argue or resist. He promised to plead with the leader for leniency if he demanded more money than we could collect. We could now see the village of Ma Letto and as we neared the village we saw the gang leader with a carbine slung from his shoulder standing straight on the landing with hands on his hips Dempsey moved to the fore of the boat to get a closer look, but the group leader pushed him back. As the boat pulled alongside, Dempsey jumped onto the landing and ran to the gang leader and hugged him. The gang leader slapped Dempsey several times on the back and bellowed, "Dempsey, I can't believe it. Very happy to see you, old boy."

"Good to see you, Reggie. You're some kind of Captain Cook or what?" Dempsey asked.

"Hey, it's a nice way to make money, my friend. I don't shoot or kill anyone or sink boats like the other gangs, you know. I just collect taxes and guarantee the travelers their safety," he told Dempsey.

I walked up slowly to Reggie and offered my hand.

"Hey, Spence," he shouted but ignored my hand and hugged me instead. Reggie Unger, an Anglo Karen, and Dempsey shared the same room at the hostel in Judson College and they attended the same classes. We did not have to pay any protection money to Reggie. What a wonderful answer to our prayer.

One hot summer day someone came and told us that a poor villager had just died. He had no relatives and his wife was away. Dempsey and I went over and we made a coffin out of some spare boards that we had and placed the man in it. The village pastor came and conducted a funeral service. The pastor wanted the funeral to take place the same day as the weather was hot and the body would decompose quickly but some of the man's friends said they wanted the wife who was traveling to another village at that time to see the husband before he was buried. A messenger had been sent to inform the wife of her husband's death but it would take two days for her to arrive. Dempsey and I protested because, we said, after two days she will not recognize her husband because of decomposition. Dempsey and I went ahead and dug the grave in the nearby wood and came back and insisted that we would burry the man there and then. But the friends stood their ground. So Dempsey went and bought a large quantity of wood resin and came back, took the corpse out and sealed the cracks and crevices in the coffin and made sure that it was air tight and replaced the corpse in the coffin.

That night it was very hot and humid. The next day the temperature soared to maybe at least a hundred degrees. When we went back, the corpse seemed to have begun to decompose. The wife was arriving the next morning, we were told. But Dempsey insisted to close the coffin and seal it shut. The wife should not see her husband's corpse Dempsey told the friends. She should remember her husband as he was when he was alive. So in spite of the protests Dempsey closed and nailed the coffin shut. The next day the wife had not arrived. We waited till afternoon and the wife still had not arrived. So the pastor and Dempsey decided that we had waited long enough and would only wait for the wife until early the next day and whether she arrived or not the burial would take place early the next morning. When we went again to the hut early the next morning we realized immediately that the seal that Dempsey applied did not work as we could smell a strong odor of decomposition coming from the coffin. After a very short service Dempsey and I and two other young men from the CE lifted the coffin and placed it on our shoulders and marched to the grave we had dug three days earlier. Slowly our shoulders began to get wet and we realized at once that fluid from the corpse was seeping through the cracks in the coffin.

After the funeral we burned our clothes before we got home and had our bath three or four times a day for the next few days. We learned later that the messenger never caught up with the wife to give the message. She returned a few days later to learn only upon her arrival that her husband had passed away while she was gone.

CHAPTER 9

AIR RAIDS OVER RANGOON

RUMOR WAS CIRCULATING THAT THE British had dropped spies in some villages in the Deltas and that some spies had also landed from Submarines. Heijima had not been visiting for a while and we wondered if he was busy deploying his men in search of the spies. He turned up a couple of weeks later. Everything seemed normal as he continued to take his English lessons.

One day some acquaintance from the Delta area came to inform Dad that Captain Ba Thet Gyi, of Special Force 104, had been captured by the Japanese and was now in custody in Rangoon. The news was a shock to our family because we knew Ba Thet well since he and Nita, our oldest sister, had begun dating before war started. Ba Thet was an A.B.R.O. (Army of Burma Reserve Officer) and retreated with the British to India. He parachuted down near a village in the Deltas. The Japanese found out about him and threatened to kill all the village elders and burn the village down if they did not surrender him. To save the villagers from being punished by the Japanese Ba Thet surrendered. The news was devastating to Nita who insisted on going to Rangoon to try to see Ba Thet.

At that time Saw Ba U Gyi, cousin of Ba Thet, was living in Rangoon. He was an English educated Barrister who received his bar in London. He was in Rangoon working closely with General Aung San in a reconciliation effort with the Burmese community after the terrible communal clash that killed thousands of Karen and Burmese people in the Deltas. He owned a house in Sanchaung quarters of Rangoon but did not live there. He pleaded with the Japanese authorities to allow Nita to see Ba Thet. When the Japanese agreed to the visitation he invited Nita to come and live in his house in Sanchaung. I accompanied Nita to Rangoon to stay with her. The Japanese allowed Ba Thet to visit Nita during the day on Saturday and Sunday under escort. After several weeks Nita made an impassioned appeal to the Japanese officials to allow them get married. The Japanese eventually gave Nita and Ba Thet permission to be married. But the Japanese warned Ba Thet that if he tried to escape his wife would be arrested. After they got married, the Japanese allowed Ba Thet to spend weekends at the house without guards. I accompanied Nita to Rangoon because Nita needed me to stay with her during the week as Ba Thet was allowed to visit only on week ends. Nita was intensely afraid of bombs. She would tremble violently when an air raid siren sounded and kept trembling even after the all clear sounded. I was glad that I came along with her to Rangoon.

During my first week with Nita I heard a woman next door playing her piano which was outrageously out of tune. This was a great chance for me to make my trade known – piano tuning and repairs. I offered to have her piano tuned at a very reasonable cost. She was very pleased with the result and the moderate fee I charged and told a few of her friends about me. I soon began to have many people visit me (there were no telephone services in some areas in Rangoon) to engage my services for tuning or repairing their pianos. I only accepted appointments on days and times when bombings were unlikely because I wanted to be with Nita during air raids. Air raids usually came after eleven in the morning, never earlier and never after three o'clock in the afternoon. My business hours were from eight to eleven in the morning and in the afternoon from three to seven.

Besides repairing pianos I also tried to look for other opportunities, like buying some goods cheap and reselling them at a profit like Dempsey did when we were in Insein. I tried to look out for items that people were looking for most but couldn't find. One of these items was a material called voile. Women were crazy about the thin see-through voile for making jackets and it was the one material I came across occasionally and made some money on. One day when I was in the city the air raid siren sounded. A man at a corner fabric store began to close the shutters to avoid possible looting. I stepped inside before he pulled together the last shutter and asked him if he had any length of voile. He probably thought that I was about to rob him. Without saying a word he reached up to a top shelf and brought down a bolt of voile and asked for a ridiculously low price for the entire bolt. Fortunately I had enough money and paid him and placed the bolt on my bike. I waited in an alley behind the shop for the bombs to fall and was thinking of Nita at the same time. But nothing happened and about forty five minutes later the all clear sounded. Sometimes there were false alarms and the all clear sounded shortly after. As soon as the all clear sounded I quickly rode across the city to a woman whom I knew wanted several lengths of voile for an up coming wedding of her daughter. I expected to make a good profit but did not expect to make three times what I thought I should fetch for the material. The lady had to be in a generous mood prior to her daughter's wedding. She bought the whole bolt.

A visitor arrived one day. He came from Bassein to deliver Saw Ba U Gyi's car buthe had no place to stay for the night. Saw Ba U Gyi sent him to the house to spend the night. Soon after he arrived he developed a very high fever. There was no telephone and I had no transportation to take him to the hospital. I went to a nurse a few doors away but she was on duty at the hospital. Someone suggested cold compress while we waited for help. The man's fever continued to rise and there was nothing we could do. I sat down with my sister and we prayed for the man whose name we didn't even know.

Nita took a basin full of water and with a wash cloth applied cold compress to his forehead. After a few minutes the water in the basin turned almost as hot as the man's forehead. We had to keep changing water every so often. I sat up with the man through the night but fell asleep in the early hours. When I woke up in the morning he was already dead. We prayed again this time for his family. There was no way I could contact Saw Ba U Gyi because I didn't even know where he lived. I went to the ward official down the block to report the death and asked him what I should do. He told me, "Just take the body to Tamwe cemetery, and dump him in the common grave." He gave me direction to the cemetery.

I didn't know how to take a dead body across the city. I didn't know where to buy a coffin. There were no taxis and I had no transportation except my bike. I walked along the neighborhood around the block and found a two wheeled cart with a broken platform. I didn't know who it belonged to but I took it home anyway. I brought the body down from upstairs but had difficulty placing it on the platform of the cart which was like a see-saw. The load had to be dead center to balance well. He was a big man, about a hundred and eighty pounds, and I was only five foot five and a hundred and thirty pounds. Finally after a long struggle I managed to place the body dead center on the cart and started on my way across the city, a distance of at least three to four miles. I passed buses and bicyclists and pedestrians on the way. No one paid me any attention. A couple of truck full of Japanese soldiers passed by, pointed at the corpse on the cart and waved at me. I kept my head down in embarrassment as I pushed the cart along the pitted road and over pot holes. It must have taken me a good two and a half hours to get to Tamwe cemetery. I wondered how I could bury the corpse. I saw a high mound of dirt straight ahead and figured there had to be some kind of a ditch beyond it. I pushed the cart toward it. Sure enough, when I got close I saw the ditch, about fifteen feet or so deep, fourteen or fifteen feet wide and perhaps thirty feet long. I looked down and saw scores of corpses, some of them fully clothed while others were partially clothed and a few had no clothes on. I got a whiff of odor from the decomposing bodies below and nearly threw up. There was no one around, no attendant, no ground keeper. I guessed this was where everyone came to burry their dead, a common grave the ward official told me about. I pushed the cart right to the edge of the pit and said a quick prayer. I raised one end of the platform of the cart to let the body slide down into the pit feet first. I didn't look down the pit. I quickly turned round and returned home. I took back the cart to where I had found it and got back to the house as it started to get dark. I must have looked terribly ashen and spent. Nita came and hugged me and said, "You poor boy. I'm sorry I brought you here to go through all this."

I pushed her away and said, "Don't touch me. I'm filthy. I just handled a dead man and came back from a stinking ditch full of dead bodies. I stink. I need a bath." I threw away the clothes I was wearing and had a bath.

Bombing was now becoming more intense. Whenever we went into the shelter Nita would shake so badly it even shook me while I held her tight.

"Nita, do you want to go back to Twante where it is safe from bombings?"

"No, I'll stay here. I need to be with Ba Thet," she cried.

"Of course you do. I'll stay with you," I reassured her.

It was touching to see the two of them, during weekends, holding onto each other, not letting go until early Monday morning when the Japanese soldiers took Ba Thet back to prison. It was good that Ba Thet had a very good sense of humor, laughing and telling jokes especially when his cousin Saw Ba U Gyi was visiting. The two cousins would talk for long hours sitting together on the couch, Nita sitting on the floor between

Ba Thet's knees. That's a picture I'll never forget. I was glad that Nita got to see Ba Thet and married him and I thank God that they were able to spend time together and share their love for several months.

Several weeks later someone brought an envelope addressed to Nita. She read from the small piece of paper inside the envelope and immediately threw herself in my arms and cried, "They've taken him away, don't know where." I remember hearing people talk about the Japanese moving troops out of Rangoon for several days now. Were they deploying troops or retreating, I had wondered. Later Saw Ba U Gyi came and told us that the Japanese had indeed moved all prisoners including Ba Thet out of Rangoon. It was likely that the course of war was turning against the Japanese. In any case it was wisest now to be with family. I took Nita back home to Twante and not any too soon.

Our two years agreement with the Japanese Imperial Air Force with regard to Grandpa's house at Insein was approaching. I accompanied Dad to Insein to have the contract renewed. We stayed at one of Dad's friends in Nanthagone village. We went to Grandpa's house to meet with the Japanese officers. We knew none of the officers that we met, but Dad showed them a copy of the contract. An officer asked us to return the next day when we would be able to see some officer familiar with the matter. Most officers were away at a meeting at the Air Force office. On our return the next day we were fortunate that one of the officers who had been my student was there to take care of the matter. He told us that it would take a week or ten days before a new contract was ready and for us to return in two weeks. Dad did not want to stay that long because of the frequent bombings so the next day we returned to Twante. At about noon when we were about ten or twelve miles away there was an air raids over Rangoon. Many river traffic stopped and passengers got out of the crafts and ran ashore for cover. Where our boat was there was only an open rice field. So we just got off our boat and sat on the bank and watched the air raid. A week later Dad and I went to Insein again and this time Dad was able to sign the contract extendidng the lease for another two years.

Dad returned to Twante alone as I had to stay back to tune a piano at one of the churches in Ywama, near Insein. I returned a few days later only to be caught in an air raid, this time over the the river traffic. As we were nearing Twante, a British fighter bomber, made a couple of passes over the traffic allowing the passengers to get off. All or most of the passengers left their boats and took shelter away from the bank. Seeing the R.A.F. insignia on the plane, I stayed put on the boat not expecting an Allied pilot to fire on civilians. But I jumped out of the boat when I saw the plane turn to make a third pass. It was flying low and it looked like it meant business this time. Then it opened fire with it's cannons. I could see the rounds hitting the muddy bank in a straight line, about ten feet apart, each round throwing up a column of mud and water a several feet into the air. It was too close for comfort for me and I thank God that the plane did not turn back.

Air raids on the city were now heavier and more frequent. Heijima was visiting less frequently. Japanese soldiers were passing through the village more often on patrol duties. Otherwise life went on as usual although there was an air of suspense that reminded me of the days before we left Prome just before the Japanese entered Burma. Dad began to worry that there could be a battle for Rangoon fought in or around Twante since the canal was the main artery between the Deltas and Rangoon. The Japanese called on the community elders to help law enforcement officials to try to maintain law and order and Dad had to go to township meetings every few days.

Allies were now using a larger number of bombers in their raids. In earlier raids they used B-17 Flying Fortresses. Later more B24 Liberators were flying, especially when they were carpet bombing with a dozen or more bombers. The close formations whch consisted several bombers never broke up as they flew high over Rangoon and unloaded their lethal cargo. I was glad that Nita and I were not in Rangoon anymore. I will never forget the heaviest bombings ever in which the most number of bombers participated. I am not sure whether they were B29 Super Fortresses or a mixture of both B 29 and B 24 Liberators. Many seemed to be larger than the bombers before them. There must have been at least thirty or forty bombers flying in formations of five or seven escorted by scores of Spitfires and Hurricanes while Japanese fighter planes flew in circles around the bombers chased by allied fighters which swooped and dived to get their sights on the Japanese planes that were attacking the bombers trailing white smoke behind them. When a Japanese fighter was chased it made something like a long backward flip that usually ended up behind it's pursuer. Today's attack was on a very clear sunny day and we had an unobstructed grand stand view of the air battle. It was like having a very large TV screen in front of us without a border. Exploding anti aircraft shells peppered the sky with puffs of black clouds as the dog fights painted the sky with circles and streaks of white clouds.

Anti aircraft shells popped continuously while sounds of cannons from fighters and exploding bombs could be heard faintly over the heavy drones of the bombers and the high pitched roars of fighters. At times a Zero or an Allied fighter was shot down trailing black smoke as it dived and screamed to it's grave below. Then an amazing thing happened. A formation of seven bombers was flying through an anti aircraft barrage while at the same time being attacked by a few fighters. A bomber in the center of the formation suddenly exploded and the aircraft emitted black smoke which trailed behind as it turned westward and headed out in the direction of the gulf. Then two other bombers on either of it's flank were also emitting black smoke. Whether they were hit by debris from the bomber that earlier exploded or by anti aircraft guns we couldn't tell. These bombers also headed west towards the gulf. Yet another bomber in the same formation or another formation caught fire but this time that bomber continued heading toward Rangoon perhaps to try to release bombs over it's target before crashing. It began to loose altitude. Finally it disappeared beyond some tall trees on the horizon. A few seconds later we could hear a faint rumble. Perhaps the plane exploded with all it's bombs onboard.

Now we believed that it was only a matter of days before the Allies recaptured Burma. Our only worry was that the Japanese might put up a strong defense at Twante. They certainly were very good fighters and would readily die for their emperor instead of giving up the fight or surrendering to the enemy. But where they would make their defense we couldn't tell. Meanwhile Heijima had stopped visiting us. A week went by with no air raids on Rangoon. Then a few days later there was another raid with less number of bombers. But this time it was early in the morning, the first time ever that bombing took place in the early morning. The bombers were neither met by anti aircraft fire nor by fighters. A couple of hours later there was another air raid on Rangoon, again with no resistance from the Japanese from the ground or air. There was yet another raid on the city while we were having lunch at noontime still with no resistanc from the ground or air.

That afternoon Major Heijima came and brought a box of Japanese cookies. He said he was wishing us good bye. He then asked Mom to pray for him. Mom read Psalm 23 and prayed. He asked for May Paw and Pauline, kissed them and turned to attention and gave Dad a salute. The girls were teary eyed and silently prayed for Heijima as he bade farewell to them. As he left he called Dempsey and me and told us to go to his room early in the morning. He would leave two samurai swords for us on his table. When we got to the building early the next morning we knew that there would be no samurai sword for us. Looters had already been there. The whole building had been completely ransacked.

As we sat for breakfast some one came and told us that Japanese were approaching the town in a boat. The township alarm sounded at the same time. So Dad hurried to the township office to find out what was happening. He met a police officer.

"Everyone had left, sir," the officer told Dad, "I'm leaving now myself, and here is the key to the armory." He gave Dad a bunch of keys.

"But what is happening?" Dad asked.

"The Japanese are attacking the town. We stand no chance," he said and left without another word. Dad came back with a bunch of keys and told Dempsey to get his buddies to come along as he went to the police armory to see what he could find. Dempsey ran around the refugee village and rounded up twenty young Karens. They followed Dad to the armory. Dad had a hard time opening the armory because he did not know which key was for the armory. When they finally got the armory door opened they found about twenty five rifles and boxes of .303 ammunitions. Dad told the men to help themselves. Dempsey took two rifles and some ammunition. Dad then told the men, "Dempsey is in charge. You will take orders from him."

They marched back to the village. Dempsey gave me a rifle and some ammunition and told me not to leave the family and to be with them at all times. He left with the men to the town square to find out what was going on.

What really happened was, a woman was said to have seen Japanese soldiers boarding a boat and were preparing to proceed to Twante. She concluded that the Japanese were coming to Twante to attack the town and she set off the alarm. When Dempsey and his men reached the river front they found that there were some twenty five young Burman from the town all armed with rifles that had taken up positions and were waiting for the Japanese boat to arrive. The boat soon appeared. It was a small motor craft that could not have held more than fifteen or eighteen Japanese soldiers. Dempsey told his men to hold their fire and to wait and see what the Japanese would do. He would give the order to fire. As the boat drew close, the Burman boys opened fire. Japanese soldiers jumped off the boat and tried to swim across the canal. Some who made it climbed up the opposite bank of the canal and ran into the rice field.

The Burmese contingent rushed to the river, jumped into sampans and crossed over to the opposite bank in pursuit of the fleeing Japanese soldiers. Dempsey told his men not to fire. "These Japanese soldiers are trying to get back to their units in Rangoon. We're not going to shoot them in the back" he told his men.

At home we were waiting in suspense not knowing what was going on. After more than an hour Dempsey came back with some of his men and told us what happened. Dad agreed with Dempsey that the Japanese were just trying to get back to Rangoon to rejoin their units and there was no need to ambush them. There were no more Japanese in town now and also there was no civil administration. But the town was quiet with people walking quietly from place to place, house to house, chatting in small groups. We were all wondering when the Allies would show up. The day passed quietly into night with no more exciting incidents.

Next day we were sitting out in the morning sun on the bamboo benches by the duck pond after we had had breakfast and talked about the previous day's excitement. We were all certain that none of the Japanese soldiers who ran across the rice field on the other side of the canal could have survived. We wished that there had been no ambush so that they could at least have rejoined their units in Rangoon and eventually return home to be reunited with their families. But this was war. These soldiers had placed their lives on line for their country as did British and American soldiers and others who were fighting in the war.

Just then we heard the sounds of motor launches chugging along the canal. Soon the town alarm sounded and we stood up to look around. Dempsey ran for his rifle and started to run to round up his men. Almost immediately we saw an aircraft approaching, this time from the east. It came in very low and fired a long volley from it's cannons. As we made a dash for the shelter Dempsey shouted, "It's a British plane. It's RAF."
Mom ran into the house and brought out a large Union Jack at least ten feet by fourteen feet, and spread it out on the front yard. Where, when and how she got hold of that huge flag we didn't know. We were all excited and looked all around us to see if there were already Allied soldiers in town. We stayed by the shelter and watched the aircraft as it turned around and made another swoop over the canal and fired several bursts again. Obviously the chugging boats had been the target. Probably it was more Japanese soldiers trying to reach Rangoon. As the plane flew away it dipped it's wings in a victory sign.
"He saw the flag! He saw the flag!" Mom screamed.

"I really feel sorry for those Japanese boys," Dad said.

"The boats we heard chugging along the canal earlier must have been carrying remnants of Japanese soldiers on retreat, like the one yesterday," I said.

"They had to be. Or they wouldn't be attacked. I feel so sad for the Japanese," Audrey said. "They must have been trying to catch up with their units in Rangoon."

"Even if they made it to Rangoon, they couldn't survive," Dad said, "because Rangoon is already in Allied hands"

"How do you know?" Audrey asked.

"Remember the last three bombings in one day over Rangoon yesterday?" Dad asked. "There was no resistance from the Japanese, no anti aircraft guns, no Zero fighters in the air. The Japanese had abandoned Rangoon."

"Yes, I think Rangoon is retaken already," Louise said. "The plane that came just now came from the direction of Rangoon and returned the same way."

"Aren't you girls going to finish preparing lunch?" Mom called out. "I'm hungry."

"We're almost done," Nita called out from the kitchen. "May Paw and Pauline, help us get the tables ready for lunch, please."

Just as we were about to finish lunch, one of the town elders came to see Dad.

"Do you know that Allied troops are in town already?" he shouted before he even got to the house. We jumped up nearly upsetting the table. The man came and leaned against the rail of the landing as we sat around facing him to hear the news. He had just spoken to one of the officers who just got into Twante with a company of soldiers. When some of the Allied troops came from the sea in landing crafts, they didn't find any Japanese in Rangoon. Another detachment marched down from the north and met with no resistance. Rangoon was now reoccupied by the British and Allied troops. We were laughing, yelling and cheering now that the war had ended. Then I looked around and noticed that Nita was not with us. I looked in the kitchen but she was not there, either. I became very close to Nita from the days we were together in Rangoon before Ba Thet was taken away by the Japanese. I then went into the girl's room and there found Nita crying over a pillow she placed over her knees. I knelt down beside her but could not come up with any comforting words to say to her. I just held her shoulders and let her cry.

Someone must have found us out. The merry making outside stopped and everyone started to talk in whispers. We were together for a whole half hour until Mom and Dad came in and started to talk to Nita. Dad broke down as he tried to say something to Nita and never got the words out. Mom was the stronger of the two. She took her eldest daughter's hand and said, "You know, Nita, Dad and I, apart from our devotional prayer, pray every night on our own for Ba Thet and I know the Lord is with him. We also pray for you for we know what you are going through. Just remember that we all love you and most of all God loves you, dear." As Mom and Dad left the room I released my hold on Nita's shoulder and looked down to see her face. She wiped her tears with the edge of the pillow slip and gave me a faint smile.

"Thank you, Spence," she whispered and held me for a whole minute. I was worried that she might start crying again. But instead, she got up smiling and pulled me by the hand and went out to the landing to join the rest of the family. The town elder who came to give us the good news had left. Now the family was discussing our return to Insein. Louise brought us up to date.

"Dad wants to return to Insein as soon as possible," she said. "So Dempsey is going to try to hire a large boat. The day after Dempsey gets the boat we'll leave. We don't have much personal belongings so we don't need much time packing. The problem is to get a boat soon. There will be a rush of refugees returning to Rangoon and the suburbs. So it will be quite difficult to get a large boat within days. We may have to wait a week or even longer."

But we didn't have to wait a week. Dempsey knew the boatman who took our CE group to a wedding several months ago. He went to the boatman's house. The boatman was on a trip to Rangoon but would be returning the same night with the high tide. Dempsey told the boatman's wife that he liked to reserve the boat and he even made full cash payment in advance. We were to leave the day after the boatman returned. Dad was pleased. He called the family together after lunch because he had something to say. We were all wondering what announcement dad was going to make.

"First of all," he started to say, "I thank the Lord for His blessings. We endured the war and have not only survived but have grown in strength and experience in faith. I am proud of every one of you for doing your part, sharing in your responsibilities, without complaining. And I didn't have to lift a finger to take care of the family. Once we get back into our own lives and go our own ways don't ever forget your family, and your heritage. Above all, let the Lord be your guide in everything that you do. Take strength in Him in troubled time. Share your time and talents with others, especially those who need you most. You girls, including the little ones (meaning May Paw and Pauline), have done a great job taking care of Mom and me and running the home. Dempsey and Spencer, the two of you, just out of your teen, exceeded my expectation in protecting and providing for the family during these hard times. I have not heard a word of complaint from any of you."

Mom interjected, "We have spent almost four years together – they were four glorious years with all our children. There was no arguing, no fighting."

"But Dempsey and Spencer had a fight over the shelter, remember Mom?" Audrey quipped.

"Don't forget you slapped Nita in the face, Audrey," Dempsey told her. Everyone laughed.

"What your mother tried to say is," Dad said, "that we are very proud of our children. We thank you. We say it now because once you go your own ways we may not have the chance to say this."

"We thank the Lord," Mom said, "that we can be proud of all of you. Our prayers will be with each one of you no matter where you are."

Nita went to Mom and give her a hug and then to Dad. One by one we followed suit.

"Meeting is adjourned," Dempsey said as he walked out to make a last trip to fill up the jars in the kitchen.

"Don't forget, Penn, you have two more trips to make," he reminded me.

CHAPTER 10

BACK HOME AGAIN

WHEN WE RETURNED TO INSEIN, Harry, Grandpa's younger brother, was there to greet us. The gardener had left, he told Grandpa. Harry couldn't keep vandals from running through the house carting away lighter furniture and breaking others they could not carry. A few windows were broken, otherwise the house was intact. The old piano was missing but the long teak dining table remained intact and suffered no damage at all. We started to clean up immediately, throwing away broken pieces of furniture and debris out and sweeping the floors. Nita and Audrey went into the detached kitchen to take a look.

Audrey came back immediately. "You won't believe it," she said, "nothing is taken from the kitchen. Everything seems in place as the Japanese must have left them. There are even new pots and pans." Mom made a list of things we needed the most – a 180 pound bag of rice, a four gallons tin cooking oil, four gallon kerosene oil, salt, sauce, sugar, brooms, dish cloths, bar soap, etc. Dempsey and I were given the responsibility to get these articles immediately while the girls had to go to the market each day to buy fresh meat and vegetables. My brother and I, with the help of our new male servant, also had to clean up the well because the Japanese had neglected to clean it periodically like Grandpa did every year. Once a year before the monsoon, silt at the bottom of the well had to be cleaned out to keep the water clean and the spring running. Grandpa and Grandma were returning from Twante so we wanted to have everything in order before they arrived.

Meantime Dad was anxious to return to civil service as soon as possible. He had to go to Rangoon to report to the Civil Affairs Service, CAS(B). He took Dempsey with him because Dad had never taken public transportation before and would never be able to find his way around. He came back rather late in the afternoon in a car that he had just bought, with Dempsey at the wheel. He was asked to return to CAS(B) in ten days to get his posting order as mail service was not yet reliable. Then Dad read a letter brought by some one while he was away in Rangood that day. The letter was from Uncle Albert. After reading the letter Dad said, "Penn, this letter is from your Uncle Albert. Do you know anyone by the name of Harry?"

"Yes, I told him. "I know a few Harrys, but Harry who?" I asked.

"You uncle didn't say. But he said this man is Arakanese and he went to Univeristy College before the war."

"I know him. What about Harry?" I asked.

"Albert's niece, he didn't mention her name, supposedly allowed the man to live on the landthat belong to Albert and Richard. Can you find out if the man is the Harry you know and if so under what kind of agreement ishe living on the land Albert could not find any document relating to the property. No map, no deed. Nothing."

"I'll go and see Harry tomorrow, I replied, "if you tell me where he lives.'

It looked like alarge property but it was completely fenced in with bamboo stocks. It looked more like a stockade. I looked through the crack in the gate. A man was walking up and down inside the gate. A watchmanm? Or a guard? He was carrying no weapon. I picked up a stone and knocked on the gate. The man walked over, peeked through the crack and asked me what I wanted.

"Is Harry home?" I asked. The man didn't recognize the name Harry, a western name.

"Is your boss in? I asked

"What do you want with him?" he asked back. "Who are you?"

"I have a business to talk about," I replied.

"He won't see anyone. He is in a bad mood now," he told me.

Just then someone called out from the bamboo hut inside.

The man walked back to the hut and after few minutes returned to open the gate for me. He pushed the gate open just a little because the bottom of the gate was dragging on the red soil. I squeezed myself through the narrow opening and walked over to the hut. Someone came out to meet me.

"Hey, Spencer, what the hell are you doing here?" It was Harry alright. "I was expecting someone else," he said.

"Just thought I'd drop by to see you." I said. "You got a nice piece of land here. Want to sell me a part of it?" I asked.

"I don't actually own the damn property yet. I hope I will soon," he replied.

"Know where Iris is?" I asked him.

"Come on, let's talk about something else," he told me. Iris, a beautiful Burmese girl, was his girl friend in college.

We started talking shop, about the war and the future of Burma.

I looked out and studied the land from where I was sitting. A young girl brought a tea pot and pour out tea for us.

"You've been excavating and selling earth and rocks?" I asked. There were mounds of red soil and piles of rocks or stones. There were also a couple of trucks.

"You can say that," he answered."

"But you said you don't own the land yet, Harry," I told him.

"The property belongs to someone, a girl. You won't know her. I hope I find some way of getting a parternership with her. Now that I have excavated so much off the land I am thinking of filling it up when the rains came and have a fish farm."

So Harry is making money out the land he did not own and planning to make some more dough out of it.

"So you leased the land from the girl? Who is she?" I asked.

."Not lease the land from her. We're doing it together. She's Karen, you know. You won't know her," he said.

"Have some more tea. I've got to go in a while. Nice seeing you again," he said, dismissing me.

I went home and reported to Dad that there was no legal agreement between Harry and Uncle Albert's niece. Harry was just taking advantage of the girl. I don't know what happened to the land later. I never followed up on the matter.

There was no phone at Zion Hill. Contact with another person was only possible by a visit in person. One of Dad's friends in Nanthagon, a village about a quarter mile to the north, came to see Dad to bring tragic news to the family. There were just the two of them in the sitting room. Mom was in the kitchen with the new servant girl. Dempsey and I were clearing trash in the back yard with the male servant. The girls were out visiting somewhere. The friend told Dad that a messenger was sent from someone in an army unit in Moulmein to tell him that Captain Ba Thet Gyi had been shot and killed by the Japanese near Papun at a Force 136 Camp. But Dad told the friend that Ba Thet was a prisoner taken away by the Japanese on their retreat.

"Yes," explained the friend, "Ba Thet was taken by the Japanese but he jumped off the train while the train was moving and managed to find his way to the camp near Papun. One night about two weeks ago as he was preparing to retire in a hammock someone called out his name. From the assassin's pronunciation of the name, it was thought that he was Japanese. Ba Thet sat up and there was a burst of gun fire. He toppled to the ground, dead. Men from his unit combed the area all night but the assassin managed to get away."

Just then Dempsey and I came into the sitting room but we stopped short when we saw Dad sobbing with both hands pressed against his face, his whole body shaking. The friend rose from his seat and walked over to Dad and placed a hand on his shoulder. Dempsey asked Dad's friend, "What's wrong? What happened?"

"Your brother in-law, Captain Ba Thet Gyi is dead. Shot and killed by the Japanese."

Dempsey was very close to Ba Thet long before the war when Nita and Ba Thet were dating in Rangoon. Ba Thet used to take him out to movies and dinners and they became very close.

"No, no, no," Dempsey cried and went over to Dad and knelt down by his chair and wept over Dad's knees.

It took me a little while for this tragic news to sink in. It was so unreal. My first thought was Nita. I knew she was not home but I worried for her. Poor Nita. What could I say to her? I ran into the house as Mom was returning from the kitchen and was heading for the sitting room. I said, "Mom," but couldn't say another word.

"What's the matter? Why are you crying?" she asked.

"Ba Thet,..." was all I could say.

Mom looked over into the sitting room and saw Dad sobbing with Dempsey crying at his knees. Dad's friend now was standing awkwardly behind Dad. Mom walked over to the sitting room, taking me along, her hand around my shoulder and walked straight to Dad's friend. Addressing the friend, Mom said, "Can you tell me what happened?"

The friend slowly repeated the story. Mom didn't cry.

"God has a purpose to let that happen. I just feel concerned for my daughter at this time. She had gone through so much."

"I'm sorry that I had to bring you this tragic news," the friend told Mom. "We will be thinking of your family in our prayers." He touched Dad on the shoulder again and left.

By now Dad had regained his composure. He looked at Mom. "What are we going to tell our daughter?" he asked Mom.

"Just tell her the truth," Mom replied.

"The girls are back," I told them.

I heard talking and laughing as the girls made their way into the house and were now walking up the front stairs. Dempsey rose from Dad's side and headed for the stairway. I thought he was going to meet the girls but as the girls came into the sitting room he abruptly turned and retreated into the bed room and threw himself on the bed burying his face in a pillow.

"What's wrong with Dempsey?" Louise wanted to know.

Without saying a word Mom motioned to the girls to take their seats.

"Another conference?" Audrey asked.

"Why all the long faces?" Louise asked, then, "Dad, you've been crying."

Nita took the chair next to Dad and asked, "Dad, what happened to Ba Thet?"

"He's no more with us," Mom told her and moved over to Nita.

Nita put up a hand. "It's alright, Mom, I'll be all right. Just tell me what happened."

Mom slowly repeated the story. Audrey began to cry quietly. Louise wanted to know who brought the news. Dad told her. Nita leaned back in her chair, looked up at the ceiling and blinked several times. But there were no tears. She sighed and said softly, "I knew this was going to happen. I was expecting something like this, knowing Ba Thet. But I was also hoping that I'll see him again though I had accepted the fact that we may not see him any more. I'm strong, Mom, like you." She reached out to hold Mom's hand and squeezed it lightly.

The following week Dad got his orders from CAS (B) to resume service with the Burma Civil Service. He was to be Deputy Commissioner of Insein District. That meant that he could stay on at Grandpa's house. Dad didn't drive and he did not want Dempsey and me to be tied down with having to drive him to office and back each day because he wanted us to be free to do what we had to, to go back to school or look for jobs. So Dad hired a chauffeur. Audrey went to live in Rangoon as she had just started working as assistant manager for a Chinese company.

Dempsey and I decided that we would go back to school. We went to the University to find out when college was opening. While we were at the university someone told us that young men were lining up at Bombay

Burma Trading Company on Phayre Street in Rangoon to apply to join the British Navy as cadets. We took a bus to Phayre Street to find out. We saw the long line of young men patiently waiting for their turn to get into the building.. We took our place at the end of the line while discussing if this was what we really wanted. We wondered if we should go back to school instead. Every now and again we watched naval officers as they walked past in their white uniform, with peaked caps on their heads and gold stripes on the epaulettes showing their ranks. I thought they looked really smart.

Let's just see what happens, Okay?" he told me. "We may not even get the chance to get into the building. The line is so long."

Forty five minutes later we were almost at the entrance. We looked back and found that there were at least some forty or forty five young men behind us. Ten minutes later when the two of us were already at the door a hefty uniformed navy man began to close the door.

"That's all fellas." He called out. Just as the door was closing Dempsey pushed me hard and we both stumbled inside. The man looked at us, shook his head but said nothing. He showed us where the applications were and made us sit at a bench to fill out the papers.

"Phew!" Dempsey said, "we just made it."

"Thanks Dem," I replied and began to fill up my application form.

We had to go back in ten days for the results which would be displayed on the bulletin board placed in the hallway. After ten days, as we entered the hall of the building, Dempsey told me, "Don't look all over the board for your name. Look at the end of the list under 'Z'." Of course I knew that. We both looked and we found only two names under 'Z': ZAN, DEMPSEY and ZAN, SPENCER. We made it! There were only about thirty other names on the board out of at least two hundred that lined up ten days earlier. A date on which we were to report at the Navy Base at Monkey Point was shown at the bottom of the notice. We rushed home with the good news. Mom and Dad were very pleased. On the appointed day we went to Monkey Point to report and a Petty Officer issued us with a kit bag, some uniforms and a pair of boots. "The leading seaman will take you to your boat," we were told.

We had to wait for three or four more 'cadets' before a leading seaman took us to our training ship, ML 418. It was a Fairmile Class coastal patrol boat with twin screws that ran on 100 Octane. It looked dirty and some of the structures were rusty with paints chipped in many places. There were large and small patches of red lead on the superstructures.

I was quite disappointed. The leading seaman led us into the foc'sle, or seaman's quarters, which would be our home for the next several months. We went down the gangway into the foc'sle, our new home, and found that there were some cadets already there. I walked over to a bunk that was still unoccupied and placed my kit bag on it. Dempsey and I looked around to see if we knew anyone when a couple of them called out our names. They were friends we knew back in college. The leading seaman turned to leave and then looked back and said, "The Chief Petty Officer will be with you in an hour." Then he disappeared up the gangway. An hour later another leading seaman came down the gangway followed by five more cadets. "The Chief will be here in an hour," he told us and left.

We tried to strike up conversation with the other cadets as we waited for the Chief Petty Officer. One of the cadets brought some snacks and passed them around as we talked and tried to get better acquainted. It was more than one and a half hours before the Chief Petty Officer came down to the foc'sle, a clip board under his arm. He was accompanied by the first leading seaman who brought us to the boat. Some of us stood up while others continued to sit on the bunks.

The Chief surveyed the group, his eyes traveling from one cadet to the next. It took a whole minute before he narrowed his eyes and barked, "Stand up, you idiots."
Those who were sitting quickly scrambled to their feet. I pulled myself up straight. Another minute of silence went by as he continued to shift his stare from one cadet to the next.
"I don't think any of you will make it to become officers of the navy. You look a pathetic lot," he said quietly and shook his head in disapproval. Then he said, "My name is Ray. I am the Chief Petty Officer on this boat. I will be your instructor until you graduate. That is, if you graduate. I am not a commissioned officer. You don't address me as 'Sir'. You call me 'Chief'. Again he surveyed us, resting his eyes momentarily on each cadet. There was a long silence.

Then he said, "I'm looking for someone with guts. Any one here who has any guts, step forward." No one stepped forward. After a while he said, "You must be a bunch of sissies. You won't make it to officers. Now, any one with any spunk at all?" he repeated. At this point Dempsey was wondering if he was calling for a fight just to show us who the boss was. If so Dempsey thought he could handle him. Dempsey was in the school boxing team in his high school days. He was debating whether he should step forward to accept the challenge when Ray called out again, "I want someone with any guts at all to step forward."

Dempsey took a step forward. Ray took a step closer to Dempsey and looked him over.

"What's your name?" he barked.

"Dempsey Zan," Dempsey answered.

Ray looked at his clip board and studied it for a few seconds.

"Zan, see those heads over there?" Dempsey looked puzzled.

"If you don't know what heads mean, it's the toilet, stupid. They are blocked and need to be cleaned out. See that bucket and the brush over there? Pick them up and get to work."

Someone giggled.

"Who was that?" he asked. "We don't want any women in here. Then he spoke to the rest of us. "I'm your instructor for the next twelve months of your training. Not all of you will make it to officers. But if you try really hard, work hard with perseverance and discipline, you will get there. Your training starts tomorrow after breakfast," he said and he went on explaining in more detail what we'd have to learn – starting with seamanship, while we would also have to chip, and paint the super structures, the hull and water line, and scrub the deck with the holy stone. Later we would have small arms and gunnery training, learn communications including Morse codes, signaling by semaphore and then complete our course in navigation and pass the exam to qualify for our commission.

We had good comradeship and our training went pretty smoothly with no problem for Ray to complain about although he would frequently give one or the other of us a hard time with harsh or foul language that only drill sergeants could come up with. Sometime later we were taken out to sea on a maneuver with a squadron of other ships and we thoroughly enjoyed that new experience although a couple of cadets became sea sick the first few days. Next we were transferred from ML418 to a mine sweeper for mine sweeping training for two weeks. After that we were returned to ML418 to resume painting the boat. With most of the paints applied to the superstructures and the hull, the boat now looked quite beautiful. I even commented to Ray about it thinking he would appreciate it. He didn't as much as smile. That next week end, after we returned to the boat, I went on liberty and came back with a bad cold. I also returned late because of a city wide bus strike.

"I'm sorry chief," I told Ray, " I couldn't get back in time because of the bus strike."

"I'll take care of you later," he replied shortly.

During a break in the afternoon he took me aside and told me to paint the water line which involved getting wet in the water.
"Chief, can someone else do it?" I asked Ray. "I have a chest cold."
"Go down and paint the water line," he ordered.
Well, I thought, that's how he's taking care of me.
Dempsey walked over and said to Ray, "Chief, let me do it. My brother has a cold."
"I asked your brother to do the job and he will do it."
"Please Chief, he has a bad cold. Let me go down and paint the water line, Okay?"
"You don't get me," he replied. "I asked Spencer to paint the waterline. Not you."
A couple of cadets now stopped working and were watching us. I became very uncomfortable because I knew that Dempsey, when pushed, could be very short tempered.
"Never mind, Dempsey, I'll do it," I told him.
Dempsey roughly pushed me aside, moved a little closer to Ray, reached out and grabbed a fistful of Ray's shirt front, and very quietly said, "Chief, I'm going down to the waterline."
Oh, boy, Dempsey, you did it, I said to myself. Now he'll get you. Ray gave a faint smile with a sideway glance and said, "All right. You do it." Then as Dempsey let go of his shirt front, he slowly walked away. Those cadets who were watching were stunned. We were all afraid of Ray except Dempsey who picked up the gear and disappeared over the side to paint the waterline. When we got back into the foc'sle after work that day a fellow cadet told Dempsey, "He's going to get back at you, pal. You better hold your horse."

Months after that incident we were transferred to the flag ship *HMS MAYU*, which after independence was renamed *UBS* (Union of Burma Ship) *MAYU*, for our navigational training. It was a beautiful Frigate. Here we did not have to do seamen's duties any more but had to attend navigational classes every day conducted mostly by a young Lieutenant, named K. T. Lwin and sometimes the captain, Commander Bo himself. This was the last stage of our training. We were often taken out to sea for practical navigational training to get to learn to use the sextant to take sights to pin point our position on the chart among other things. After our last training trip out at sea we had to take our exam on the *MAYU*. After the exam we were returned to ML 418 where we resumed our seamen's duties while we waited for the results. About a week later, Ray came into the foc'sle to announce the results. He read out the names of successful cadets and since our names start with 'Z', we had to wait till the end of the list to learn if we made it. At last Ray called out, "Midshipman Spencer Zan,...," and then continued, "that's all folks. Congratulations to all of you. The rest of you who didn't make it, pack up your uniforms in your kit bags and return them to base. And good luck." He then came over to shake our hands. I felt like Ray had just hit me in the pit of the stomach. Poor Dempsey, I thought. I couldn't even look at him. I walked over and sat on my bunk after I shook hands with Ray and looked at the new midshipmen who were still shaking hands with Ray. Then my eyes shifted to the others who didn't make it. My eye caught Dempsey shaking hands with them and smiling. I walked over and offered Dempsey my hand but couldn't say anything. He must have noticed my eyes welling.

"Don't worry, kid. I'll be all right," he told me as he started to pick up his uniform to stuff into the kit bag.

"See you at home this week end," he told me. Later I walked with him to the gangway as he left for the base to return the uniform. He turned back and raised his hand in a mock salute before he disappeared round the building.

CHAPTER 11

SERVICE IN THE NAVY

THE FOC'SLE WAS NOISY WITH all of us talking and speculating about where we might be posted. There was a loud thud. The foc'sle was suddenly quiet. Ray had jumped down from the last four rungs of the gangway. Everyone stood up.

"You don't have to stand up for me, gentlemen," he said. "You are officers and now I have to call you 'sir'. I want to celebrate with you tonight so I have ordered some food for dinner." A seaman came down the gangway holding a two gallon jar of Jamaica rum. "Get your mugs, gentlemen," he said and opened the bottle. He filled up a mug for himself and poured the rum into our mugs. Then he held up his mug and said, "Cheers, gentlemen, and congratulations."

We drank for several minutes before the food arrived. There was roast duck, roast pork. By that time most of us were getting quite merry. Some were singing while others were moving around and talking aloud to each other so they could be heard.

"You know," Ray said aloud, "I do feel very sorry for those who didn't make it. Some of them did very well in many areas but not in all. You see, you have to score high marks in all subjects to pass."

I was sitting at the table next to Ray. He placed a hand on my shoulder and said, "You know, your brother actually did better than you did."

"Then why didn't he pass?" I asked him.

"Insubordination! Insubordination my friend, is not tolerated in the navy," he replied.

"Food is running out, Ray, I mean, Chief," someone shouted.

"Hey, you can call me Ray. It's okay," he said, then turned to climb up the gangway. He missed his step and nearly fell backwards but managed to regain his balance, walked up and disappeared up the deck.

"The son of a gun is already drunk," someone observed.

"Let's get him really drunk tonight," another said.

Actually we were all getting tipsy ourselves and we agreed to get Ray drunk that night.

Ray came back. "Some more food coming up," he said. The singing and shouting went on as we kept pouring more and more rum in Ray's mug. The stuff was strong and we were drinking neat. I knew I was already tipsy in spite of the fact that I was going slow with my drink. I wanted to stay sober to enjoy the evening so occasionally I walked away and diluted my drink with water or emptied it into the sink when no one was looking. Now Ray was slouching over the table but was still trying to talk. We ignored him. Someone suggested we went up to the deck. We didn't realize that it was already dark outside. Someone knelt down in front of the long box that housed the spare Bofors gun barrel.

"What are you doing?" I asked him.

"Trying to pick the lock. Let's throw the barrel over the side and get Ray in trouble"

"Throw the whole box overboard," someone suggested. Another made a nasty remark that angered the cadet who was picking the lock and a fight broke out. Somehow we all ganged up against the cadet who just made a nasty remark and held him down on the deck and stripped him stark naked. While he was being held down I got hold of a can of gray paint and a brush and painted an underwear on his bare lower torso. When we finally went back into the foc'sle Ray was still slouched over the table singing to himself. The stronger guys lifted him up and placed him on an upper bunk and tied his hands and legs to the bunk support chains to keep him from falling off. It was past midnight by then and we decided to call it a day. When I woke up early in the morning I saw that Ray was sleeping in the bunk below the one he was placed in the night before. Someone had mercifully untied Ray and carried him down. We never found out who it was.

We went on liberty that morning leaving Ray still sleeping in the foc'sle. When I got home in Insein the family already knew that I had made it to midshipman because Dempsey was home three days earlier. Dad was not disappointed that Dempsey did not make it because he believed that Dempsey would make a better army officer than he would a navy officer having had the experience of being a corporal in the UTC in college. There was a visitor at the house at the time I got home. Colonel Marcus Paw was visiting Louise. He and Louise were studying together in England before the war. He graduated from the Medical College in Rangoon with M.B.B.S. and went for further studies in England where he received his M.R.C.P. (Member of the Royal College of Physicians) and F.R.C.S. (Fellow of Royal Colllege of Surgeons ?)

While Louise returned to Burma at the outset of the war, Marcus joined the Army Medical Corp and served in the South East Asia War Theater as a medical doctor during the war. Louise and Marcus were engaged while I was in training in the navy and in October 1945, the same month that I became a midshipman, they were married.

Upon our return from liberty we were given our postings. I was posted as Number One on HDML 1462. A 'Number One' was a second in command of a ship. No matter where we were posted we were still under training until we became sub-lieutenants, and in this case I was being trained to learn the nitty-gritty of running a coastal patrol boat like ship handling and managing the crew, etc. My first post on the HDML was in a combat zone on the Arakan coast where the Fourth Burma Regiment consisting of Gurkha troops was engaging communist rebels led by the Arakan communist leader U Sein Da. The navy's chief duties were to transport troops or escort them to combat zones. Every four or five months I was transferred from ship to ship under different commanders, serving in the Deltas or the Tennasserim Coast, and again back to the Arakans in operations against communist insurgents.

During my early service in the Arakan, I had a rather unusual pet, an otter I named Silver, given me by an Arakanese friend. I occupied an end cot in the officer's quarters and next to me was Lieutenant Douglas Pe Tha, the only surviver of the Saw Pe Tha family. Douglas survived only because he was in India serving as a midshipman in the Royal Indian Naval Reserve. He also had a pet, a monkey he named Bayoke, which got along very well with my pet, Silver. Douglas fed his pet monkey with bananas and fruits. I fed my otter with live fish because it refused to eat dead fish. He wanted to play with a live fish in a pool on the beach before he made a final meal of it. Douglas and I used to take early morning walk along the beach accompanied by our pets. At times when we woke up late, our pets would take the walk by themselves. One day we got up late and we knew that the odd couple had taken a walk. But this time the monkey came back alone, jumping and screaming to get our attention. "Where is Silver?" I asked, but Bayoke the monkey, just kept jumping and screaming.

We knew that something was wrong. Bayoke led us back to the beach. After walking for a half mile, the Bayoke stopped and kept jumping near a pile of what we thought was a jacket washed ashore at high tide. It turned out to be the remains of the otter - pelt, head, tail and bones. The otter had obviously been attacked by jackals which were roaming wild in the nearby woods while Bayoke managed to escape.

While I was on my second assignment in the Arakan I received a telegram from Dad that Marcus, my brother in law was in the Military Hospital in Rangoon suffering from concussion. His jeep driven by an army driver went off the cliff and landed some twenty feet below. The driver died. Marcus was returning to Myitkyina where he headed the Army Medical Unit when the accident occurred. He was discovered unconscious only the following morning and immediately flown to Rangoon. He was in a coma for fourteen days. When he regained consciousness he never remembered that he was married although he remembered Louise and the rest of us. I asked for a transfer to be with the family. He was in the military hospital for several months and after he was discharged he returned to service and was posted to Meiktila. Louise was able, very slowly, to nurse him to regain most of his recent memories. Although he was suffering from a degree of memory lapse, he functioned extremely well in his job.

By the time I returned to my assignment in the Arakan, we were all promoted to Sub- Lieutenants and then I was sent to Ceylon (now Sri Lanka) along with two other officers for training at the British Naval Base in Trincomalee. Upon my return I was posted to the only mine sweeper the navy had, under the command of Lieutenant K. T. Lwin who was our navigation instructor on the *MAYU* during our training. I learned later that Lt. Lwin, we called him K.T., asked for me specifically to be his Number One. I did not know the reason he chose me but I knew from the first day that I liked him and we became very good friends. We read the same books and listened to the same kind of music and liked to watch the same movies. It turned out we had a lot in common and we got along very well. There was a third officer, a sublieutenant George Daing, or K. D. who was commissioned after our batch of officers. K.T. had Burmese crew he carefully selected as half of the crew on the mine sweeper. They were hard working, intelligent and young. The existing Chief Petty Officer was a Karen by the name of Henry Saw Oo. K.T. asked me to select the other half of the crew. So I selected Karen young men, who were bigger and stronger knowing that we would also need muscles on the ship. Serving on the minesweeper was one of the highlights of my naval career. I believed that we had the best run ship with some of the best crew in the navy. K. T. certainly a very good skipper.

I was posted to the mine sweeper at a time when political maneuverings were gaining momentum in Burma. The Burman political movement under the leadership of General Aung San was demanding for independence from the British government. At the same time, the Karen community in general was wary of their safety and security in an independent Burma under a Burman administration after the horrible experience at the hands of the B.I.A. when Japan invaded Burma. They were afraid that under independent Burma they would be treated as second citizens. They also felt that the British owed them one, having been loyal during the war. Also during the Japanese occupation many villages were torched, village elders and other Karen leaders were executed by the Japanese army for their loyalty to the British and for their help supposedly given to British agents during the war. The Karen also believed that they were the main force that helped the Allies regain the country from the Japanese which fact had been testified or confirmed in accounts retold and in books written by former British soldiers and other notable journalists and authors. All these led to the decision to send a delegation led by Saw Ba U Gyi to petition the British government to create a separate Karen state for the Karen which would remain within the British Commonwealth. Saw Ba U Gyi set up the Karen National Union Head Quarters at his house in Sanchaung where my sister Nita had lived with her husband Ba Thet during Japanese occupation. Nita helped Saw Ba U Gyi with many of his busy schedules, making appointments or setting up interviews in an unofficial capacity, typing memos and directives and in time became close to him which ultimately led to a civil marriage, conducted by Rev. Maung Bu of the Karen Theological Seminary, Insein.

There was an air of suspense because of the complex political situation with many parties trying to jockey for positions of advantage to participate in the new independent government. There were the Communist Party, Myo Chit Party, Do-Bama Asi-Ayone, and the P.B.F. to name just a few and there also was the question of Karen aspiration for their own state. General Aung San had envisioned a program of autonomy for the minorities which in his view would prevent the nation from disintegrating. However, on July 19, 1947, General Aung San was assassinated along with most of his cabinet members while the cabinet was in session. U Nu who was next in line in AFPFL leadership took over the rein of the Party but he rejected the program of autonomy for minorities as envisioned by General Aung San, for he believed that it would instead result in disintegration of the Union. It is my belief that U Nu considered the ethnic minorities inferior to the Burman race and I had wondered whether U Nu and General Ne Win could have something to do with the assassination of General Aung San or at least knew about it. Both were dead opposed to the granting of full autonomy to ethnic minorities.

As I can see today U Nu was wrong. Under Aung San's plan, the nation would certainly struggle with many problems that could be faced by the central government and the different states within the Union but the country would still remain strong and united and continue to progress as the government and people learned to deal with those problems democratically. Today, run and mismanaged by the generals beginning from Ne Win to today's military dictators, the country has been reduced to one of the poorest and most underdeveloped and impoverished nations in the world, down from a position of one of the most advanced in the east before the army took over. According to the Asian Development Bank, Burma's economic development was lagging way behind the rest of South East Asia. Prosperous and developing Burma was reduced within a few years of army take over from riches to rags.

I was later posted to a Flotilla operating in the Deltas. I was Number One on an HDML under Lieutenant Tin Thein Lu and our duty was to take cabinet ministers on their tour of the regions in the Deltas visiting Burman and Karen villages One of the ministers that we had to take was Thakin Tin who was visiting the villages in the Deltas to try to ease the tension now building up between the two ethnic races. He spoke to village elders of both races and asked them to control their villagers to make sure that no clashes would take place. He wanted to make sure that no village instigates a clash that could escalate into an all out communal riot. We stopped at dozens of villages. I admire Thakin Tin's tact as he responded to questions posed by village heads very patiently. He would quietly admonish those who were out of line. He never used any harsh language. We also stopped at Bassein, a large town in the west where there was a large population of Karen. There he held a town meeting which I did not attend because I had an old classmate visiting. It was from this classmate that I learned that Uncle Albert's niece Chris, the lone survival of Uncle Richard's family, who was missing after the communal riots in Myaungmya, was living with a friend. This little girl had been wounded and was abandoned by her nanny. A Burman Buddhist priest found the wounded girl outside of the monastry. He took the girl in and hid her under a basket when the B.I.A. searched the monastry. He treated her wounds and took care of the child till she recovered. Later he handed over the girl to a Karen friend who recognized the little girl. She was now about seven years old. I had no time to get to see Chris as our boat was scheduled to sail that same day after the town meeting. I got her address, however, and when I returned to Rangoon, I wrote to Uncle Albert that Chris was in Bassein in the care of a friend. Later Uncle Albert went to Bassein and fetched Chris and took her home with him. Today Chris and her husband are happily settled down in North Carolina, and believe it or not, her husband is Burman, and I cannot name a more happily married couple if I tried. They now have three grown children with their own families and are all doing very well in the United States.

I was later posted to Akyab Naval Base as Senior Officer, Arakan Flotilla. I left my Delta Flotilla to take over my new job in Akyab. Although in charge of the base, I also commanded my own ship, an HDML with mostly Karen crew. All of our actions against the insurgents were along the coasts and in rivers and even in creeks. This time we were fighting the Mojahids, hard hitting Moslem separatists, demanding their own homeland. I had only three HDMLs under my command and all three would be involved in combat at one time or another under very able officers and crew. We also had to escort troops as they were transported to their bases or to combat zones and thus occasionally we would get drawn into fire fights when we were ambushed along the narrow upper reaches Kaladan River, the Naaf River or even in the creeks along the coast. Sometimes we had to provide covering fire with our twenty millimeter Oerlikon cannons as troops were landed to attack rebel strongholds.

One such combined operation took place not long after my arrival at the base. We escorted a company of Fourth Burma Regiment troops in landing crafts to the estuary of the Naaf River on the Arakan side which was the boundary between Burma and East Pakistan (Bangladesh, today). The Fourth Burma Regiment was now replaced by Burman soldiers as all the Gurkha soldiers in the regiment had been disbanded soon after independence. This was the elite Burma Army soldiers under well trained officers with fighting experience against tough communist insurgents. The air force bombarded the defenses as troops prepared to land. We then opened fire with our Oerlikons to pin down the defense while the troops made their way to the heavily fortified village. The counter attack from the insurgents was heavy and many rounds screamed past or ricocheted off our boat's superstructures. To be able to get as close to the shore as possible without running aground, I hired the services of a serang, a local pilot, who knew the waters in the area well. I had the quarter master man the starboard twin Vickers machine guns and I asked the serang to take the helm. The serang, being a civilian had no helmet, so I gave him mine to put on which he did. Both our fore and aft Oerlikons were firing non stop as I watched the action on my binoculars.

Then I felt a very tremendous velocity of wind between my legs just below my crotch. For a second I wondered what that was but I was distracted by the boat swinging around as it began to drift downstream. I turned to the serang to see what was going on. I saw him leaning halfway across the helm and against the bulkhead of the bridge and slowly slid down as his knees buckled. I reached out to him and saw a bullet hole just below the helmet in the back of his head. He was a huge man. I ordered the quarter master to take back the helm and bring the boat back to position and yelled for the P.O. to help me lay the serang down on deck. We turned him over and saw that his left eye was bulging almost out of it's socket. The P.O. quickly ran into the wheelhouse and brought back a vial of morphine and gave the serang a shot on the arm. He was still breathing. There was no way to save his life except to try to get him to a hospital. I signaled to the other boats that I was returning to base to take the wounded serang to hospital. After all, the operation had been a success. After an hour before we reached base we received a signal that the village was retaken without a single casualty on our side. The serang however died before we reached the base.

Many days later I remembered the very strong velocity of wind that I had felt between my legs under my crotch during action on the Naaf River. I searched for a fragment of bullet that might still be on the deck somewhere but I found none. Of course by this time the deck had been washed down several times. But among the other marks left by flying bullets I saw the mark of a bullet on the bulkhead on the bridge behind where I was standing at about the precise height of my crotch. That certainly was a close call.

Apart from the Fourth Burma Regiment, the Union Military Police was also stationed in Akyab as a support unit. They certainly were neither well trained nor well equipped. A few months after the Naaf River operation, we had an urgent call from the Fourth Burma Regiment outpost at Buthidaung on the northern reaches of Kaladan River. The outpost was besieged by Mojahids, and the platoon was running out of food and the outpost was in danger of being over-run if no help arrived soon. I escorted a steamer full of U.M.P. troops to retake Buthidaung. There were perhaps a company of them. I noticed that after each couple of miles we made up the river a wisp of blue gray smoke rose through the tree tops into the open blue sky. Obviously signals were being sent to warn the insurgents of the approaching government forces. Each village we passed was unusually quiet and even looked deserted. Whenever our boats passed by before, kids used to come out to the river bank to wave or to just watch. I kept the crew on the alert throughout and when we came to about three miles before we reached Buthidaung I had all gun positions manned. The wireless operator was at his station so he could send signals out as I yelled into the tube. Other seamen were all excited and ready in the event one of them had to take over gun positions should a gunner got hit. We were now less than a mile from Buthidaung.

"Sir, the channel is blocked," the quartermaster reported. I immediately brought the boat to slow ahead. It was about four in the afternoon. In the valley surrounded by high ranges it got dark early. There was no sun now. Indeed, just fifty yards ahead I could see a cable strung across the channel and kept afloat by what seemed to be jerry cans. The navigable channel was narrow and there was no way we could get around the obstacles without running aground. My P.O. came running to tell me that he would try to cut the cable if I could get the boat close enough. Just then the insurgents opened up with all their fire power from both banks and from the villages in the distance. Some fired from ditches not too far from the boat, some from as far as the edge of the woods and even from the village upstream. They were so spread out that it was not possible to concentrate our fire to knock out any one position. The Vickers gunners took care of those in closer range while the Oerlikons crew sought out farther targets.

By this time I was able to maneuver the boat so that the bow just touched the cable. The P.O. could now cut the cable but it was easier said than done. I was also worried that a bomb might be attached to the cable to blow up the boat. The P.O. was pinned down by a concentrated fire in his direction and he was really lucky that he was not hit. A couple of other seamen tried to help the P.O. but were also pinned down at the bow. It became too dangerous that I ordered them to call it off.

"The U.M.P. boat has left, sir" reported the quartermaster. I turned around to see the steamer about half a mile downriver and slowly disappearing round the bend. The serang of the steamer later reported that he was ordered at gun point to turn round and leave. It was getting dark and we could see tracers coming our way from every direction, many whizzed past just above us. Meanwhile I sent the following signal back to base.

"ATTEMPT TO REACH BUTHIDAUNG UNSUCCESSFUL DUE TO CABLE LAID ACROSS CHANNEL. UMP RETREATED WITHOUT ENGAGING ENEMY. ATTEMPT TO CUT CABLE FAILED DUE TO HEAVY ENEMY FIRE. WILL DISENGAGE ENEMY AND WITHDRAW TO AWAIT FURTHER SUGGESTION FROM BURREGT"

Fifteen minutes later I received a signal from base advising that Fourth Burma Regiment would be deployed to Maungdaw by way of Naaf River escorted by the navy and have troops march to Buthidaung, which would take about an hour or maybe two, to surprise the insurgents from the rear. I withdrew to a few miles below Buthidaung and remained there after disengaging the enemy to give them the impression that I was waiting for reinforcement. The strategy was a success as the insurgents at Buthidaung were completely unprepared for an attack from the rear. The siege of Buthidaung was broken as Mojahid rebels were driven off after suffering some casualties.

Meantime back home, Dempsey had joined the army and was now a captain serving somewhere in Upper Burma in a Karen Battalion. My younger sister, Caroline, was now the only sibling living with our parents in Insein. In late 1948, Dad was transferred to Pegu as Deputy Commissioner. At the time, Pegu, fifty miles or so north of Rangoon, was a hot bed of communist insurgency. Dad had seen a cyclostyled copy of *Operations Aung San*, said to be a secret government directive (definitely not written by Aung San) to eliminate Karen army and civil officers, which somehow got into the hands of some high ranking Karen officers and clandestinely passed on from hand to hand. The directive suggested that both Karen army and civil officers were to be eliminated in ways that would not arouse suspicion or point fingers at the government. For fear of his life Dad resigned from civil service after serving less than a year in Pegu and returned to Insein to retire. At that time I had not yet heard of *Operation Aung San*. On Christmas eve that year, local militias known as *Sitwundan* attacked a Karen congregation at worship in a church at

Palaw, in Mergui District in southern Burma killing some eighty people. They threw hand grenades into the church while the congregation was celebrating Christmas. There were other attacks in surrounding villages where hundreds of Karens were killed by the same local militias.

Now the situation in Rangoon was getting worse between the Karen and U Nu Government. Since U Nu renounced Aung San's appeasement with the minorities, the A.F.P.F.L. seemed to maintain an attitude of superiority and was imbued with ideological zeal and was determined to ride the high horse. At the same time the Karen refused to back down, not trusting U Nu to keep his promise of 'Burmese one kyat, Karen one kyat' equity between the Burman and the Karen. It is my belief that U Nu and Burman politicians of those days would certainly short change the Karen. The A.F.P.F.L. had a private army named the People's Volunteer Organization (P.V.O.). The K.N.U., wary of the P.V.O. and U Nu's honesty and sincerity in dealing with the Karen problem, organized a defense force it named the Karen National Defense Organization (K.N.D.O.) to protect Karen villages from possible attack by Burman villagers incited by petty political hirelings. Dad wrote me a letter warning me to be wary of my Burman colleagues. He told me that Saw Ba U Gyi and Nita had come to stay in Insein with the family. And Louise and Marcus who happened to be on vacation were also with the family in Insein. A contingent of K.N.D.O.s was brought into Insein to protect the townspeople. He said the government had deployed the P.V.O.s in a ring around Insein who were patrolling the perimeter of the town day and night. The K.N.D.O. was under strict order from Saw Ba U Gyi not to fire at the P.V.O.s unless they were fired at first, and even so, not without the direct order from Saw Ba U Gyi himself. Grandpa and Grandma were moved for their safety to stay with Aunty Gyi in Ahlone, near Rangoon. I wondered why Dad was so worried about my safety because I knew I was among people I considered my friends. I could take care of myself. But I became very worried for my family in Insein. I trusted the K.N.D.O.s to be capable defenders of the town but I still worried because I did not want anything to happen between our two peoples. We didn't deserve it. We were only pawns in this political drama. I did not hate the Burman then, nor do I today. I grew up with Burman kids, played with them, fought with them, I was cursed by them and I cursed back in return. I did not consider myself their enemy, nor do I regard them mine, just because we spoke different languages. I always believe that we should and can live together in harmony as we are all Burmese.

Dad wrote to me again, this time telling me to be extremely careful, because he was worried about my safety. I was angry and disturbed that Dad was concerned for my safety. He wrote that the P.V.O.s had fired into the town several times and thank the Lord, he wrote, no one was hurt. It was obvious they were trying to instigate the K.N.D.O.s to retaliate so that they would have an excuse to attack the town. But the well disciplined K.N.D.O.s held their fire. I was the only Karen officer on the entire base in Akyab and I had only twelve Karen boys on the base. I was not expecting any problems at the base. But I worried for my family because of the situation in Insein. I knew that the P.V.O. could not be trusted.

One day near the end of January in 1949, the Deputy Chief of Navy, Commander Than Pe, flew in from Rangoon to visit our base and make sure that the base was calm. He took me aside and told me that he was worried about me and my men and wanted me to know that he was always there for me to call on if I had any problem. I was really touched by his concern for my safety and that of my men. I assured him that I and my men had no problem and that we got along very well with the rest of the personnel at the base. I also assured him that my men would not create any problem for the base. He thanked me for my assurance and left on the return flight back to Rangoon.

Frustrated that the Karen had not retaliated in Insein, the PVOs then surrounded Thamaing, a small Karen village, approximately half way between Rangoon and Insein, and demanded that the residents surrendered their arms. The residents replied that they had no weapons except private hand guns or shot guns. Nevertheless the P.V.O.s gave the villagers something like forty eight hours to surrender weapons the PVOs insisted that they had. Runners were sent to Insein for help but the villagers were disappointed to learn that the K.N.D.O.s would only come to their aid if the PVOs attacked them first. The PVOs did attack. They, the PVOs, U Nu's private army, fired the first shot and forced the Karens to retaliate and defend the village. Thus began the Karen insurrection. Thamaing was torched by the PVO and many Karen young men trying to defend the village with small arms were killed.

I was still in bed when the quarter master brought me the January 30 morning paper.
"FIERCE BATTLE ERRUPTS BETWEEN GOVERNMENT TROOPS AND KAREN REBELS IN INSEIN. BASSEIN, MEIKTILLA, MANDALAY, MAYMYO OCCUPIED BY KAREN REBELS" the

headline of the Nation read. I didn't think that things would happen so fast. I had to think hard and do the right thing without creating any undesired situation for the base. My first responsibility was to keep the base calm and safe. This was a critical moment in my career. Dad always told me, as long as I earned a living, my first loyalty was with one who paid my salary. If I wanted to do anything different, "Get out. Resign," he had said.

I knew in a situation such as this there was no question that I and my men would have to be disarmed – both for our protection and the protection of the base. I decided I would not allow myself be disarmed by my officers. I would disarm myself. I got up and got the safe key and took out the armory keys and laid both set of keys on the table, laid back on my bunk and waited. I knew my officers would by now have received instruction from Rangoon to disarm me and would soon be on their way to my boat to carry out their orders from Head Quarters.

The officers came. I could hear their footsteps on the deck above as they came on board. The quartermaster announced that they wanted to see me and I asked them in. They were all my friends. I wished them a good morning and gave them the keys and told them that I had my own plan to be discussed with Head Quarters in Rangoon. One of them volunteered to take me and my Karen crew wherever I wanted to get off on the Arakan coast and he would just let us off and report that we had deserted. But then I quickly thought, if we had left the ship as suggested we could have made headlines such as, "Karen Navy officer and twelve seamen killed after deserting ship". I didn't really believe that was the intention of the officer. But I also didn't relish the possibility of being shot in the back. I was just not taking any chances.
"Hey, wait a minute," I replied. "Let me take care of myself and my men." We continued to make polite but strained conversation. There was a strange air about the wardroom that I could not describe. We tried to make friendly talk but we seemed to be talking to each other like we were total strangers. I suppose they felt bad for me and of course I felt the same way because of what was happening. When they finally left I sent a signal to Head Quarters addressing the Commander requesting permission to return on leave to Rangoon with my men. Almost immediately a reply came.
"PERMISSION GRANTED. COMMANDEER A VESSEL AND RETURN IMMEDIATELY."

I could now return openly having had permission from Head Quarters and I could go on leave and now join forces with my people. I put on my uniform and drove to commercial the jetty. I saw a LCT loading rice for Chittagong.

I asked to see the skipper and told him that I would take over his ship to go to Rangoon.

"You can't do that. Can't you see, I'm loading cargo for Chittagong," the Skipper protested.

"I know that," I replied, "but I'm still taking your boat. So top up fuel, water and ration for the trip. I have twelve men with me."

"No, sir," the skipper pleaded, "I have a contract to be there in three days. I am leaving tomorrow."

"I'm sorry. But I taking your ship tomorrow," I told him.

This is a drawing of the house Dempsey and I built. We cut down the two dead trees in the background for firewood. The earthen 20 gallon jar in the foreground was to collect rain water from the bamboo gutter that ran along the eave. The jar on the opposite end by the 2 step ladder also collected rain from the same gutter and the water was used for washing the feet before entering the house. On the left behind the house is the out house that accommodated two. The little circle in fornt of the house is the sun dial.

This was how we transported water from the well to the homes. During hot weather we wore loin clothes like the Japanese soldiers did

Sailing down the Irrawaddy River in a country boat.

After the battle for Katha our family took refuge in this house which belonged to the village headman. Dempsey and I had to find our own places to sleep at night.

This family picture was taken just a couple of months before our journey to freedom.

CHAPTER 12

FROM NAVY TO PRISON

WE LEFT THE NEXT MORNING after bidding farewell to officers and men at the base. For me it was a sad parting but at the same time I was happy and excited because now I was free and could return to join my family and my people. The sea was rough and it took us five days to reach Rangoon. I went over to the naval base and walked up the two flights to my boss, Commander Bo.

"Good to see you Spencer," he shook my hand after I saluted. "You don't have to report, and I won't list you and your men as deserters. I understand that you will be worried about your families. Just throw away your uniforms and try to look for your families. And I wish you good luck, Spencer. You are one of my best officers." The last he said was to make me feel good I'm sure. Anyway, we all loved Bo. He was a perfect gentleman.

"I appreciate what you are doing for me, Sir. Thank you very much." I gave him a salute and he offered me his hand.

"Good luck, Spence," he said as we shook hands.

My men were waiting for me. They were happy to hear the good news that they were free to go any where.

"Good luck, fellas," I told them, "you're on your own now."

I took a bus to Pegu Karen High School in Ahlone where I was told Karen soldiers who were disarmed from the War Office and other military departments were interned. When I arrived at the school I saw that the whole compound was barb wired. An army truck was just entering with a load of young Karen soldiers apparently just disarmed, who were showing 'victory' signs to the curious crowd outside of the school compound. I still had my uniform on and so was not stopped as I walked through the gate. There were tents all over the school compound. Obviously families were also interned because there were women and children in many tents. I found a tent in which a lot of young men were playing cards and asked them if they knew of any navy personnel in the camp. They pointed to another tent nearby.

As I approached the tent someone called out, "Hey look. See who's here."
"Hey, Spence, what are you doing here?" greeted one lieutenant, "I thought you were in Akyab."
"Hey, watch it guys. The guy is still in uniform. We have a government spy here," quipped another officer.
I was overwhelmed. We shook hands all round. I told them about ourselves and listened to them as they told their stories. Here was a whole bunch of us, over eight hundred in all, behind barbed wire enclosure, not being able to contribute to our cause while our other forces were trying to fight the government for our right. We sat at a long table and continued with our conversation. A woman overheard that I was free to go about. She asked me if I could please look for her ailing mother whom she knew was taken to a civilian refugee camp. It was only then that I was told that the P.V.O.s had attacked Karen quarters in Thamaing and torched the entire village. Ahlone, Karen quarters nearby, was also attacked and the P.V.O.s burned down many homes there. Refugee camps were set up to house the thousands of homeless from Thamaing and Ahlone. Not being able to make the Karen to rise up in arms U Nu's government had deliberately provoked the Karen to rise up in arms.

I remembered Dad wrote and told me that Grandpa and Grandma had been moved to Ahlone to stay with Aunty Gyi. I was worried now for my Grand Parents and wanted to look for them. So I told the woman who asked for my help that I would certainly try to look for her ailing mother and I took down details from her. Another woman, a navy seaman's wife, came and told me that she wanted part of her husband's salary to be allotted to his father who was sick in a refugee camp and I agreed to go to the Navy Base to arrange that for her. I asked to see her husband and took down details from him. I was glad that the Lord had allowed me to stay out of the camp so I could look for Grandpa and Grandma and Aunty Gyi at the same time try to help these poor people with their needs. I went to the War Office and saw a senior colonel I knew at the

Adjutant General's office and asked him if I could be officially appointed liaison officer to take care of the needs of navy families who had various problems because there were no more navy officers free to run around for them. His reply was that as long as I was wearing a uniform I could try to help the navy personnel as well as their families. But he could not give me anything in writing. I understood this to mean that I was still in service and could carry on my duties as an active officer. I did not tell him that my commanding officer had allowed me to quit. I kept my uniform and stayed on in the camp and the guards allowed me to walk in and out at will.

There were many civilian refugee camps in and around Rangoon. The camps I visited were all in deplorable state. Refugees brought their own blankets and meager belongings and laid on the hard floor in huge ware houses that had poor ventilation. Other refugee camps were old empty office buildings with broken windows that gave no protection from sun and rain. Many families had been separated and were trying to find each other which was difficult because movements were restricted and a curfew was also in force. I finally found Grandpa and Grandma after visiting three different refugee camps. My heart sank when I spotted them in this old office building. Grandpa was lying on an old blanket on the hard wooden floor obviously asleep while Grandma was massaging his leg. I choked as I knelt down by Grandma. We held each other for several moments before either of us could speak.
"Don't worry Grandma, I'll get you out of here," I told her, though I did not know how. "Where's Aunty Gyi?" I asked her.
"We couldn't get a place together. Aunty Gyi is on the upstairs floor. There were so many people and we had to stay where they placed us. But I'm glad they placed us here because we can't climb up the stairs anyway."
"I'll go see Aunty Gyi later," I promised. "Now what do you need, Grandma?" I asked her.
"My bedroom," she smiled and a tear fell on my hand as I held her.
"Do you think you can take me back there?" She was just kidding, of course. "Do you know if the house is still standing?" she asked.
"I don't know, Grandma," I told her. "Now, don't worry about that. Just tell me what you need."
"No, I don't need anything. But your Grandpa doesn't feel too good. He has problem urinating," she said.
"He needs a doctor. I'll try to get our family doctor, Dr. Suvi or Dr. Raj, to come and see him," I told her. "You remember them, don't you?"

"Of course I know them," she replied. "Do whatever you can do to help your Grandpa."
"Tell me, Grandma, what can I bring you?"
"Get us some blankets and pillows. Can you get your Grandpa some fruits too? We are all right with food because your aunty Gyi is taking care of that for us. And you'll get Dr. Suvi to come and see your Grandpa, won't you?"
"Sure, Grandma," I told her."

I left after taking a mental note of what else they would need to make their lives in this deplorable old abandoned office building more comfortable. I thanked God for keeping me free. I couldn't find the woman's ailing mother. I asked everyone everywhere who would talk to me. I walked up to next floor to look for Aunty Gyi and found her. Her son Bobby and daughter Maggie were with her, sitting on the floor by her and chatting with each other. Bobby was with them and was able to run around, as circumstances would permit, to make them quite comfortable.
"Just do what you can for your Grandpa," Aunty Gyi told me. "Bobby is here to take care of us and he is also taking care of Grandpa and Grandma downstairs."
Now I remembered that Audrey was not living in Insein any more but had moved to Ahlone, a large part of which was burned down during the P.V.O. attack on the Karen community there. I asked Aunty Gyi whether she knew where Audrey was. She didn't know. So now I had to look for Audrey too at the same time continue to look for the woman's mother.

Next I went to the Naval Base to see the Pay Master about allotting part of a seaman' salary to his father who was sick in a refugee camp. He was very helpful. He gave me a few forms for the man to fill up and sign. I was shocked however to learn from the Pay Master that we would all be paid only two third of our salary while we were interned. I came back to the camp quite dejected. I later started to look for Audrey when someone told me that she was in a home with friends she stayed with whose home was not lost in the fire. I was relieved and happy that she was not in a refugee camp. I was soon able to contact my sister and was happy that she was safe although, she told me, she went through some terrifying moments during the P.V.O. attack, which was 'much worse than the fighting in the jungle of in Katha.' She said the whole assault on the village lasted over five or six hours and the army rounded up those who lost their homes and hauled them into army trucks and took them away to place them in camps. Many families got separated and it took some many days or even several weeks to finally find each other.

A few days later as I was returning to the camp, I noticed several army trucks outside and inside the camp and scores of armed Burman soldiers positioned in and around the camp with their rifles at the ready. The army was loading men from the camp onto trucks. I was not wearing uniform that day so I was able to watch with the crowd of curious onlookers to see what was going on inside the camp. After about an hour or so all the trucks left. I had no idea where the men were taken to. I waited for some time before I ventured into the camp to find out what went on. I learned that the men were taken to Rangoon Central Jail. Only families were left behind. Now I began to think what I should do – go underground immediately and join the forces in Insein or remain as long as I could to help as many needy people as possible including my family. I decided to do the latter because one more person wouldn't be of any help to the defenders of Insein but my being out here would be more helpful to others who needed me. Unfortunately that was not going to happen because a few days later a jeep load of MPs came to look for me. The major accompanying the MPs had an order from the War Office to take me to Central Jail.

One end of the jail in the exercise area was full of tents like huge mushrooms on a large plot. As I walked into the yard the officers and men who saw me clapped and cheered. I bowed, acknowledging the thunderous applause I was receiving. I got into an officer's tent which had four cots and a desk.
"Sorry, no room for you here, buddy" one told me.
I sat down anyway and we just chatted.
"We are all too crowded already. I don't think you'll find a place in any ofthe officer's tent. Go and stay with the Colonel over there," an officer toldme and pointed to the far end of the yard. There was a large tent next to a white one story brick building.
"A Colonel? Colonel who?" I asked.
"Colonel Po?" He told me.
"Orville Po?" I asked.
"O, you know him?" the officer asked.
"Yes, I do," I replied. Colonel Orville Po was the brother of Colonel Lionel Po with whom we stayed in Prome before we evacuated to Katha.
I walked over to the Colonel's tent. He was doing crossword puzzles from an old news paper.

"Good morning, Sir," I greeted him. He looked up and I saluted.

"Hello, Spence. Come in and sit down," he said, "what the hell are you doing here?"

"Just like you, Sir. Prisoner, I guess," I answered.

"No, call it detainee. We are not charged with any crime yet. We're only detained because the son of a bitches are afraid of us."

He filled up a glass with whiskey and shoved it in front of me. He lifted his glass and said, "Cheers, Spence. And welcome to the club."

I raised my glass and said, "Cheers," and drank.

"Where are you staying?" he asked me.

"I don't know yet. I was told that the officer's tents are all full. I wonder if you can order me a tent. I can share it with a few of my navy officers."

"What's wrong with that old building over there?" He pointed to the white building next to his tent.

"Who lives there?" I asked him.

"No one," he answered.

"Then why doesn't any one stay there?" I asked him.

"Because they're afraid," he replied.

"Afraid of what?" I asked.

"They think it's haunted," he replied. "It's a condemned cell. Prisoners convicted to be hanged are kept in there during the last few days before they're hanged."

"Can I stay there?" I asked.

"I don't see why not, if you're not afraid of ghosts," he said.

"I'll stay there," I told him.

So I moved my little duffle bag in there while the colonel ordered that a cot be put in the condemned cell for me. The cell measured about twelve feet square with two barred windows facing each other from opposite walls. Three cement steps led up to the red painted iron barred door to the cell. I loved my new home, ghosts and all, although I never met any of them because they never visited me.

"Sir, the colonel wants you," an orderly came and told me.

I walked over to the colonel's tent.

"Yes, Sir," I addressed the colonel as I entered the tent.

"Let's have lunch, Spence," he said.

"Thank you Sir, but I'll have lunch with the other officers," I told him.

"You'll have lunch with me from now on. It's too damned boring eating alone. And stop calling me 'Sir', damn it. Call me what you used to call me."

"Uncle?" I asked.

"Yes, I like that. You call me 'Sir' when it's official."

"By the way, where is your brother Dempsey?" he asked.

"He's now a captain in the army in Upper Burma somewhere," I told him.

"I hope he'll give those bastards what they deserve. Both Mandalay and Maymyo are taken, do you know that? Dempsey must be in the thick of it."

I didn't say anything because I didn't know.

A few days later I had a visitor. I'd been thinking of this person, wondering what he was doing and how he felt about the whole situation. What were his duties now, I wondered. Was he still on the mine sweeper?

"Hello Spence," he greeted me.

"Hello, K.T., how are you doing?" I asked my old C.O. from the mine sweeper.

"Okay. You need anything Spence?" he asked.

"I'm all right, K.T. I'm so glad to see you," I replied, "I don't think I need anything right now. And thanks for coming. How's George?" I asked.

"O, he's fine," he replied.

I had a feeling that he wanted to say something but he couldn't bring himself to it. I was sure he felt the same awkwardness I felt.

"You know, Spencer, if there's anything you need, just let me know."

About ten days later K.T. visited again. This time he stayed longer and we were more relaxed.

"How's your family?" he asked me.

I had introduced K.T. to Audrey and he had also met Dempsey.

"Audrey is in Ahlone, remember? She's still there. And Dempsey is with the army somewhere in Upper Burma," I told him "but the rest of my family are still in Insein as far as I know."

"I'm on the *MAYU* now," he told me. "You know we are shelling Insein with our Bofors and our four inch guns," he said quietly almost in an apologetic way.

He continued, "You know, the Karen are good fighters. Almost everyone of our soldiers hit by the Karen were hit in the head."

"How do you feel about all this, K.T.?" I asked him.

"You know I don't like it, Spence," he replied.

"I know you don't, K.T.," I told him. I told him that I felt the same way too.

We continued to talk of old times, being careful not to say anything that
might make the other feel awkward

"I'll come and see you again, soon," he said.

"Thank you, K.T., for coming. Tell George I asked," I told him.
K.T. dropped by to see me a few more times.

Karen troops in upper Burma were trying to move down to the south
to relieve Insein from government onslaught. I heard in the news that
the government redeployed it's elite Fourth Burma Regiment from the
Arakan to stem the tide of Karen advance toward Rangoon. If Karen
troops were able to join forces with the K.N.D.Os at Insein the safety
of Rangoon would be in jeopardy. The Karens troops however could
not make any progress as they were met with heavy resistance from
government troops at Meiktilla which was recaptured from the Karens
sometime earlier. Meanwhile they were also running out of ammunition
while suffering heavy casualty at the same time.

Because Rangoon was still threatened Prime Minister U Nu sent out
urgent appeals to India and other countries for help. In the following
months Burma began to receive ship loads of arms, ammunition, trucks
and other needed equipments as many nations responded to U Nu's
appeal for help. It saddened me and every Karen that one of the countries
that sent help to U Nu's government was our old friend, Great Britain,
and also the United States of America, with whom the Karen had fought
shoulder to shoulder during WWII. Dozens of Karen villages were
torched, and many of our elders were accused by the Japanese army of
having harbored British agents, and jailed or executed. Thousands of
Karen boys shed blood on the Burmese soil to help free Burma from
Japanese occupation. In time the tide slowly turned against the Karen.
The Karens have been fighting alone from the beginning without any help
of any kind from any nation. But U Nu's government had the support of
the international community and therefore was able to keep the Karen
from taking the capital city, Rangoon.

In April the British Ambassador and Bishop West, the Anglican bishop
of Rangoon, attempted to broker a truce between the K.N.U. and U
Nu's government. U Nu took this opportunity to try to end the Karen
insurgency once and for all. U Nu responded by calling for a three
day truce and asked Saw Ba U Gyi to come out to Rangoon for a peace
negotiation. It was touching to hear that during the truce, Burman
and Karen soldiers would walk to each other's lines and have friendly
chats, at times even exchanging jokes, food and cigarettes. I can truly
say that ordinary Burmese, whether they are Karen or Burman or any
other ethnic race, can co-exist without any help from politicians. It
was moving and heart warming to hear of such stories reported by the

media and I believe the stories were true. I also heard that U Nu was planning to invite the Karen soldiers to come out of Insein en masse and that army trucks would pick them up if they so wanted or something to that effect. Later on a young Karen captain, whose name was Kino who was still attached to the War Office came and told Colonel Po that U Nu was planning to move us out of jail and place us in a barbed wire secured camp somewhere to make room for the KNDO soldiers he was planning to bring into the jail. Because this young officer was still on active duty in spite of the fact that he was a Karen, many Karens did not trust him and suspected that he was a government agent. He was a close friend and when he brought this information to Colonel Po, I knew that he could be trusted. The army meantime took advantage of the three days truce to re-deploy and re-enforce their troops around Insein. But no one knew of U Nu's plan to try to corral the Karen troops from Insein into Central Jail except the few officers in Central Jail including myself.

Colonel Po called for an emergency conference of six or seven selected officers, myself included. He told us that he was informed of a plan by U Nu to move us out of jail to make room for the KNDO in Insein. We agreed that we could not let that happen. We had to stop the KNDO from becoming victim to U Nu's plan to capture Insein. We considered many options including raiding the jail armory and staging a break out just to spoil the government's plan. Then navy Lieutenant Douglas Pe Tha informed Colonel Po that one of his wireless operators had managed to smuggle a radio transmitter into the jail. He offered to check and see if the radio transmitter was working. What happened afterward I did not know because I was not in on the next meeting. Lieutenant Douglas Pe Tha, son of the late Saw Pe Tha, a Karen leader who served in the cabinet in the British colonial governemt before the war, and who, together with his entire family, except Douglas who was in India during the war, was killed by the BIA in Myangmya, later told me that he was asked by Colonel Poe to send a message to Insein to his uncle Saw Ba U Gyi, warning him that U Nu was planning to place the KNDO into jail in order to retake Insein and end the resistance. He asked his uncle not to let the KNDOs out of Insein if invited by U Nu. True to information received from Captain Kino, we were moved out of Central Jail and into a camp the army named Armed Forces Rest Camp (A.F.R.C.). Thank God that the empty space we left behind in Central Jail was never filled by the KNDOs. Saw Ba U Gyi however, did meet with U Nu and Geneal Ne Win for a serious peace talk but they failed to come to an agreement that would bring about an end to the fighting. Did Saw Ba U Gyi get the message from his nephew? I never found out. No one except those few officers at the meeting with Colonel Po knew about this ploy by U Nu to out maneuver the Karen. There were varying versions given by the press for the failure of the peace talk, one being that U Nu and Ne Win did not accept the K.N.U. demand for an autonomous state which I believe was true. U Nu's plan to outwit the K.N.U. did not work and the battle for Insein resumed unabated after the truce ended.

A.F.R.C. was a huge camp. It was on the shore of the Royal Lake not far from the Boat Club, which used to be a British club but now used as a club for service officers. Even families of married personnel were brought into the camp. I was given an end room in a bamboo and wood barrack and had to share the room with an army major. Colonel Po was no more the commandant. He had a large tent and his wife came to live with him. The new commandant was Colonel Calvin Ogh, a Karen, who parachuted down with the Allied troops under General Stillwell in Northern Burma during the war. I was given an orderly whose name was Maung Lone. That was one of the best things that happened to me in the camp. Here was a private from the army, someone I never knew before, who took care of all my needs like he was, believe it or not, my wife. He was a good cook and sometimes he cooked special dishes for me so I didn't have to go to the officer's mess for my meal. He washed and ironed my clothes, mends my socks and sewed buttons on my shirt. Best of all, after dinner when I would be relaxing and reading from the faint light above my bed - no cot, only a thin mattress on the cement floor - he would massage my back and my legs until I fell asleep and he would blow out the lamp before he left the room. The major once asked him to give him a massage.
"Sorry, sir, I am not your orderly," he politely answered.

I did not have to eat at the mess too many times nor did 'my man Jeeves' have to make special food for me too often because Colonel Po's wife told me that I was always expected to have meals with her and her husband because Colonel Poe told her how he had enjoyed my company when we were in jail. She said she considered me a part of their family. Colonel Po and Hilda did not have any children.

Life in the A.F.R.C. was different from life in jail. Now we were returning to service routine. Colonel Ogh was a very able and efficient commander. He was very strict and every so often we had a hard time pleasing him. He disliked Karen rebels because he believed that they should not have revolted. Perhaps he had his reasons. He called my father a rebel many times in conversations in front of other officers, and came out with outbursts like, 'Your father is a rebel,' 'You are the son of a rebel' etc. But other than that I considered him a nice person, but a hard man to deal with because he was a man of discipline, a perfectionist and somewhat eccentric. Perhaps he realized that we were all struggling to cope with the situation and under pressure for not having our families and worrying about them and not being free to do anything about it. In our first year at the camp he organized a beautiful cantata for Christmas, staged just outside the camp, using the adjoining hill and woods as a back drop, with lights, costumes and live animals, like sheep, goats, camels and donkeys loaned from the Rangoon Zoo. We had to rehearse for a whole month. It was the most beautiful show I had seen in Burma. It was a real extravaganza. All big shots of the city of Rangoon were invited, including army brass, civil officers and other notables. It was a smashing success.

I was able to get my jeep back from a friend who had kept the jeep for safe keeping while I was away in Akyab. I spent a lot of time with Douglas Pe Tha working on the jeep. We considered each other relative since his uncle, Saw Ba U Gyi, was my brother in law. Together we took my jeep apart, cleaned and lubricated all the parts and reassembled it during our spare time. Naturally Douglas had the freedom to use my jeep when I was not using it to drive over to his girl friend and spend time with her. All of us were allowed to go out Saturdays and Sundays from seven in the morning till seven in the evening. We had to obtain passes issued by the security officers at the gate. However, we were wary of some rash kids and hard heads in the camp who wanted to break out to join the KNDO in Insein. We could not let that happen because it would only jeopardize the well being of the entire camp, families included. A group of ten or even twenty, even if they could break out, would be no help to the KNDO in Insein. They didn't have guns or ammunitions to take with them. They would become extra mouths to feed and certainly a burden to the already beleaguered townspeople of Insein.

One of our standing orders to officers was to keep a close lookout for those youngsters and ensure that they stayed out of trouble. Our discipline was so good that the War Office allowed weekend passes for officers from seven on Saturday morning till eight on Monday. Men were now allowed overnight passes on Saturday and Sunday at the discretion of their company commanders. This privilege also encouraged our young men to observe the rules as they valued this time out which was a break from the otherwise meaningless and monotonous life in the camp. Later, week end passes were also allowed to the men. Doctor's and hospital visits were allowed but had to be escorted by a medical sergeant and an NCO. Dependents were free to go in and out any time but had to carry passes with them just like the rest of us for their own security. Sport was allowed. There was a soccer field just across from the camp and inter company football tournaments were held during football season.

At about this time, William Paw, younger brother of Marcus Paw, Louise's husband, returned from England after receiving his M.B.A. in London. He married my sister Audrey several months later. William became a professor at the University of Rangoon in the Commerce Department while Audrey joined the teaching staff of the University in the English Department. They were now living in staff quarters on the campus.

One day I was asked to come to the Security Gate. I was told I had a visitor. It was the wife of the Deputy Forrest Officer Poferio Po Ba, who was stationed in Akyab when I was serving in the navy in the Arakan. I visited them often the last time I was at the Base in Akyab and had meals at their house many times. They had five lovely young children with whom I used to play on my visits during week ends. Mrs. Po Ba was teary eyed as she shook my hands.
"I heard you were here and thought I'd drop by to see you," she told me.
"Thank you. How are you doing?" I asked her.
"O, I'm fine and the children are doing all right too. They always ask about you," she told me.
"How about Uncle Po Ba, is he back in Rangoon now?" I asked.
Mrs. Po Ba immediately burst into tears. I had to hold her for several minutes until she could speak again.
"He died. He took his own life," she sobbed.
"But why?"
"I don't know. He never left a note nor was there any hint that he had problems. He shot himself while we were away."
It was a short visit. I was shocked to hear of Uncle Po Ba's suicide and could say nothing to comfort Aunty Po Ba. I thanked her for visiting me and told her that I would be praying for the family and also that I would be visiting her and her children soon.

Karen forces fighting their way to reach Insein started to run out of arms and ammunition and finally had to retreat into the Pegu Yoma to the east and to the Deltas to the west. Morale of the K.N.D.O.s in Insein was also running low as they also were slowly running out of ammunition besides having lost so many young lives trying to defend the town. But the government still could not dislodge the K.N.D.O.s from Insein.

However on May 24, 1950, we woke up to read in utter disbelief news paper headline that said, "INSEIN RETAKEN BY GOVERNEMNT TROOPS." I did expect the fall of Insein sooner or later. But the fact was the government never retook the city. The KNDO left town the night before. They completely withdrew on the night of May 22nd. When Dad and a few elders came out of the town early on the morning of the 23rd waving white flags to let the government know that the KNDO had left town, army officers did not believe them. They probably thought that it was a ruse. It was not until after noon when the troops cautiously ventured into the town that they realized that the KNDO had indeed left Insein. In spite of the fact that Insein was retaken by government forces we were still kept interned in the camp. We had thought that after Insein was retaken all the service personnel in the camp would be released. We had to remain in the camp for two more years.

While in the camp I was able to visit Grandpa and Grandma occasionally and took them apples and grapes and other necessities which they also shared with Aunty Gyi. Grandpa was visited by Dr. Suvi and Dr. Raj and later was admitted to the General Hospital for surgery for enlarged prostate. After a few weeks he died from complications. Grandma moved to live with Aunty Gyi who was allowed to move back to her house in Ahlone a few months after Grandpa's death. The house somehow escaped the fire set by PVOs. I wondered about my family in Insein. I wondered if I could get special permission and return to Insein and find out how they were doing. A couple of weeks after the fall of Insein, Dad wrote me a letter addressed as follows:

Lt. Spencer Zan, Burma Navy
Concentration Camp, Rangoon.

All mail was held at the security desk at the gate. The mail was not opened but addressees had to come and collect the mail themselves. When I went to the gate the Police Security Chief himself was there. He was a perfect gentleman, well polished in words and manners. He was also very understanding of our situations and tried his best to accommodate us. He smiled at the address on the envelope as he handed me the mail himself. I asked him if he liked the address, 'concentration camp' he replied, "It's all right. But I want to talk with you," he told me and took me into his booth.

"I met your father in Insein. He asked about you and I told him that you are doing well and for him not to worry about you. He told me that he would be asking you to send him a few things that the family needed especially for the baby."

"What baby?" I asked him.

"Your sister's son. They named him Samuel," he said. "He was born during the height of the fighting. I offered to take the articles to them."

"Where are they now?" I asked him.

"In Insein jail," he told me.

"Why are they in jail?" I asked.

"I can't tell you. But they will be fine. You don't have to worry for their safety. I'll see to it that they are well taken care of. Just get them what they need."

Dad and Marcus were in one cell, Dad wrote. Mom, Louise, the baby and Caroline were in a cell in the women's block. They were allowed to visit Dad and Marcus every day. They needed milk powder, glucose, soap, material for diaper, scissors, needle, threads, slippers etc. Nita had left with her husband Saw Ba U Gyi but Dad didn't know where they were now. Dad wanted to know about Grandpa, Grandma, Aunty Gyi and Audrey. I managed to get most of the things they wanted. I wrote back a long letter and brought them up to date about the family, that Grandpa had died and Grandma was living with Aunty Gyi in Ahlone and that Audrey was safe and still living at the same place. I did not seal the envelope. I gave it to the security chief to read if he had to. He sealed it without reading and took the letter and the parcel. Mom, Louise, the baby and Caroline were released from jail ten months later but they were not yet free. They were confined in a camp, which was an old warehouse they called *Dan-O-Set,* in Thamaing.

Our family was struck by yet another tragedy. Lt. Douglas Pe Tha woke me up one morning to show me a morning paper. The headline read, "SAW BA U GYI KILLED BY GOVERNMENT TROOPS IN AN AMBUSH." He was on his way to Thailand with a group of his men including Saw Sankey one of his most trusted friend and leader. My thoughts went immediately to my sister Nita. I wondered if she was with him at that time. But since the paper never mentioned her I figured that she must be in the jungle or already in Thailand somewhere. I had no way to find out but prayed for my sister. She went through a lot of heart ache and tragedy during the past few years. Now she lost a second husband.

One morning I was summoned to the office of the Commandant together with an army captain, Tha Shwe. The two of us were to move to another camp adjacent to the present camp. Captain Tha Shwe was to be the Commanding Officer of the new camp called the A.F.R.C. Buddhist Camp, for Buddhist personnel, and I was to be the second in command. I asked my orderly Maung Lone to pack my things and his so that we could move to the new camp the next morning. Next morning I saw that Maung Lone had already put my meager belongings into the jeep. I then asked him, "What about your stuffs, aren't you taking them with you now?"

"I'm sorry, Sir. I will not be going with you to the Buddhist Camp."

"Why not? You are my orderly and you are going with me."

"I'm sorry, Sir. I'm going to get baptized so I can't go to the Buddhist Camp."

I was surprised. Maung Lone was a devout Buddhist and now he was going to get baptized. He never mentioned to me that he was planning to do that. I never spoke to him about religion, leave alone tried to convert him. Of course I was happy that he was going to become a Christian but that need not prevent him from coming along with me to the Buddhist camp.

"Maung Lone," I told him, "I am happy that you are getting baptized. But that should not keep you from following me to the Buddhist Camp. Get your things. I'll wait for you. You are coming to the other camp with me. I don't want any other orderly but you,"

"I'm sorry sir," he replied, "I'll just stay back here. I already told the Adjutant and he said he will let you know and get you a new orderly."

He was so determined that I had to let him go. I shook his hand and wished him a 'God bless' and left. As I left I noticed tears in his eyes. Maung Lone, my man Jeeves indeed. There would never be anyone like him for an orderly. God bless him.

When I arrived at the Buddhist camp and stopped in front of my quarter which was a bamboo hut, there was a soldier waiting for me. He gave me the usual salute and told me he was my new orderly. His name was Maung Tin. He carried my things into the hut and set the table because he had already cooked. That was great. Another good orderly, I thought. After lunch and clean up Maung Tin came to me and gave me another salute.

"Sir, can I have the day off?"

"Yes, why not?" I let him take off. After all I had no need for some one to take care of me hand and foot, day and night. I had to go and see Captain Tha Shwe, the camp C.O. He was married and had a larger hut some distance from my hut. Captain Tha Shwe was a very disciplined and hard working man.

"I want you to take full charge of the single men. That'll be your responsibility. I'll take care of the married men and the families. We'll have a lot of problem with them especially the wives. I've been in this business long enough. I know how to handle these women. You just take care of the single men."

We asked for some more officers to run the new camp. A few more officers were sent the next day. One of them, an army lieutenant, Bob, who had just returned from the U.K. after training, came and billeted with me. We both shared the same orderly and developed close friendship. Bob and I worked together as assistant to the camp C.O. We had no problem with our men except for occasional breaking of curfew, or gambling. We had more freedom and were able to leave camp almost at will albeit the security at the gate. We were getting regular ration from the army but we supplemented occasionally with our favorite meat and vegetables which we asked Maung Tin to get from the market. However, after a couple of months we noticed that our food was not what it used to be and Bob questioned the orderly about it.

"I think somebody is stealing our ration, sir," replied Maung Tin.

We did not worry too much about that because we usually went out and had our meals elsewhere, either at friends' homes or at restaurants. We also noticed that Maung Tin was asking for permission more often now to take off. Bob and I went out together one day and returned late at night. The orderly was sitting up clutching a machete.

"What are you doing up so late, and what's that machete for?" I asked Maung Tin.

"I'm watching out for the thief who's been stealing our ration, sir," he said.

"Go back to your quarters and put away that machete before I take it from you," I told him.

One morning a week or ten days later, the gate security officer asked me to come over to the gate. I wondered why the security would want me at the gate. Bob and I walked over to the gate where we found our orderly, Maung Tin, detained by the guards.

"What happened?" I asked.

"Is this your orderly?" I was asked.

"Yes. What has he done?" I asked him.

The officer showed us bags of potato, onion, rice, lentil and some meat that Maung Tin was trying to sneak out of the camp.

"Now we know where our ration has been going," Bob said.

Then Bob asked Maung Tin, "What are you going to do with these? Sell them?"

"No, Sir," Maung Tin replied, "I take them to my girl friend."

We found out later that his 'girl friend' was a prostitute. He was paying for his pleasure with our ration! I didn't charge him with anything. I just wanted to give him another chance and warned him not to steal our ration any more. Needless to say the quality of our meals improved after that.

Dad and Marcus were released a little over one year after Mom. They were all allowed to return home now. But Grandpa's house was a heap of rubbles after it took repeated direct hits during the last phase of the battle for Insein and there was no place for them to go to. So William and Audrey invited them, as well as Marcus and Louise, to stay with them on the campus.

I was visiting the main camp one day and saw a group of officers in the mess hall crowding over a bunch of papers and I asked what they were reading. Douglas told me, "You won't believe it. You've got to read it." I waited for my turn and finally was able to read the cyclostyled copy of what seemed to be government paper titled '*Operation Aung San.*' Without elaborating, the gist of the government directive said that the Karen were becoming a menace to the stability of the country and had to be eliminated from the top down both in the armed forces and in civil service. The manner of elimination ranged from making a set up assassination appear as a result of a robbery or accident, or tampering with a vehicle to make an assassination look like a car accident I didn't get to read the entire directive. Someone snatched the papers away while I was still reading it a split second before Colonel Ogh walked into the Officer's mess and asked, "What are you people doing?"

"Just talking, sir," someone answered.

"No, you were all looking at something. What was it?"

"You don't want to see it, Sir," Douglas told him, "they're pornographic photographs. Would you like to have a look, Sir?"

"No! You disgusting people. And you call yourselves Christians and you go to church on Sunday. Get rid of that dirty thing. Now I want to see all the officers in the assembly hall in an hour." Then he walked out. I didn't get to read the papers again. Now it all seemed to make sense. I had wondered why Dad was so overly worried about my safety while I was in service in Akyab. He must have known something about this paper. He probably was worried that I would 'have an accident'. Then my thought went back to where one of my officers offered to drop me and my men off at any spot on the Arakan coast and report that we had deserted. I couldn't dismiss that thought from my mind. I wondered whether that was a close call for me and my men.

An hour later we were in the assembly hall. We were all wondering what the commandant had to say to us.
"I have good news for some of you. I have bad news for others," Colonel Ogh told the assembled officers.
"I have a list of you," he continued, "who will be allowed to return to service on full salary. There is another list of you who will be released from service and may leave this camp within one week. I have still another list of officers who will remain in this camp until they are cleared by the War Office before they are released from service. Your company commanders will be given the list shortly and you can contact your company commander to find out where you are listed. I also have a list for the other ranks. The adjutant will take care of that. By the way, that dirty material you were looking at earlier. Get rid of that immediately. I don't want any pornographic material in my camp. That's all, gentlemen. Officers, dismiss."

It was late in the afternoon when the company commanders called all officers to the mess hall. He read out names of officers who would return to service. Then he read out the lists of those who were released (honorable discharge) from service. As expected, I would remain in the camp until I heard from the War Office and so would Douglas Pe Tha and about seven or eight other officers. The next day we wished farewell to Lieutenant Raymond, who returned to the navy, and about twenty other officers who returned to the army. None of the Air Force officers were returned to their units.

The following couple of weeks the camp was busy seeing men and families off as they left the camp. Some were picked up in private cars and others hired taxis, depending on where they were heading. It was several more days before all those who were allowed to leave finally left the camp, and there were only ten or twelve of us left in the camp including Douglas and myself. There were no more other ranks. We had nothing to do in the camp. We became quite friendly with the security staff at the gate and asked if we could go out everyday. To our surprise the security allowed us to leave and return any time we wanted, but we had to sign in and out so that they would know who was away from the camp at any one time. We spent our days watching movies and visiting friends and families. I even went to the Naval Base and visited some of my old friends. A couple of months later we were all cleared by the War Office and released from the camp.

CHAPTER 13

RELEASED FROM DETENTION

AFTER DROPPING OFF DOUGLAS AT his girl friend's house, I drove off not really knowing where I wanted to go to. I had nothing planned because I didn't know what I wanted to do. I was now free and was overwhelmed by the thought, but at the same time I realized that I was also worried because I needed to have a job. I was lucky that I was still single and had no responsibility for a family. I had to see Dad and ask for his advice. So I drove to Audrey's house.

Mom, Dad and my sisters were surprised, overjoyed and excited to see me. I never warned them that I might be let out of the camp anytime soon. There was a happy reunion with their long incarcerated son and sibling. William asked me to stay with them until I could find a place of my own. We talked about our experiences over lunch and through out the day and well into the night. There was so much to catch up on what we all went through over the past four years. Finally Audrey asked me what I planned to do. I told her I had not thought about it but that I would look around for a job as soon as I could get myself back together. I took it easy for a couple of months trying to unwind from traumatic experiences of the past few years in the detention at the camp.

Meantime I had a chance to talk to Dad who wanted to know more about me and my plan for my future. I told him in more detail about what I went through, the life in jail and at the Camp and about U Nu's plan to coral the KNDO into jail after moving us out of there. Then he asked about a friend of his, Poferio Po Ba, the D.F.O. in Akyab who, he heard, committed suicide. I told him that I knew no detail except that he took his own life and that I only learned about his death from his wife. "Do you think he really killed himself?" Dad asked me.

"That's what his wife told me. The whole family went out except him and when they returned home much later, they found him dead on the floor with his shot gun lying next to him."

"Have you heard of *Operation Aung San*?" Dad asked me.

"I read a small part of it when I was in the camp," I answered. "Wait, do you think he was murdered?" I asked Dad.

"He could have been. Look, why would he kill himself during the tense political climate leaving his wife and five young children to fend for themselves in a place where there were no other Karen families? It didn't make any sense. He was happy and content with life, had no financial problem or any other kind of problem that his wife could think of. Think about it."

"Yes, it's possible. But we can't prove it," I told dad.

"Don't mention it to anybody. It's just a nagging feeling. Of course he could have killed himself too. But for what reason?" Dad asked.

"You know," Dad continued, "if I hadn't resigned from service after I served in Pegu for several months I might not be alive today. I might have been killed by the communists, just the way they wanted. Communists were very strong, very active, in Pegu District. And they had no use for government officials. Burman DCs were afraid of the communists and they declined to accept postings to Pegu."

Several months later we heard news that Capatain Kino, the young Karen Intelligence Office attached to the War Office, was killed by drug smugglers in the Shan States where he was sent to investigate the activities of opium smugglers. However, some Karen nurses believed that he was killed by his own troops because the bullet that killed him entered the back of the head. Then Capatain Lloyd Kaing, a close friend of mine and former ADC to General Smith Dun, the former Commander in Chief of the Armed Forces, was killed by a gang of robbers while traveling in Shan States. He was singled out from among the passengers in the bus he was riding in and was shot dead. The bandits did not rob the passengers and allowed the bus to proceed. But these were stories I heard second hand from a third party. Then there was Captain Nelson, also a friend who was returned to his old unit after internment at AFRC, who was later killed in action. But according to nurses that saw his corpse the bullet that killed him entered the back of the head. These were all my friends and after having read *Operation Aung San* I wondered often whether they had been the victims of this despicable directive.

A couple of months later while Dad and I sat talking in the dining room about midnight, after everyone else had left, I heard a familiar whistle. I put my hand up and asked Dad to listen.

"Did you hear that, Dad?" I asked.

"What was that?" he asked me.

"Listen," I told him again. But we didn't hear anything for a while. Then it sounded again, the familiar whistle Dempsey and I had agreed on during the war to warn each other of possible danger. It sounded again and this time Dad also heard it.

"That's Dempsey," Dad said.

"Shh!" I told Dad to be quiet.

I got out of the side door of Mom and Dad's bed room and peered into the dark night but couldn't see anything. I whistled. Then Dempsey came running out of the shadows and right into my arms. We held each other for a several minutes. I loved my brother. We were very close. I felt so bad when he walked away from the training ship back in 1945.

"Are there any guest in the house?" he asked me in a whisper.

"No, come inside the house. Mom and Dad will be so happy to see you," I told him.

We walked in by the side door where Mom and Dad were waiting. Immediately Dempsey threw himself into Mom's arms. Dad came over and placed his arms around him. They held on to Dempsey for several moments. Mom was crying. Mom heard that Dempsey had died in a fire fight with the government forces sometime back. We learned later it was another person by the same name. It took several minutes before they could regain control of their emotions and begin to talk.

"I can't see too well," Dempsey whispered.

"Why are you whispering, son?" Mom asked.

"Oh it's a habit. We always had to talk in whispers as government troops were everywhere near where we were," Dempsey told Mom.

"What's wrong with your eyes?" Dad asked.

"I don't know. I can't see very well. I can't see the sight of my gun, or read news papers," he said. "I need treatment. Otherwise, I think I'll go blind."

"Don't worry, we'll take care of that. You'll need a rest. Get ready to have a bath," Dad told him.

At the sound of our noisy conversation Audrey and William came into Mom and Dad's bed room followed by Marcus and Louise.

"We'll have to keep this from the servants," William said. They mustn't know that Dempsey is back from the underground."
Naturally William was worried because he was a government employee and it would jeopardize his standing with the government and he'd be in trouble if it was found out that he was harboring a rebel.
"Bill," Marcus said, "Don't worry about it. Tomorrow I'll go to Douglas Blake to ask for Dempsey's protection." Brigadier Blake, the garrison commander, was a very close friend of Marcus.
"Douglas has a lot of clout in the War Office," Marcus added.

The next morning, true to his word, Marcus went to see Brigadier Blake regarding Dempsey. He came back with news that Brig. Blake had arranged for a quick debriefing and an intelligence screening for Dempsey. Dempsey went through all intelligence processes and debriefing and in just two days was pronounced clean. Dempsey was now able to freely go anywhere including being able to see his fianceé, Doris Aw, after eight long years of separation. Marcus took the responsibility of having Dempsey receive treatment for his eyes to restore his eyesight. Several months after his eye treatment which restored his sight, Dempsey got a job with Motor House, a British compsany. After nine years of engagement Dempsey and Doris finally got married. Marcus became the Director of Social Security Services while Louise went back to study Law. After she received her bar she joined the Burma Baptist Convention as Legal Advisor, and later became General Secretary of the Convention.

Dad later built a cottage on Zion Hill adjacent to where Grandpa's house used to be and bought shares of Aungmingala Ice and Refrigeration Company, to become one of the senior business partner of Saw Benson, a Jewish Karen businessman. I applied for a position at the United Liner Agencies, a British shipping agency, and got a job as covenanted assistant and became manager of the company's import department. I used to have my lunch at one of the small Chinese shops a few blocks away on Strand Road but later found a place to eat at an apartment nearby where a friend who was a widow, offered to cook lunch for me everyday. I rented a small house across from Inya Lake on Prome Road. Now our entire family had all been blessed with good jobs, except of course Caroline, who always stayed with Mom and Dad.

I occasionally went to the United States Information Service Library, only a block from my office, after lunch before I returned to work. One day I was surprised to see this young lady. The last time I saw her she was just about seven years old. Now at eighteen, Nu Nu turned out to be a very beautiful young woman. Later I saw her a few more times at a Chinese shop where I usually had my lunch and later invited her to join me for lunch at my friend, the widow's flat. I was enthralled by the stories she told me about how her family went through some tragic and terrifying periods from the time the British tried to recapture Mandalay to the time of the Karen insurrection.

Weeks before the Japanese withdrew from Mandalay the Allies intensified their final assault on the city. To give the impression that there were many Japanese soldiers defending the city, the Japanese would fire at Allies' position from one spot with their weapons and move several hundred feet to another area and did the same, and moved still to another area and fired at the Allies who were stationed on Mandalay Hill which they had recaptured a few weeks earlier, making it appear like Japanese soldiers were spread out over a large area. They did this many times in the proximity of the trench in which the family was taking shelter. The Allies retaliated by lobbing artillery shells into the area. Nu Nu's family would remain in the trench for long hours and only came out occasionally during a lull to fetch water or cook. One day during a lull in the shelling, her grand father, Reverend Ba Te, , and a few of them left the trench temporarily to stretch and relax after having been cooped up in the crowded trench for several hours. Among them was June, Nu Nu's youngest sister, who was now seven years old.

Suddenly a shell exploded right next to them, instantly killing June and an uncle, and wounding Nu Nu's father who took a shrapnel in the chest under his right arm. The shrapnel exited in the back on his left side. Nu Nu, then twelve years old, and her older brother Mike, who was fourteen, dragged their seriously wounded father into the trench and waited till the shelling stopped. Then they dug two graves to burry June and the uncle. The children had to rush into the trench several times before they finished digging the grave and were finally able to bury June and the uncle. Meantime, her mother tried to dress her husband's wound. The wound was so large that the gauze simply dropped into the gaping hole in his side. But she managed eventually to place a proper bandage over the wound. The father regained consciousness but started to feel the pain which later became so acute that he asked for the ball of opium that they had saved for emergency. It was a practice of many families to keep a ball of opium handy for medicinal purposes. The ball of opium can sometimes be as large as a marble. Mom used to make us swallow a clove of garlic embedded with opium slightly larger than the size of a grain of rice and lightly roasted over fire to treat dysentery. It worked like magic. Or one could swallow a small amount of opium the size of a small pea to reduce acute pain. Opium was used in a variety of combinations to cure many maladies and also to ease pain. Nu Nu's father asked for the ball of opium – perhaps the size of a small glass marble used in the game of Chinese checkers – and swallowed it all and soon lapsed into unconsciousness. They remained in the trench for three more days. Then on the third day they heard footsteps outside. Someone called out in English, "Are there anyone sick or wounded that needs to get to the hospital?" It was the Red Cross. Finally the British were back. Her father was immediately taken to the military hospital.

When he fully recovered, he was posted to Pyinmna where they lived in a large teak bungalow on stilts. This area was heavily infested with communists and communist sympathizers. The administration was not fully in control of the area yet at that time. One night after dark dozens of shots were fired at the bungalow and when the firing ceased, a man called out, "Open the door or we will burn the house down."
The father got out his shot gun and stood ready to shoot if the door was forced open. Her mother however asked him not to resist because there seemed to be many of them. So he opened the door to let the men in. Only a couple of them had rifles and the rest had machetes.
"Give us your money," the leader demanded.
"We don't have any money. We lost everything during the war and we have just started a new life," Nu Nu's mother told them.
"Then give us your jewelry. And hurry," the leader demanded.
"Look at my ears. And the children's ears. They are not even pierced. We don't wear any jewelry," she replied.
Then the men started beating Nu Nu and her mother with the flat side of their machetes and stopped only when one of the men found the shot gun leaning against the wall by the door and showed it to the leader. The leader looked at it and found it loaded.
He then turned to the father, and said, "So, you're planning to shoot back at us. Come along with us, you and your wife."
He picked up a flashlight he saw on the table and pushed him and Nu Nu's mother in front of him and marched them out of the house and into the dark night. Using the flashlight to light their way they walked along the foot path through the sugar cane field for about twenty minutes when the leader stopped and told his men that he'd like to test to see if the shot gun worked. They were all watching the leader as he prepared to fire into the air. Nu Nu's father took advantage of this distraction and pushed his

wife into the grove of sugar canes where they remained crouched and kept absolutely quiet and perfectly still. They silently prayed as the leader of the gang pointed the gun up in the air and fired.

"Where are our hostages?" one of the men shouted.

Instead of looking for them in the immediate area, they back tracked and shone the light everywhere thinking that their hostages had run back home. After about fifteen minutes they returned and on their way walked past their hostages without seeing them. Nu Nu's father waited several minutes to make sure the men were gone before he took his wife back to the bungalow..

In 1949 when the Karen insurrection began, Nu Nu's father was still in Mandalay when Karen troops occupied the city at the outset of the uprising. Karen troops were ordered to march down to Insein to the aid of the beleaguered KNDO who were defending Insein. However, if the bulk of the Karen troops marched to Insein, many dependents in Mandalay would be left behind with few soldiers to protect them. At that time government troops were already attacking Karen positions in Mandalay to retake the city. It was therefore decided that dependents of servicemen and Karen civilians would be moved to Maymyo, a military base on the Hills of western Shan State, where they would be safer. A Burman Buddhist monk offered to hide Nu Nu's family in his monastery in the event government troops recaptured the city and rounded up the Karens. But then, my brother Dempsey, now captain in the First Karen Rifles, turned up in Mandalay and moved all Karen families to Mauymyo, and housed them in the army barracks there which were vacated by Karen soldiers who were marching down to Insein. The battle to retake Mandalay by government forces intensified and many Karen soldiers were wounded or killed. They were sent to Maymyo military hospital to be attended by Karen doctors and nurses. Civilian girls including Nu Nu were recruited to help at the hospital. Then the government, after retaking Mandalay, and knowing that Maymyo hardly had any sizeable Karen troops left to defend it, sent a Kachin battalion to retake the City. However, the Kachins were in sympathy with the Karen and wanted to avoid bloodshed. They therefore told the Karens remaining in Maymyo to leave the city before they marched in, or they would be interned. At that time rumor circulated that the government had ordered all Karens to be killed. There was a general panic and many families started to move out of Maymyo very quickly. Nu Nu's mother prayed that the Lord would let them know whther to leave or to remain in the city. That night she dreamt that just as she was to step on the gang plank to get on the boat taking people out of the city, the boat moved away leaving her standing on the shore. She believed that the Lord told her that the family stay put. Then a man came and left a jeep saying he had no use for it now and left on foot. Later another man came and left a jerry can full of petrol as he was leaving with his family. At that time, Mr. Muni, a friend of the family heard that his friend was in Maymyo. He searched for them and finally found then in the barracks. He invited them to stay at his house. Nu Nu's family moved in with the Munis who hid them in their vacant bedroom upstairs.

Later after Maymyo was fully evacuated by the Karens and was taken over by the Kachin troops, government soldiers came to the house to check a few times.
"Do you have any Karen living in this house?"
"We don't have anyone living with us," Mr. Muni replied.
Then he was asked, "How about the room upstairs?"
"O, that's empty. We keep it locked all the time," he answered.
After proper administration was restored, the family came out of hiding.

Nu Nu was very matured and level headed even at eighteen. Nu Nu was named after her paternal grand mother Daw Nu. Her grand father was Reverend U Ba Te who left his law practice because he was disgusted with the corruption that plagued the profession. He became a minister and preached all over the Shan States walking on foot from village to village and even reaching Yunan in China and preaching there. During his lone mission he learned several languages including Chinese. He even preached among the Wa head hunters. He told us the story about the time when he arrived at a Wa head hunter village one night and needed some hot water to take some medication. However the not so hospitable host told him that there was no hot water. Reverend Ba Te said it was alright. He decided instead to take Eno's Fruit Salt, the effervescent antacid, like Alka Seltzer, which foams and bubbles when mixed with water. He asked for some water and poured the contents into a mug. When the villagers saw the water foaming they thought the water was boiling and marveled at his ability to turn water instantly into hot water. Not only that, they saw him drink the 'hot' water while it was still boiling! He got many conversions from that village. He was well known for his lone mission work among the hill tribes from Eastern Burma in the Shan States to Yunan in China.

When Nu Nu and I talked, we would exchange views about our goals and outlook in life and our likes and dislikes. I was surprised that her views seemed to be identical with my own to the last detail, which was independence of thought and action. We both wanted to be independent of others, including family and prefer to make up our own mind about things that mattered most to us. I believed that if I asked someone for an advice and made a decision based on that advice I would hold myself responsible for my decision no matter what the outcome would be. Nu Nu also felt the same way.

"And I do not cry over spilt milk," she told me, "but try to avoid making the same mistake twice."

These were some of the conversations that brought us very close which over time led to a point of intimacy. Later I began to have romantic feelings about her and realized that I was in love. I was engaged to be married at least twice and had dated many girls and quite a few times seriously enough to think of marriage but our relationships seemed to lack the important ingredient I needed to make a decision for a lasting relationship. There was always something, family, outlook, taste or something else that was in the way for me to make a final decision about marriage. Because of that I always hesitated to go through to the end with a relationship and allowed it to disintegrate.. We were married on April 6, 1954.

We were blessed with two lovely sons, Lester and David, born in 1954 and 1957 two and a half years apart. As I discovered, children were the joys of our lives. I remember the thrill and excitement I had when Lester was born. I took Nu Nu to the Duffrin hospital late at night but came home because the doctor said she was not ready yet to deliver. When I went back to the hospital early the next morning I was told that she had already given birth to a baby boy earlier in the morning. I ran up to Nu Nu's ward and saw Nu Nu nursing the baby. It was such a joy seeing your little offspring cuddled in the mother's arms suckling away. I left her bedside telling her that I was rushing home to give Mom and Dad the good news. In my excitement I never thought of using the phone. I was singing all the way to Audrey's house where Mom and Dad were living. Dad was looking out of the window of their ground floor bed room at that time. I stopped the jeep right in front of the window and yelled, "It's a boy," and drove off again to the hospital. I was so anxious to see Nu Nu and my son again that I drove over the speed limit without realizing it. A motor cycle cop followed me and signaled me to stop. As I pulled over, the officer came alongside and asked for my driver's license.

"I'm sorry officer, my wife just gave birth to a son and I was in a hurry to get to the hospital," I told the officer.

The officer said, "It's better to slow down and avoid any possible accidents. That way you can be sure you'll see your son."

I took out my driver's license and handed it to the officer. He looked at it and smiled. He handed me back my license and surprised me by giving me a salute instead of issuing me with a violation ticket. I wondered why and then realized that my driver's license still had my picture in navy uniform.

When Lester was about six years old I took him to a movie. There was a preview of a forthcoming Italian movie by the name of 'Pani amore e". What that meant I don't know. After each shot clip a male voice would announcw, "Pani amore e." It went on for about four or five times. But after the last short scene there was no follow up of a male voice Instead, in the still silence of the darkened cinema hall, a small shrill voice cried out "Pani amore e" followed by a loud roar of laughter from the audience.

The following year I attended night classes at the Adult University where I met many of my contemporaries from the old days. We enjoyed getting back together again, older, and perhaps a little wiser. We had a lot of stories to exchange at the restaurants where we usually ate together before attending classes. It was here that I leared of the death of at least a few my friends, both Karen and Burman, while defending their families during the communal riots that took place in the Deltas. Our Burman friends expressed their anger at the BIA. One of them was in Wakema when the Japanese reached the Deltas with B.I.A. troops. He said one night they heard gun fire. The family took cover under a storage platform. The next thing they knew a group of a dozen Karen entered their house and asked everybopdy to come out of hiding. Then they herded the family into an open lot. They also herded other families to the same open lot. They lined up all male adults, sixteen of them, and shot them all. My friend was spared because he looked much younger than eighteen. He put the blame on the B.I.A. who he said were the ones that started the communal clashes in the Deltas. The open discussion of the incidents never ruined our friendship. These were the friends whose friendship I treasured, with whom I attended classes together in the Adult University and planned to graduate and then go into business together. We even talked about getting into import/export business together after we graduated. However, things didn't work out that way for me. On the week of the final exam I was taken to the hospital for an emergency surgery to remove my ruptured appendix.

1957 Nu Nu gave birth to David at the Seventh Day Adventist Hospital. People say that after the first child a person loses some enthusiasm. But for me it was with the same thrill and excitement that I rushed to the hospital from my work when the hospital called to say that Nu Nu had just given birth to a boy. I ran straight up to Nu Nu's private room but found her alone without the baby.
"David has to be in an incubator," she told me, "because he weighs only four pounds six ounces."
A nurse took me down the corridor to take a peak at David. He was so tiny I could hardly see all of him in the incubator. When I got back after seeing David I called Mom and Dad and told them the good news. They were just as excited as I was. As soon as I left office, I returned to the hospital to see Nu Nu because I was worried about David who was so tiny.

Several months after David's birth Nu Nu left her job as librarian at U.S.I.S. to work for Asia Foundation under Jim Dalton and David Steinburg, the director and assistant director of the foundation. Two years later she decided that she wanted to start her own business and went to Singapore to take a course in dress making. While she was away I was invited by my old friend K.T., my old C.O. on the mine sweeper, and another ex navy officer and a close friend, Kin Oung, who wrote "Who Killed Aung San", to join them and others to start a steam laundry business, the Rosebank Steam Laundry Company, with the plant on Rosebank Road. Among the senior partners were the Mahadevi of Yawnghwe, wife of the first president of independent Burma, U Tin Maung, an insurance executive, Jimmy Yang, an ex member of parliament from Kokang in U Nu's government and now founder and director of East Burma Bank, and a few other better known personalities among Rangoon's elite. The business only catered for large establishments such as hotels, hospitals and ships in harbor for their heavy linens like sheets, blankets, draperies etc. Since this was the only laundry business of it's kind, we had a monopoly of the business. The business flourished and within the first year we were able to collect dividends regularly every quarter.

When Nu Nu returned from Singapore David, not yet three years old, didn't recognize her and refused to go to his mother.
"Why," Nu Nu asked David "why won't you come to mummy, son?"

"You're a stranger. You're only a visitor." Nu Nu had been away almost a year.

Then David called out to the nanny, "Paw Say, I want to go potty. Bring me my reeder diger."

"What was that? What is reeder diger?" Nu Nu asked me.

"Oh," I answered, "that's Reader's Digest."

"You mean David can read?" Nu Nu asked.

"You'll see," I told her.

After a while Nu Nu went and took a peek at David sitting on the pot in the bath room. She came running back to the bed room, laughing hysterically.

"He is holding the magazine upside down!"

Nu Nu rented a space at the Student's Center, a Chrisitan student center on Prome Road right across from the Judson College, and started a dress shop catering mainly to college girls who lived on the campus just across the street. There was the Benton Hall of Judson Colege and Inya Hall, of University college on the campus. She hired two girls as help. Boy friends would escort their girl friends as they came to have their jackets custom made. We had a small cafeteria in one corner of the shop, serving coffee and tea with snacks. The young men enjoyed the games we placed in the cafeteria as they sipped their coffee or tea while they waited for their girl friends.

Now we were living in a rented house on Dubern Road at 7th Mile Prome Road. From our house we had an unobstructed view of General Ne Win's mansion on Ady Road across a short stretch of Inya Lake. Our house also overlooked a small stretch of shoreline where staff of the American Embassy, like O'Brian, Landry and others was living. Beyond our house was a piece of empty land called Dubern Beach, a popular picnic ground which was crowded every weekend during summer.

My work at United Liner Agencies involved taking care of all aspects of inbound shipping including cargo discharge, delivery, inspections and claims. I also had to handle passenger services which we had very little of. I also had to take care of the welfare of ship's crew and crew transfers etc. One day my director told me that there was trouble on board one of our Swedish vessels at a pier. An unruly Swedish seaman who was drunk was giving the custom officers onboard a difficult time and the captain asked for help from the agents because even ships officers couldn't handle him.

"Spencer, go down and take care of the matter," my director told me. I didn't have my driver with me that day. I drove my Volkswagen to the pier and parked the car near the bottom of the gangway. There was a huge crowd of stevedore laborers watching what was going on on the ship. It was high tide and the gangway was at an angle of at least fifty five or sixtydegrees. I strained to look high up and saw a huge seaman, perhaps six foot two or three and weighing perhaps three hundred pounds.

"O God, please help me," I prayed. How wasI going to handle this giant of a man, I wondered. The seaman had in his hand a large fish he obviously had just bought from the market and was slapping with his fish everyone who came within range. Ship's officers had the wicket door locked so that the seaman could not get into the ship. I told myself, "I had a job to do. I'm going up," then prayed, "God, help me." It was the shortest prayer I ever said. The gangway must be a good twenty five feet up. I climbed up and when I got near the top I looked up, reached up to offer my hand to the seaman to shake. He bent down and nearly lost his footing. Then he grasped my hand and shook it with just a gently squeeze.

"Who are you?" he asked me in heavy Swedish accent.

"I'm your agent. How are you?" I asked him.

"Fine," he answered "These men won't let me into the ship," he complained to me.

"Okay then, you can come with me," I told him.

"Where are you taking me?" he asked.

I didn't lie. He needed to sleep it off.

"To the police station," I said as I turned and began to climb down the gangway. I looked back. He was coming down with me. I yelled at one of the stevedore's men to call ahead to the Port Police Station to have a cell ready for a drunken seaman. When I landed on the pier and turned round to look, the seaman was still coming down the gangway rather unsteadily as the gangway swayed and rocked under his weight. When he landed on solid ground he asked again, "Where are you taking me?"

"I'm taking you to the police station," I replied.

I opened the door of the Volkswagen for him and as he got in the Volkswagen rocked to one side and sank a couple of inches.

I got into the driver's seat and drove to the Port Police Station which was only a block away. As I pulled away I could hear a thunderous hand clapping from the laborers on the pier who were cheering me. When I got to the police station, all the policemen drew back as I led the man into the building. The cell door was open and I told the seaman to step in. He stepped in like a lamb walking into its pen. Only when I locked the cell door did the police officers come over to talk to me. But before they could even say anything to me there was a crash. The cot the seaman sat on broke in the middle. The seaman then started laughing and I told him we'd get him a larger cot.

"I'm hungry," he said.

"I'll bring you dinner," I told him and left for the Strand Hotel which was right across the road from the police station. I told the policemen to get another cot for the seaman. I bought two orders of steak for the big man. When I got back to the police station the seaman already had a new cot. His feet stuck out a good twenty inches over the end.

"I'll take you to court tomorrow and bail you out and then take you back to the ship," I told him. The policemen brought him a table and before he started to eat he offered me his fish. I gave the fish to the policemen. I got back to my office and told my Mr. Clunie, the director, that I had taken the seaman to the police station.

"Did you have any problem?" he asked me.

"No problem at all," I replied.

He smiled. "I knew you could handle it," he commented. He didn't know how scared I was when I saw that big man I was to take care of. The Lord heard my prayer and helped me. The next morning I bailed the man out and took him back to his ship.

CHAPTER 14

THE COUP

1958 WAS THE YEAR THE Shan and the Karenni, two of Burma's ethnic minorities, had a choice to exercise their rights to secede from the Union as guaranteed by the Panlong Agreement. Prime Minister U Nu now was facing two major problems. The political situation was unstable and domestic problems led to the split of the powerful AFPFL party into two factions, the Clean AFPFL under U Nu and the Stable AFPFL under Kyaw Nyein and Ba Swe. U Nu also was worried that the Shan and the Karenni might just exercise their rights to succeed from the Union thus, in his short sighted view, disintegrate the Union. In September of 1958 he handed the rein of the government to General Ne Win citing deteriorating law and order as the reason. He asked Ne Win to restore law and order and prepare the country for a new general election. The army did a fine job of house cleaning under the supervision of Brig. General Aung Gyi. Rubbish disappeared from the streets, houses and public buildings along highways were repainted and cosmetic improvements were made to parks and other public places around the city. The army also removed all squatters living in squalid hutments, the Kwethits, which were public eyesore in and around the city, to new satellite towns of Okalapa and Thaketa. The city was a lot cleaner and much pleasant to look at. Aung Gyi also placed senior army officers in charge in many important government offices to clean up the mess and back logs. One such office was the office of the Port Commissioners.

When posted to these offices to clean up the mess, army officers believed that they had all the answers for improvement. They thought that they could do better jobs than civilian officials. For instance at the port they tried to change the systems that had hitherto been used. They ordered heavy machineries under tarpaulins in the open yard to be taken inside the sheds. To make room for the machineries they had cases of exercise books for schools taken out of the sheds and placed in the open yard and had the cases covered under tarpaulins. As a rule these cases were stored in the shed for protection from rain and moisture. The result was that when school reopened, students found that the pages in the exercise books were stuck together from being moist and therefore not usable. Another example was when car tires arrived at the port, army officers had the tires stacked up high to make more room in the shed. Civil Supplies, who were the consignees, usually took a little while to clear their cargo and by the time the cargo was cleared it was discovered that the tires at the bottoms turned to giant washers under the weight of tires on top. Army officers also ordered that cases of sardines, also for Civil Supplies, were stored tight together to provide more space in the sheds. That left no room for air to circulate to keep the cases cool. Inside the sheds the cans of sardines were exploding like grenades. However, the army quickly learned to stick to established systems of storage. There were improvements in other areas as well. Government departments were running more efficiently than before with fewer graft. The army also cleaned up the economic mess and greatly improved the economy. However, the majority of the work forces who had lived as squatters in the city and had been moved to the satellite towns were not happy with the army because the move had caused them financial hardship especially now when they had to travel a long distance to the city to work. But the overall state of the nation had improved enough to enable Ne Win to declare that the country was ready for a general election which was held in April, 1960. Kyaw Nyein and Ba Swe's Stable AFPFL which had the backing of the army, and U Nu's party, renamed Pyidaungsu party, were the two major parties that ran for election. U Nu's party won by a comfortable margin.

Friday March 2, 1962 was just another day as I got into the car to go to work. I picked up a day old 'Nation' on the seat and began to scan the pages as the driver drove me to work. A few minutes after we got to center city the driver slowed down the car.
"Why are you slowing down?" I asked.
"What are the soldiers doing there sir?" he asked.
I looked up from my paper. "Where?" I asked and looked straight ahead but saw nothing unusual.
"Over there at City Hall," the driver answered.

I turned to look toward City Hall and saw a dozen soldiers or so and a couple of army tanks at the front entrance of City Hall as we drove round Sule Pagoda.

"Maybe the Prime Minister is visiting at City hall," I told the driver.

By this time we were approaching my office.

"Sir, there's a tank in front of Union Bank," he told me. "There are soldiers in front of our office too," he continued.

The bank was right across from my office.

As the car pulled up in front of the steps leading up to the office a soldier walked up close and peered inside. I got out of the car and ignoring the soldier walked up the steps and into the elevator.

When I got into the office I saw that the staff were gathered at the large window in the director's office watching the scene below.

"Anyone knows what's going on?" I asked.

"I don't think anyone knows for sure," a clerk responded. "I saw soldiers everywhere along the way as I came to work."

Nothing was going on except a few soldiers and a tank parked in front of the Union Bank. A few minutes later, Mr. Clunie, the director, walked into the office. Everyone hurried back to their desks. The director came out of his office after a while.

"What's happening out there?" he asked me.

"Maybe the army has taken over like they did the last time," I told him. Someone had a radio on loud and we could hear an announcement that General Ne Win would be speaking shortly. Just before nine Ne Win came on the air and announced that the army had taken over the government for the sake of security and stability. He asked the population to remain calm and to go about their business as usual.

As it turned out the coup was bloodless except for seventeen year old son of Sao Shwe Thaike, the ex president of Burma, who was shot and killed by the army in the early hours of the coup. Prime Minister U Nu together with Sao Shwe Thaike and the entire cabinet members were taken into custody. As I saw it, the real reason for the coup was political. The late General Aung San, architect of Burmese independence, had envisioned a free and unified Burma, with autonomous states sharing man power and resources with the larger Burman state and in that spirit the Panlong Agreement was signed in February 1947. But Aung San was assassinated on July 19 of the same year and U Nu became the prime minister. The draft constitution being prepared for independent Burma was completed without the inclusion of the spirit of Panlong Agreement. That naturally displeased the ethnic minorities. So sometime after U Nu was reelected in 1960 minority leaders were attempting to revive the spirit of Panlong by proposing to amend the 1947 constitution as a mean to preserve the Union. Ne Win evidently feared, as U Nu did, and as did many politically short sighted Burman leaders, that granting of autonomous states to ethnic minorities would result in the disintegration of the Union. The contrary is true. With the minorities running their own states Burma would still have to struggle to grow both economically and politically. But both the central government and the states would be able to learn to solve their domestic problems through democratic process and be able to maintain political and economic stability for the nation. Had the ethnic minorities been given true autonomous states, Burma today would retain it's prestige of being one of the most advanced nations in Asia and would not have to swallow it's pride and apply for the status of one of the poorest nations in the world like it had to under the army administration. The Burmese polulation had a high level of literacy, man power, fertile land and rich natural resources and was developing economically.

Ne Win staged the coup to circumvent any movement by the Shan and the Karenni and other minorities to press for autonomous states. Many people however, were hoping that the army would restore political stability and bring about law and order which had eluded the civilian government for a decade and a half since independence in 1948. They hoped that the army would bring about law and order as promised by Ne Win and also bring an end to insurgency and improve the economy. But it came as a shock to all when Ne Win unceremoniously suspended the constitution. Soon we began to hear of people being arrested for speaking out against the army. Tea shops used to be great for hangouts. Men would sit at tea shops and discuss politics or just talk shop. However now, men were known to have been taken away for interrogation from tea shops, some never returning home. Government informers were everywhere. A couple of my friends were taken into custody for reason unknown to their families.. Some people were picked up from their homes and not heard of again. The Military Intelligence Service and their agents were everywhere spying and eavesdropping on people.

University students were in the middle of their exams at the time of the coup. General Ne Win told them over the radio to carry on with what they were doing. After the exams the students returned home for the summer holidays and were back in school by June. University students were always at the forefront of any national issues and this time it was no different. With widespread arrests of those who were critical of the military government people began to realize that the freedom that they once enjoyed was now gone. Sometime later students heard rumors that a couple of students were shot by police in a confrontation. The rumor turned out to be correct. This gave the students a legitimate reason to demonstrate against the military government.

On July 7, 1962, speeches were made by student leaders at the Student's Union Hall condemning the military coup and calling for a return to democracy. Nu Nu and I were at Nu Nu's Dress shop which was across the University College on Prome Road. We heard speeches blaring over loud speakers but did not pay much attention to what was going on. However, later in the afternoon we were startled by salvos after salvos of heavy gun fire coming from the direction of the University. We looked out but saw nothing going on. Several minutes later a group of students came running into the shop and told us that several students were hit in the shooting at the Student's Union Hall. Shooting continued for several minutes. After a while all was quiet. The next morning the Student Union Hall was reduced to rubble by dynamite set off by the army. News paper and government reports stated that a dozen or so students were killed. But according to the students and other independent observers the death toll was much higher. The army shut down the university until further notice.

I was still working for United Liner Agencies when in September of 1962 I was offered an attractive position with a national firm of Let Ya and Company, whose director was Bo Let Ya of the famous Thirty Comrades. The CEO was Brig. General Saw Kya Doe, a career soldier and a graduate of the military college of Sandhurst in England. They wanted me as export manager for their timber department. So in early October I started a new career in timber exporting business with buyers both in the Far East and in Europe. The company was one of the major timber exporters. After a few months I noticed that Bo Let Ya was not attending office any more and I soon learned that he had gone underground. One day he sent word to me to meet him at a secret location. He wanted to know if I would be able to recruit among ex-service officers from all three services to organize a resistance army to stage a coup within a time frame of four to six months. If the coup was a success, he would take over the government and return the country to democratic rule. He also wanted my father to be a part of his political 'team' representing the

Karen in his cabinet because he did not trust other Karen politicians. Coincidently, an ex service friend of mine had earlier contacted me and suggested that we got together with other ex-officers to organize a resistance. So I promised Bo Let Ya that I would try to get hold of some ex-service officers and find out if they would be willing to get involved. I promised to let him have my answer in a week or so. Then we had another surprise in February of 1964, when all foreign banks and most foreign companies were nationalized following an earlier announcement by the military government that all major industries would be run by the army. There was no compensation paid for any of these take over.

Meanwhile I and a friend managed to get together about seven ex officers from all three services to meet separately at different times at different locations. We all agreed that things did not look good and that something needed to be done but we lacked intelligence and leadership. I mentioned about Bo Let Ya's plan to the group and there seemed to be a lot of enthusiasm. Our secret discussions were centered on how to recruit supporters for resistance without attracting attention of the army intelligence because MIS spies were everywhere. We also agreed that we had to explore the possibility of inside help. I talked to Nu Nu about my involvement and she wasn't happy at all because of the danger involved. I also spoke to Dad about joining Bo Let Ya but Dad declined because he did not believe in an armed uprising until all other possible means to persuade the army to return the country to democratic rule had failed. He asked me to tell Bo Let Ya to get together with other political leaders and make a united overture to Ne Win calling upon him to prepare the country for another general election like the one he had done two years earlier. That way, Dad believed, Bo Let Ya would receive the support of not only the Burman majority but strong support would also come from the Shan, Karenni, Kachin, Karen and other minority leaders. If Bo Let Ya agreed to do that, then Dad would be willing to join him.

Weeks went by and I began to notice that wherever I went my car was tailed either by a black Austin, a jeep or a white Volkswagen with Inya lake Hotel logo on the door. I dismissed my driver for security reason and also because I didn't want him to be picked up for what he knew nothing about. I asked a member of Bo Let Ya's family to let Bo Let Ya know that we would try to organize a resistance force but that progress would be slow because we were being watched.

Next the army closed Dubern Beach to the public as they tightened security around General Ne Win's home on Ady Road. A military check point was then set up on Dubern Road and each time we returned home from work our car would be stopped and we had to produce National Identity Cards. Because the university was closed Nu Nu prepared to shut down her shop since her customers were college students who have all returned to their home towns. However, one of her customers was the Mahadevi of Yaungshwe whose orders were still being taken care of by the girls at Nu Nu's Dress shop.

"I think the Mahadevi is skipping town," Nu Nu told me.

"The Mahadevi skipping town?" I asked.

The Mahadevi was also our business partner. She was a major share holder in Rosebank Steam Laundry Company.

"Yes," Nu Nu replied. "She ordered lots of blouses and skirts made. You know that Burmese women do not wear skirts and blouses. Thai women do. She must be planning to skip to Thailand. She wanted her order completed before the end of next week so I had to ask the girls to work overtime."

Nu Nu was able to close her business a week after the Mahadevi's order was completed. .

Meantime we continued to meet but made little progress in recruiting more ex officers from all three services because of the watchful eyes of army intelligence. Now almost every morning, the black Austin that took turn tailing my car would break down in front of our house. The driver would get out and pretend to tinker with the engine. He would tap the engine with his screw driver to make some sound and wipe the radiator with a dirty rag. From my porch I could see with my binoculars what he was doing. One day I walked over to ask the man if he would like a cup of coffee or a drink of soda. He declined. I told him how unfortunate that his car had to break down in front of my house almost every day. He smiled wryly and shook his head. Then he said, "Sir, what can I do? I have to carry out orders." A couple of weeks later as I was returning home from work I saw eight or nine officers and NCOs leaving our house with our friend the driver of the Austin bringing up the rear. The officers ignored me as I walked past them. I asked our friend the Austin driver, "What is this all about?"

"They just searched your house for weapons," he told me in a whisper.

Things were getting hot. But if I had arms, which I did not, the house would be the last place I'd hide them in.

As I walked into the house Nu Nu came out to meet me.

"Did you see those army officers?" she asked me.

"Yes, I did. We've got to talk about getting away..." I started to say to Nu Nu.

"No so loud," Nu Nu told me. "The servants are in the house," she warned.

The very next day I took Nu Nu out of town and drove toward Pegu, a town some forty miles north of Rangoon so that we could discuss the situation as we drove along. However we could not concentrate on our discussion. The white Volkswagen was right behind us. I slowed down the car several times to let the Volkswagen overtake us but it just slowed down to remain behind us. Then I increased speed only to see the Volkswagen increase speed to stay on our tail and kept up with us. Suddenly I turned into a rice field and got onto a cart track and drove a hundred yards or so and stopped under the shade of a palm tree next to a small hut. The volksvagen drove past the cart track but stopped some fifty yards on the highway beyond the track. I walked over to the hut and asked for some toddy. The man brought out toddy in a bamboo container and also beef jerky wrapped in old newspaper. I threw a blanket on the ground and placed the bamboo container carefully on an even ground. We drank toddy out of two aluminum cups provided by the man. The man later brought more beef jerky freshly roasted over fire. I was quite sure the men in the Volkswagen were watching us with their binoculars.

"What do we do?" Nu Nu asked. "I don't like what's happening."

"I don't really know what we should do," I answered truthfully. "Maybe I'll go away alone. You and the kids can stay back."

"What do you mean by going alone?" she wanted to know. "Going where?"

"Maybe Thailand. I don't know," I replied. "The MIS is on my tail."

"I know that," she said, "but you can't leave us. I won't let you go alone."

"But how can I take you and the kids?" I replied. "I don't even know how to get there."

"Have you prayed about it?" she asked me.

"About what? About escaping?" I asked.

"Yes. Have you prayed about it at all?" she asked again.

"No," I replied, "getting away never entered my mind until they searched the house yesterday."

"Then let's pray now," she said.

So we prayed together. We asked God to give us wisdom to conduct ourselves in a way that would not get us into trouble with the military authority and that if what we were doing was wrong and not God's will, for Him to stop us and show us other ways we could be of service to our country and to our people and meantime for God to protect us from the authorities. And if it was His will that we get away, for Him to let us know somehow and to lead us safely in our journey to wherever He wanted us to go. We continued to pray that very prayer every single day and night.

"Whatever it is," Nu Nu said, "I'll pack things that we will need just in case we have to leave,"

"You're really bent on going with me, aren't you?" I asked.

"Didn't we just pray about it?" she retorted. "We don't want to be separated you know, or we'll never be able to get back together."

"I guess you're right," I told her. I paid the man for the toddy and the beef jerky.

On our way back, the Volkswagen turned round and continued to follow us. As we neared home and turned into Dubern Road it drove past us and continued on it's way on Prome Road probably to an army intelligence office somewhere in Rangoon to give their report. It was getting difficult and dangerous to continue to meet with our group because we knew that we were being closely watched and it was just a matter of time before we got busted. Since we had not really accomplished anything it didn't seem worthwhile to continue to meet. At the same time we must have lost our will and enthusiasm because the group simply stopped meeting. I never contacted Bo Let Ya again.

At about this time the Karen national Union (KNU) at the invitation of Ne Win sent a delegation to Rangoon for a peace talk with the military government. The delegation was headed by Saw Hunter Tha Hmwe, Chairman of KNU. They were accompanied by four hundred fully armed Karen national Liberation Army (KNLA) soldiers. The delegation was given a red carpet treatment by the military. Lavish parties were thrown for them with a lot of fan fare and unprecedented press coverage. However Brigadier Kya Doe and I were convinced that this was a sham peace talk planned by Ne Win and we knew from the beginning that the Karen delegation had been had. I remembered what happened when U Nu tried to end the Karen insurgency by emptying the Central Jail to make room for the defenders of Insein at the height of the battle for Insein. Both Brigadier Kya Doe and I tried to reach the leadership to tell them not to continue with the talk. But with the MIS tailing us it was difficult. Brig. Kya Doe and I made our way into homes by back alleys in the dark because we did not want to be seen. We got to some leaders and told them that this was a definite set up to break the back bone of the KNU. One leader whom I managed to contact told me that the Burma army realized that the Karens were tough fighters and the army genuinely wanted to make peace with them. This, he said, was an opportunity they could not pass up to end the political stalemate between the Karen and the government. Brig. Kya Doe was furious that the Karen could be so naïve to fall for the ruse. But there was not much we could do. Brigadier Lin Htin of the famous KNLA's 5th Brigade was visiting Karen elders in the area. Lin Htin was famous for his many victories over Burma's better equipped army. During one of his visits he met Saw Benson. Benson was a staunch supporter of the Karen cause and was well respected in the Karen community. In his business he employed mostly young Karens both in key positions and in other positions as well. My brother Dempsey once worked for Saw Benson until he joined the army before the insurrection. Saw Benson invited Lin Htin to his home where he met Louisa, Benson's daughter, a former actress and a two time Miss Burma. Like her father, Louisa was an ardent Karen nationalist. The two no doubt had much in common in politics as well as national aspiration. A few weeks later they were married in a grand wedding ceremony.

The army later took delegation leaders, KNLA officers and NCOs separately to tour different military bases or other sights and places of interest leaving KNLA soldiers with no leaders. Karen soldiers were then easily disarmed by the army. Thus ended the peace talk. The much publicized peace talk dissolved into thin air overnight. No more mention of peace talk by the media. Lin Htin, irate over the dirty trick played on the Karen by Ne Win left Rangoon in disgust to return to his brigade to continue with the struggle for the Karen people. Louisa later went underground to join her husband in the jungle of Kawthulay. We were shocked to learn a few months later that Brig. Lin Htin was ambushed and killed by the army somewhere near the border with Thailand. There were conflicting reports of how he was assassinated. The popular Louisa was asked by Lin Htin's men to take over command of the brigade which she did. She rallied the troops and reorganized the brigade, picked capable officers from other areas and raised the morale of the brigade which she renamed the 4th Brigade. The brigade under Louisa's leadership continued to be Burma army's nemesis.

One day a group of four or five army officers walked into Let Ya and Company and announced that the company was being taken over by the military. A colonel sat down and had a lengthy talk with Brig. Kya Doe after which it was announced that the entire staff would remain with the company except all officers in management positions. Together with

Let Ya and Company, other large national firms were also nationalized including some smaller companies. There were no compensation whatsoever paid by the government. Now that I had lost contact with Bo Let Ya and was out of the company I felt free and relieved regarding my commitment to him but I also found myself on a loose end and worried because now I was unemployed and would have no income to support my family. However, as long as I remained a law abiding citizen now I had nothing to fear from the authorities. I was certain that they didn't have anything on me because we really had not made any real progress. Since Dad was one of the directors of Aungmingala Ice and Refrigeration Company, whose senior director was Saw Benson, I thought of approaching him about joining the staff of the Company, if there was a position I could fill. But Dad became ill at that time. No drug was available in the market at that time to treat his ailment and he passed away after a short stay in the hospital. Shortly after Dad died a grapevine passed on a message to me through a friend that my name appeared on government arrest list together with a few others. Obviously our group had been infiltrated or someone among us blew the whistle. Or maybe the MIS was just nipping a possible resistant movement in the bud. No resistance was taking shape anyway because our group had stopped meeting either from loss of enthusiasm or for fear of arrest.

I returned home that day and told Nu Nu about the new development. "This is it," was all she said looking down at the woven cane chest that she had packed.

We retreated into our bedroom and prayed together. We believed that the Lord was telling us to leave. We asked God to show us what to do and to lead and protect us on our next leg of life's journey. I spent all night praying and planning for our trip out of Rangoon without leaving any clue for the MIS about our movement in the event they were still after me. Nu Nu's father was visiting in Taungyi in the Shan States to check on a family property and fell sick and was in the hospital there. I told Nu Nu to take our two sons and go to Taungyi to visit her father for two days and on the third day to take the train to Pegu where I would meet her. I told our family that I would be in Rangoon to look for a job but told no one in the family or anyone else of our plan to leave.

CHAPTER 15

ESCAPE TO FREEDOM

ON SATURDAY, MAY 30, 1964, Nu Nu took Lester and David, who were then eight and and six years old, to Taungyi to visit her father. I went and garaged my car in Insein at Dad's house and three days later I rented a jeep and took the wicker basket containing some rare orchids that Nu Nu had collected and the cane chest to the railway station and took a train to Pegu. Nu Nu insisted on taking her orchids with her because she had taken a lot of trouble to collect the various species exchanging her collections with Dr. Suvi and others who also collected orchids. She hoped to start an orchid garden somewhere in Thailand.

Not a single member in our family knew that we were escaping. At Pegu I reserved a coach to Martaban and waited for Nu Nu's train to arrive. A coach was a first class carriage which accommodated eight passengers in the day or four passengers in four sleeping berths at night. It had it's own servant quarters and toilet and shower. The trains in Burma are narrower because they run on narrow gauged tracks and are all separate carriages by themselves so one cannot walk through from one carriage to another like the trains on broad gauge tracks. Nu Nu's train arrived on time and we quickly boarded our coach and soon our train left for Martaban. At Martaban we had to take the ferry to Moulmein where we took a room at a bed and breakfast house to stay for the night. The next morning we booked a coach to travel to Ye, the railway terminal in south Tennasserim. We left Moulmein before noon. It was a long trip and the train was slow. By the time we arrived at Ye it was getting dark. Since it was a railway terminal we were required to get off the train. But we had nowhere to go to because we did not know anyone in that small town with whom we could put up for the night. It was not a kind of town where you could find any kind of accommodation. So I decided that we would remain in the coach overnight and leave early in the morning. There was a knock on our door. I opened the door and an army sergeant climbed into the coach. I did not know until then that trains had armed guards. "Sir, you have to leave the train now," the sergeant told me. "The train will leave for Moulmein at seven in the morning."

"We have nowhere to go," I told him. "Can we leave first thing in the morning?" I asked him.

"Certainly sir, if you will allow me and my men to use your bathroom for shower?"

"Oh sure, be our guest," I told him.

The soldiers came for their showers. After the soldiers left the coach I went to buy some food for dinner. After dinner, we put our heads together and said a prayer asking for God's continued guidance and protection. We couldn't let the children know that we were escaping. We told them that we were traveling on a vacation. We woke up early in the morning and left the train. I had absolutely no idea how we would be going from there to our next destination which was Tavoy further south on the Tennasserim coast. While we were standing around deciding what to do next a man approached us and asked where we were going. I casually told him, "Tavoy".

He immediately picked up our luggage without even asking for our permission and took them to his horse drawn carriage nearby.

"Where are you taking us?" I questioned.

"I'm taking you to the ferry."

It was a short ride to the ferry. There were several sampans and dugouts tied along the bank. As the man was unloading our luggage, several men approached us offering to take us across the river in their crafts. I struck a bargain with one who promptly loaded our luggage into his sampan. Ye is on the west coast of Tennasserim. It was spring tide and the current was very strong. The tide was rising so the boatman had a hard time getting across the river in the strong current. I thought he was loosing control when he drifted about a half mile upstream. But he soon reached the opposite bank and hugged the bank and slowly rowed against the weaker flow of the tide to reach the landing.

When we got off the sampan we could see two buses loading cargo and waiting for passengers. I assumed that the buses were going to Tavoy. Four men approached us and all were talking at the same time trying to get us to take their bus to Tavoy. Then one of them tugged at my sleeve, pulled me aside and said, "I'll get you a jeep. You will be all by yourselves and you won't have to wait. But you'll have to take an armed soldier as a guard for protection. It's an order from the area army commander that all vehicles are escorted by an armed escort." It sounded good to me and after some haggling we agreed on the fare. We then bought some sticky rice in bamboo tubes and some fried chicken to have on the way. After our luggage was loaded we climbed into the jeep. We would be picking up a soldier at the outpost which was about a mile or so away. When we reached the outpost an army corporal approached the jeep, looked in and studied us without asking any question and ordered a soldier to get into the jeep. After we had traveled about three miles the driver stopped the jeep, picked up a small can from the floor board and walked away to a stream by the roadside and came back with a can full of water. Then he opened the master cylinder, poured water into it and closed the lid.

"What did you do that for?" I asked him.

"I don't have any brake fluid," he answered.

"You mean you are using water for brake fluid?"

"Water is better than nothing at all," he said.

I couldn't believe what I just heard. I was naturally apprehensive. I was worried that the brakes would not work in an emergency. I told the driver of my concern but he merely laughed. The jeep finally made it's long climb up a hill and as the vehicle started down the first steep slope the driver furiously pumped on the brake pedal. He managed to stop the jeep at the bottom of the hill where he got off again to fetch another can of water from a stream. That took place at least six or more times during the couple of hours we were on this stretch of the mountain road. But I had to give credit to the driver for his excellent skill in maneuvering the jeep over the slippery and dangerous mountain road. It must have rained a few days earlier because the unpaved road was still very slippery and there were potholes.

Puddles were still on the road, and at times there were thick brushes and rocks on one side of the road with a drop of a few hundred feet on the other side. And worse, there were no guard rails. We were on this mountain road for about two and a half hours or so before we started to descend. It had not rained in this area as we descended and the road was absolutely dry on this next stretch. Now we were driving through miles and miles of bamboo forest. I never saw so many bamboo trees in my life. We saw many pheasants feeding on the roadside as we gradually began to loose altitude. An hour or so later we emerged out of the bamboo forest and drove through rice fields which stretched as far as the eye could see on both sides of the road.

Finally we were approaching Tavoy. At the army check point the driver stopped to let the guard off. A sentry walked over and waved the jeep on. I asked the driver whether he knew where the American Baptist Karen High School was. The driver said he knew. I was hoping to find someone I knew. The driver turned into the school compound and drove straight to a huge house he said was the principal's quarters. I stepped out and immediately recognized Thra Tamla, (not his real name) one of the senior staff teaching at the high school just as he was leaving the principal's house. I knew him when he was a graduate student at Teacher's Training College where I was a high school student. I told him that I came to Tavoy to look for a job because my company had been nationalized. He invited us to be his guest and directed the driver to take us to the house. He had his wife prepare the spare bedroom for us. Later as the wife was preparing food for dinner, Nu Nu went to help her in the kitchen while I had a chat with Tamla. He told me that there were tin and wolfram mines I could work on at the border. He assured me it was lucrative business. I could have half a dozen Indian laborers working the mines for me and I could sell the ores to buyers who collect the ores and transport them across the border into Thailand. Thai buyers would then come to the border and buy the ores. It sounded interesting but since I had no intention of living in the jungles I figured I could just visit the area and find out how I could cross into Thailand.

"How far is it to the rebel held area," I asked.

"Two and a half to three hours by bus," he answered," but there are at least two army check points and that could pose a problem for you."

I didn't want to stay too long in Tavoy. If the army intelligence caught up with us, that would be the end for us. I had a responsibility for the safety of my family. I couldn't sleep all night. I sat up in the middle of the night and prayed. I thanked God for our safe journey thus far and asked Him to continue to take care of us. After breakfast next morning I left to take a look around town and to try to find a way to get out of government controlled area and get close to the border where we would be safe. I went to a bus stand. There was only one bus. I spoke to the driver and told him that I wanted to go to Myitha to pick up a parcel of tin ore. Was his bus going to Myitha? He told me that buses now do not take passengers to Myitha any more. The army only allowed Indian laborers to travel to and from a village near Myitha.

"Can I take your bus and will the army check me?" I asked.

"No, I don't go there," he told me. "I know someone who drives Indian laborers to the village and brings them back."

"Can I talk to him?" I asked.

"Stay here. I'll be back," he said and left.

In less than five minutes he came back with a man.

"This is Ba Khin," he introduced me to the man who could take me to Myitha which was a village between government controlled area and the rebel area, a no man's land.

"I can take you close to the border if that is where you want to go," Ba khin told me.

"I have my wife too, and two young sons," I told him.

He said that he would be taking a group of some thirty Indian laborers who would be returning to their village.

"Won't the Indians be checked by the army?" I asked.

"Oh no, they never check Indians. They don't check women and children either. They only check men to make sure they are not rebels."

Then he added, "Wear something simple, old and dirty," he advised, "and you'll be all right. I'll place you between the Indians and the soldiers won't even see you."

"Are you saying that you are taking us to the border?" I asked Ba Khin.

"For eight hundred Kyats, I will take you close to the border," he answered.

"When is your next trip to Myitha?" I asked him.

"Sunday. I can pick you up at the school gate at eleven in the morning."

"All right. Eight hundred Kyats, and eleven in the morning on Sunday. That's fine," I told him.

When I got back to the school I told Tamla that I had decided to take my family to the border and that a bus would pick us up Sunday morning. He asked me if I got the name of the bus driver and I told him it was Ba Khin.

"He's a good man. He is a Karen Christian," he told me.

On Sunday around eleven in the morning the bus came for us as promised. Nu Nu and David dressed in soiled country clothes, sat with the driver up front. Nu Nu had a towel on her head like the village women. To accommodate more passengers this bus was extended to the back at least six feet beyond the rear wheels. The seats were in three rows running from front to back facing inwards. The center row was a long bench with no back rest. The bus was accessible only from the open back by stepping on a foot board which hanged behind the bus a foot above the ground. Lester and I were made to sit on the center bench about the middle of the bus between the Indians. About a half hour after we left we got to the first check point. The bus slowed down almost to a halt and the driver shouted to the guard, "Kala Coolie!" (Indian laborers) The

185

guard waved the bus through. Then the bus started on an uphill climb. It was a steep climb. The driver shifted to second and then when the bus slowed down to almost stationary he shifted to first. The bus shook and groaned as it labored up the rest of the steep hill for several minutes till finally it made it to the top. And then it was downhill but not for long as the wet road started to gradually rise. I was beginning to get worried. Lester complained about the bad smell coming from the Indians and the fact that he could not lean back. The next climb was not steep and after we made a bend round a hill we came to a second check point. Again the driver shouted to the guard after slowing down, "Kala coolie." The guard waved the bus through. Another half hour brought us to a small village sitting in a valley where all the Indians got out. But there were almost as many more people waiting to board the bus. They were bound for our destination, Myitha. The boys were getting hungry and edgy so the driver asked us to eat but we brought nothing with us to eat on the way. There was no shop that sold any kind of food at the small village. I asked around to find if any one had any food to spare that we could buy. One woman came to me with some sticky rice in a joint of bamboo. She refused to accept money from me. I thanked her and I gave the kids the sticky rice.

After twenty minutes the bus left with it's new load of passengers all of whom were Karen. This time I sat with Lester right at the rear open end of the bus relieved that we could now lean back and also view the scenes from the rear of the bus. From this rear seat I could look out and enjoy the scene of high mountains all around us with lush green pristine valleys below and the beautiful formation of clouds up above. I wouldn't mind living in these jungles, I thought, if it wasn't for the future of the children. The bus continued to slowly struggle up hill twisting and turning for forty minutes or so and then it abruptly came to a complete stop. Then it started to back up several feet and stopped again. I glanced down at the road but instead of the road I found myself staring down at tree tops several hundred feet below. The rear end of the bus was literally hanging over the precipice. Then the bus slowly moved forward and made a second turn to continue on it's way up the hill. What actually happened was, as the bus approached a hairpin bend it had to stop because it could not make the turn in one maneuver. It had to back up several feet and then make a second turn to make it round the sharp bend. There was no safety guard rail. The conductor had to jump off the bus as it backed up and place a small log about eight inches in girth behind the rear wheel about three feet from the edge of the cliff to prevent the bus from rolling off the mountain side. The extreme rear of the bus was literally hanging over the precipice.

I looked at the other passengers. They seemed perfectly relaxed and at ease as they continued to talk to each other without any concern. We had about five more such bends and I never looked down again for the life of me when we came to each hairpin bend. We arrived around two in the afternoon at a large village. I thought we came to another check point so I asked the passenger sitting next to me if the soldiers would ask us to get off the bus.

"There are no Burman soldiers here," an elderly man answered.

"This is the rebel land. You are among friends," said another.

I couldn't believe it. We made it. We were actually in an area the government considered insurgent occupied area. The driver came over and asked us to follow him to a small hut which was his house.

"Is this really a rebel held area?" I asked the driver.

"No," he replied. "The Karen rebels live just across the river. They come freely here. And the Burmese soldiers come here also but the Burmese soldiers have to leave their weapons behind when they come."

"Who runs this village?" I asked.

"The village headman. The Burmese soldiers are allowed to come here to buy stuffs from the Karen soldiers like cigarettes, radios, watches and gold which they bring in from Thailand."

As we reached a small hut he continued, "You will sleep here tonight. Early tomorrow I'll take you up the river to the foot of the mountain from where you will have to find your way to the border."

I thought that we were already near the border now. And I knew nothing of any trip up the river.

"You mean we have to travel by river to get to the border?" I asked him.

"You have to travel by river for half a day," he answered, "and then climb up a mountain two days to get to the border."

"And how do I travel up the river?" I asked.

"I'm taking you up the river."

"How much more will it cost me?" I asked.

"You already paid me," he answered.

Addressing Nu Nu, he said, "This is my wife," as the wife brought him water in a coconut shell. She was a good looking jungle girl in her early twenties and was carrying a month old baby. We stepped into the hut and she showed us where we were to sleep. It was the same landing that we were standing on, all bamboo floor and walls. It was a very small hut with just the landing and the bed room. The kitchen was outside on the ground.

"Do you know any of the Karen soldiers across the river?" I asked Ba Khin.

"Their commander is a captain by the name of Tha Sein. They now have a political official visiting."

"Do you know his name?" I asked.

"Yes. Spurgeon," he answered.

"Spurgeon Pu?" I asked.

"You know him?" He seemed surprised.

"He's an old friend. Is there a way I can send a message to him?" I asked.

He gave me a sheet of paper and a ball pen. I scribbled a note to Spurgeon to tell him that I was passing through with my family on our way into Thailand. Ba Khin asked a boy to take the message to the Karen camp across the river.

Ba Khin's wife cooked chicken curry for dinner. It was a very simple meal but we were so hungry we that we thought it was the best meal we ever had. After dinner, Ba Khin's wife prepared the place for us to sleep. She swept the dirty floor and unrolled a bamboo mat for us to sleep on. As she did she was stung by a centipede and was crying in pain and developed a high fever. Her husband applied some herbs on her hand and she felt better later but was still moaning all night from the pain. Nu Nu took the mat and shook it well and I checked the mat over and over again to make sure we did not get stung while we slept. Then we heard voices outside the hut. It turned out that Spurgeon sent six armed rebel soldiers to guard us during the night 'just in case'. One guard told me that he'd take me across the river to visit his chief. When I got to the rebel camp I was surprised that they had electricity. They had a generator and the place was well lit. There were several barracks and the one that we entered was the largest. There were even gas stoves and running water. Spurgeon shook my hand and introduced me to Captain Tha Sein who turned out to be a student of my sisters Louise and Nita at the American Baptist Karen High School in Moulmein. We talked shop and updated each other on news of family, friends and politics. Later Spurgeon told me he wanted me to stay with the rebels and help with the cause.

"What do you want to go to Thailand for? There's nothing for you there," he told me.

"Let me think about it. I would like to get my family to Bangkok first and try to settle them there. I'll keep in touch," I promised.. "Don't the government troops attack the Karens here?" I asked.

"No," he answered me, " their soldiers frequently come up to Myitha to buy gold, cigarettes, watches, radios other stuffs that our soldiers bring in from Thailand but they have to come unarmed. It is like an agreement between us. They don't bother us and we don't bother them. In fact when our men meet them at the village they talk to each other like they are old friends. They even play cards together.

"That's interesting," I told him, "and you said they never attack your position?"

"When their big shots come to check their outpost they fire a few rounds of mortar and opened fire with their machine guns towards the village but never directly at our position or at the village. But when that happens we are always prepared just in case. Heh Spence, your journey to the border will be safe. Don't worry. You can ask for help if you come across any of our soldiers. I'll see to that."

I thanked him, shook his hand and returned to the village with my guard.

Nu Nu didn't get to sleep at all that night because she was busy killing the bed bugs that were coming out from the mat and the floor and crawling all over us. The boys and I were bitten all over our bodies but none of us woke up. At sun rise we were given a breakfast of sticky rice and dried fish. Nu Nu was happy that the boys now had appetite they never had when they were back at home where they were given balanced and nourishing meals. But now with only plain rice and dried fish they get to eat each day they ate like they never saw good food before. After breakfast we followed Ba Khin to the river bank. His help, Saw Htay an athletic looking young man, carried our luggage and placed them in the long dug out which was about eighteen to twenty feet long. Along either side of the dug out at the water line was a bundle of bamboo tied to the hull as fenders. At the stern was a huge Johnson outboard motor. There were two boards across the beam in the mid section of the dug out for seats. Nu Nu and I sat on one and the boys sat on the other in front of us. Saw Htay sat at the bow. Beside him lay a wide bladed oar and a long bamboo pole. The boys were now obviously enjoying it, talking excitedly, laughing and singing. We prayed silently and thanked God for the safe trip and asked for His continued protection and guidance.

Ba Khin started the motor and thus began the next leg of our journey. The ever changing scene that unfolded before us was unlike anything that we had seen before. The river began to narrow after a while as the banks on either side rose higher so that it seemed as if the tall trees were looking down on us from high as the boat sped past below them. Then a new scene unfolded as the banks rose higher still on both sides lined with rocks as big as houses. A pair of peacocks flew over us to add beauty to the already awesome scene before us. Then the current became swift and turbulent. Away from civilization and from family and friends I was getting nervous and apprehensive and worried for the safety of my family. Should anything untoward happen I would absolutely be helpless. No one back home would ever know what happened to us. We left without telling any family member where we were going. As the boat started to shake and rock Ba Khin warned that there was a rapid ahead and for us to hold on tightly to the sides of the boat. I warned Lester and David that we had a rapid ahead and to be careful. At the word 'rapid' both stood up and cried, "Rapid. Rapid," and yelled in excitement. We had to pull them down to their seats as the boat shook and swerved violently over the seething waters. We both had one hand on the side of the boat and the other hand on the kid in front as we were thrown from side to side while the boat moaned and creaked through the raging river. Saw Htay at the bow was furiously working with his oar until we cleared the rapid.

"Yeah, yeah," both Lester and David cried as they clapped and cheered.

"Dad, are there more rapids?" Lester asked.

"I want more rapids," David yelled.

"You'll have quite a few more," Saw Htay told them.

"Yeah, yeah," both boys responded excitedly.

"Are you all right?" I asked Nu Nu.

"I'm okay," she answered.

"Were you scared?" I asked her.

"No," she replied. But I was scared. I was scared that something might go wrong and I'd be helpless.

The river widened into a large lake after we passed the rapid, and the water became so calm that the surface looked like a sheet of glass. The water had to be deep here. Now we had time to look around and take in the splendor of God's creation. Tall trees were reaching up to the heavens. Their trunks were completely covered with beautiful ferns and their strong branches bore sweet smelling orchids in many varieties and species, scattering their sweet scents throughout the valley. Huge honey combs hung from many high branches as the bees hummed and danced about their hives. There were birds everywhere. We could not see all of them but we could hear them sing in a cacophony of sounds that could be heard even over the roar of the Johnson outboard motor. They seemed to be acknowledging our presence and welcoming us.

The river slowly narrowed again. The current began to gather speed and the calm water once again slowly turned into a swift flowing river. A family of fox stared down at us from a rocky cliff. They were a beautiful pair with six lovely cubs. Now we were approaching another rapid. The river was not getting much narrower but the water was shallower where we were and the current was swift. I looked ahead and could see raging waters ahead. The boat once again began to shudder and rock. But this time there were no narrow gorges with high cliffs. The river was dotted with rocks of different sizes some as big as a small car. Saw Htay picked up the long bamboo pole and used it to push the bow of the boat away from the rocks as Ba Khin slowed down the speed of the out board motor. It was a rough passage through the rocks and it took the two men at least ten minutes to maneuver the boat through the rocks. Lester and David were overjoyed, yelling with excitement when each time they stood up and fell back into their seats as the boat pitched and rocked.
"Sit tight'" Ba Khin shouted and cut the engine.
We held the boys down and braced ourselves. I thought we would capsize as we plunged three feet down to the lower level of the river but Lester and David were screaming with excitement at the top of their voices. Now the boat glided into another open stretch with sand banks on both sides and once again the river was wide and calm. On one side of the bank was a dead tree with branches devoid of leaves but the tree was a caricature of Chinese art with eighteen to twenty beautiful peacocks elegantly perched on the bare limbs. We were enjoying the sight of peacocks basking in the sun reflecting their colorful plumes in the sunlit morning when Lester cried out, "Look. Mom, Dad. David, look on the other side. Deer."
Sure enough, five or six deer were on the sand bank, two of them drinking from the river as one was sedately walking away and the others staring curiously at us.

After another twenty minutes or so, the boat pulled up along the bank and Ba Khin asked us to get off. Only then did I realize that we were on the edge of perhaps a hundred feet wide water fall with a seven foot drop. We were asked to walk ahead along the bank until we got to the spot where the water was calm. I saw Ba Khin take a long rope and tie it to a tree while Saw Htay walked behind us and waded knee deep into the water at the bottom of the fall. Because of the thick overgrowth we could not see how they maneuvered the boat down the seven foot drop. As we got to the spot where the water was calm we waited for Saw Htay to catch up with us. Several minutes later we saw him emerging from the brush dragging the boat along the bank to where we were standing. Ba Khin joined us a little later. We boarded the boat and were again on our way. Soon the river narrowed to a mere fifty feet and the banks rose so high until we could not see the top. The trees on both sides of the tall banks were touching each other at the top creating a beautiful canopy over the gorge. I began to feel uneasy as the sun disappeared behind the tall trees and the high cliffs and it started to get dark and eerie.

Lester and David were standing up again in expectation of another rapid but Ba Khin told them that they had to sit tight this time. The sun could not shine through the thick forest and high banks. We couldn't even see the sky. Ba Khin turned off the motor. The river by now was only thirty feet wide. There were no rocks but the current was extremely swift and the boat was moving very violently from side to side as it was carried through the speeding waters rushing through the gorge. This time Saw Htay sat still at the bow with both his hands tightly gripped on the sides of the boat. The boys were quiet and sat still. Both were obviously scared now. Nu Nu and I both had our legs astride each boy to hold them down while we held onto the sides of the boat with one hand and had our free hand around each other. Because of the speed of the current we got out of the long gorge in just a little more than one minute. It was a wild ride like driving a car through a long and unlit tunnel at high speed. We emerged suddenly into bright daylight and at considerable speed while Ba Khin tried to restart the engine without success. So Saw Htay picked up his oar and started to row. A moment later the engine started.

"One more," Ba Khin told us.

"You mean one more rapid?" I asked.

"Yes, smaller rocks. The current is strong but we'll have no problem," he assured us.

The sun was now getting hot. It was now almost eleven o'clock. The river was still wide but it was obviously shallow where we were because water was rushing over rocks and sometimes we could even see the bottom. It was very choppy and rocks started to appear all over, some just beneath the surface. Way beyond the rocks I could see that the water was calm and this being the last of the rapids I could now relax. Ba Khin cut the enmgine off and Saw Htay pushed with his pole to keep the bow of the boat from hitting the rocks. The boat zigzagged between the rocks for several minutes and all of a sudden there was a loud crack and the boat almost turned over. The boat hit a rock smack on the beam on the left side just below the bamboo fender.The jolt almost threw us off our seats.

Ba Khin assured us that nothing was wrong and for us not to worry. But as I looked down I saw water coming in fast. I started to bale water out with a small bucket. Then I leaned forward to check the side of the boat and saw a long crack from where water was rushing through. We were now clear of the rocks and entering a relatively calm stretch of the river with high rocks on the right side and a thick wood on the left side. However the water was getting muddy with hardly any current. I told Ba Khin to beach the boat. Fortunately there was a small sand bank on the left on the edge of the wood. He brought the boat along the bank and ran the bow up the sand bank. The boat was beached a quarter way up it's length. Ba Khin came over, pulled at the broken piece of the boat. It came off. Water rushed in and the rear end of the boat immediately sank and settled down in shallow water.

"You'll have to stay here," he told me. "I'll go and look for something to patch the hole with."

"Are there any houses around here?" I asked him.

"This is a jungle," he laughed. "I don't think there is a house around here."

"Then how are you going to get any help?" I asked.

He said nothing.

"How long will you take?" I asked.

"I don't know," he replied. "I'll try to get back before it gets dark."

I looked at my time. 11:30 a.m.

"Is it safe to stay here during the day?" I asked him.

"Stay here right on the sand bank. Don't go into the forest. I am not trying to scare you. But there are tigers and bears and sometimes bison. They may come down to the river for a drink."

"What do I do to protect ourselves" I asked.

"If the animals see you they will go to a different spot," he assured me. "Only don't go into the forest," he repeated, "it is their territory."

CHAPTER 16

SWISS FAMILY ROBINSON

INDEED, THERE WERE SPOORS IN the sand leading to the water. There were large as well as small ones. But in the sand it was hard to say if they were paws or hoofs. Perhaps both. A chill ran up my spine. I brought with me a very long Ever Ready flashlight that took eight size D batteries. If an animal approached I could use that to shine on the animal's eyes to keep it at bay. We were in a valley but now with the sun directly above us it was getting very hot. I found a knife in the boat and went to the edge of the forest to cut leaves and branches.

"What are you doing Dad?" Lester asked.

"I'm going to build a shelter," I told him.

"We're Swiss Family Robinson!" he shouted and both the boys became very exited but not for long. Horse flies got our scents and were soon attacking us and stinging us even through our clothes. The boys were busy slapping the flies as they landed on them. I made a makeshift roof and placed our luggage under it for the boys to lie down on. We kept slapping and swatting the flies wherever they landed on the boys and on us. Soon both boys were fast asleep while Nu Nu and I both did our best to keep the flies off with makeshift fly swats I fashioned from leaves and twigs. Swiss Family Robinson indeed. We spent our time talking about family members and what they would do or say when they found us missing. We talked about friends and those we knew who were arrested and wondered if they have been released. We tried to talk about our future, what we thought would happen to us if the Thai authorities found us trying to sneak into Thailand. I decided that I would rather surrender to the Thai authorities and seek asylum than be discovered and deported or sent to jail.

It was now one in the afternoon and we had not eaten. We brought sardines and corned beef and decided to open a can of sardine. We had a hard time fighting off the flies as we ate. However, after we threw away the can we noticed that there were less flies to fight off and we soon found out why. They were now attacking the empty can. So we woke the boys up and opened up a can of corner beef for them. After they ate we placed the can a few feet away from the empty can of sardine to divert the flies which helped a lot.

Ba Khin and Saw Htay returned at about half past three with a piece of board and a swath of gunny. He placed the piece of board over the hole to measure and started chipping at it with a machete. He placed it over the hole again and again as he continued shaving and chipping away at it for about a half hour. He seemed finally to have chipped and shaved the board to roughly fit the hole. He then wrapped the gunny over the board and pushed the board into the hole from the outside with the gunny backing facing the inside of the boat. He trimmed pieces of gunny showing outside of the boat. Saw Htay came back with a large ball of red clay which he placed by the boat. Ba Khin took some clay and plastered it over the cracks inside and outside of the boat. He worked on it, rubbed and kneaded the clay inside and out until he was satisfied that the board held. It took the two of them a good half hour to bale all the water out. They then pushed the boat back into the water.

Ba Khin gave us a satisfied look and told us he was ready to leave again. I wasn't about to let my family into the boat without first finding out for myself if it was really safe. I told Ba Khin I would like to go on a test ride and he kindly obliged. I went with him in the boat for about ten minutes over the calm and muddy water and I was amazed that not a drop of water seeped through the patched area. It was about four thirty in the afternoon by the time we left the sand bank. After about a half hour Ba Khin stopped the boat at the bottom of a high bank and asked us to get off. Saw Htay walked ahead of us and climbed up the steep bank as we followed. When we got to the top we saw a large hut on stilts at least ten or twelve feet above the ground with a bamboo ladder leaning on the side. Saw Htay asked us to go up the ladder which we did. There was no partition. Only two sides were walled with bamboo meshing. A WWII Enfield 303 rifle, a shot gun and a long sword in it's sheath hung on one wall. And beneath, against the wall, lay a couple of wooden boxes and an old Singer sewing machine. Another wooden box lay at a corner of the hut next to a hearth. It had a lock on it. There were a few stones in the hearth amid ashes and burned out wood. There were dried red chilly, cooking oil and saffron in tin cans and withered vegetables on a small wooden table. The hut stood on about two acres of clearing surrounded by thick forest.

Saw Htay took the boys to the edge of the woods and cut a few pieces of bamboo stems and fashioned a couple of pop guns for the boys.. Then he plucked some berries and showed the boys how to use the pop guns. The boys were thrilled and started to shoot at each other with their new toys. When it began to get dark we asked the boys to return to the hut for fear of wild animals. A little later we saw a girl of about sixteen emerge from the forest with a bamboo basket slung behind her back. She was fair, very pretty and was wearing a white Karen gown. In her right hand was a long machete. As soon as she saw us she stopped short in her tract until I spoke out to her in Karen.
"We are visitors and would like to stop here for the night," I told her. Obviously relieved, she smiled. When she came up Nu Nu told her that we were passing through but had a little mishap and needed to spend the night at her hut. She immediately unlocked the box by the hearth and took out some dried meat and began cooking for us. Nu Nu questioned her about the high stilts and she explained that it was to keep tigers away and that the ladder had to be pulled up at night. She told us that her name was Naw May Paw and she and her father worked in a clearing about a mile away growing rice and vegetables. Her mother died a year ago. She had to take along the machete with her for protection against wild animals but so far had not encountered any. Her father lived in a hut at the field most of the time to tend to the crop. Occasionally people would pass by, she said, people they didn't even know. They would stay at their hut even when no one was home and would help themselves to what ever food they found and the next time they came by they would leave dried meat, eggs, chicken or vegetables. They had never been robbed and no one had stolen anything from their home. The next morning Naw May Paw gave us dried meat and sticky rice for breakfast but refused to take any money for her hospitality. Nu Nu was so impressed with Naw May Paw that she gave her a gold chain which May Paw obviously was very happy to accept.

In spite of the now muddy water the scene around us as we continued our journey remained breathtaking. We continued to see wild animals like foxes, deer and red squirrels, flying foxes, many kinds of birds like doves, hawks, hornbills, wild fowls and peacocks. The boys were really excited with their adventure and didn't stop talking and laughing throughout the trip. Now we could see the summit of a high range many miles ahead of us which Ba Khin said we had to climb to get into Thailand. The boys became more excited at the prospect of climbing the mountain. The river was now flowing at a slower rate and Ba Khin explained that the muddy water was due to rain somewhere up the mountains in the north. We were fortunate that we never did have rain once during our entire trip. At about noon Ba Khin stopped the boat.

"This is where you get off," Ba Khin told us. "I don't know how long you will be here but now you're on your own."

That certainly was not a comforting piece of news. We were dumped in the middle of nowhere, at the foot of a high mountain we were supposed to climb to get into Thailand. And we were told that we were on our own.

Saw Htay unloaded our luggage and placed them on the bank. We were in a valley, and about three hundred feet away was the edge of the forest surrounding us.

"Where are we supposed to go from here" I asked.

"See that hut over there?" He pointed to a small hut on the edge of the wood. I'll take you there. Someone may come back tonight and you can talk to that person. The hut belongs to the wife of Karen rebel Colonel Saw Noo."

He asked Saw Htay to help with the luggage and walked with us to the hut. No one was home. Ba Khin told us he wanted to go back and see how his wife was doing. We told him we would pray for her and thanked him for the trip. We shook hands and he left with Saw Htay.

We looked around. There was no one. The ground was so wet the boys couldn't run around outside. They just stayed inside the hut and soon both were asleep on the bamboo floor while we waited for someone to turn up. Around four in the afternoon a woman walked up to the hut and introduced herself as the wife of Colonel Saw Noo. She was expecting us. Spurgeon had radioed her that we were coming. She told us that we could stay with her as long as necessary but that there was someone leaving in the morning to travel to her husband's outpost and I could go along with him if I wanted to. The man would be coming later that evening to see me. I didn't want to stay here for any length of time. I would rather leave in the morning with the man. The man showed up late in the evening and introduced himself as Samuel.

"I was told that you wanted to go to the border," Samuel said.

"Yes, me and my family", I told him.

"I have to take a few things people at the out post need. You can come along with me," he said.

"What time in the morning will you leave?" I asked Samuel.

"At sunrise," he answered.

"How long does it take to get there?"

"If we leave at sunrise we'll arrive there by sunset. That's about twelve hours."

"Did you say that we can go along with you?" I asked him.

"You can, but not your wife and children. You have to go alone to see for yourself first and later make arrangement for you family to follow you."

"Why can't they go along with us," I asked.

"They won't be able to climb that mountain. You'll see after you climbed it yourself." Then he added, "If you go with me, don't take anything heavy. Just a change of clothes. You'll get very tired before long because you're not used to this kind of climbing."

Then he asked me, "Are you planning to go into Thailand?"

"Yes," I told him. "Is there any problem?" I asked.

"No, Colonel Saw Noo can arrange for you to cross the border into Thailand. You will have to talk to him," he said.

I agreed to go with him in the morning. We all slept on the bamboo floor that night. There were no walls, no mattresses, no blankets and no mosquito nets. After a breakfast of sticky rice, a can of sardine and pepper beans with salt we left for the hills. After I left with Samuel I remembered that there was no food in the hut that we could find. Saw Noo's wife was returning in the morning leaving Nu Nu and the boys by themselves in the thick of the jungle. I mentioned to Samuel that I worried for my wife and kids because there was no food in the hut except the few cans of sardine and corned beef which would last them only two or three days. He told me not to worry because there was rice and salt and some dried pepper for them to have for their meals!

Samuel was a tall and muscular man, about five eleven and already I realized that my five foot five frame would have a hard time keeping up with him. He slung on his back a huge basket containing about a dozen chickens and a large fully stuffed Karen bag to take to the outpost. Samuel walked briskly. Often I had to take a few quick steps to keep up with him. At one time he looked back and caught me doing that. "I'll slow down a little for you, Pha-ti," he told me. Pha-ti means uncle in Karen. A younger person will not address an older person by name and Pha-ti is used as a polite way of addressing an elder.

It must have rained the day before because the ground was wet and slippery but I had no problem keeping up with Samuel after he slowed down his steps. However we were soon climbing up a slope and I began to have problems. The dry leaves were wet and slippery. Each time I made several feet up a slope I slipped back half way down over wet and slippery leaves. When I looked up I could see Samuel high up waiting for me to catch up with him. It was embarrassing and also very frustrating. The climb was always steep although at times we were walking on level ground over a short distance. Occasionally we had to skirt around large rocks. Once, by the time I got around a rather huge boulder I lost sight of Samuel because he had entered a thick wood without waiting for me. I had no idea at which point he entered the wood. I stood in front of the boulder and waited several minutes until he came back for me. On the wet ground there were leaches galore. As they heard footsteps they stretched full length to reach out to your shoes. I could already feel leaches between my toes or at my ankles inside my socks.

However the leaches didn't bother me but my heels were beginning to hurt. I braced myself for the next steep slope which was about a hundred feet to the top and tried to forget about the sore heels. I kept slipping down the slope over wet leaves and each time I climbed back up my heels hurt more. I tried to grab branches or small trees to pull myself up or to keep from slipping back down but that didn't always work because sometimes the object I grabbed hold of came loose or broke away and I still slipped down several feet each time. My heels were beginning to hurt even more now. I knew they were badly blistered. Before noon I was totally out of breath and hungry at the same time. I brought a can of sardine but had no chance to have it. Samuel was moving all the time and never close enough for me to call out to him to ask for a short rest. However a little after one, in spite of the constant climb I seemed to feel less tired. But now the climb was getting even steeper and my heels hurt terribly. When we reached a spot which was reasonably level I called out to Samuel to stop while I took a look at my heels. Samuel walked back to me as I took off my walking shoes and socks. There were more than half a dozen leaches on each foot between the toes and on my anklesa but that was not my problem. My problem was my heels which were badly blistered and I knew I couldn't climb this hill much further. The only thing to do was to cut off the back of the shoes, the heels, which I did. I felt a lot more comfortable without the back on my shoes but how could I keep my feet from slipping off the shoes without the heels as I climbed the steep slopes? I had put on my socks and shoes on without removing the leaches because I didn't know how to get rid of them without letting them pull my skin off which would leave my feet bleeding in several spots. I looked at my watch. Four more hours to reach the outpost. After eight hours of climb four more hours should be no problem.

"Four more hours before sunset, Samuel," I said, "do you think we'll make it before it gets dark?"

"You are doing very well, Pha -ti. We'll make it," he assured me.

We started climbing again. The climb now was not as steep as I thought and my shoes stayed on.

I looked ahead after we emerged from some thick brushes and all I could see was a solid wall of rock a half mile away rising straight up ten or twelve stories high. Immediately I thought of my shoes. Could I make it up that high cliff with sore feet and without heels in my shoes? The cliff drew ever closer as we kept walking. I was not tired any more and felt in good shape. But I wondered how I could make it up that rock. At least the ground was now getting drier but I couldn't help thinking of Nu Nu and the boys and I knew they'd never make that climb. A good hour later we were at the foot of the rock. Samuel walked around to the right as we entered a thicket through which I could still see the high rock. I then noticed that Samuel was now walking a little faster but I managed to catch up with him. As we came out of the thicket Samuel cautioned, "Be very careful, Pha-ti. Watch your step." The high rock was now on our left and towered at least a hundred feet above us. I turned to look to the right and all I saw were tree tops and a blue green valley a few hundred feet below.

Ahead of us nature had carved a path about five feet wide around the rock. I followed Samuel as he skirted the towering rock on our left and made it straight to the narrow ledge but I dared not look down the sheer drop on the right. Samuel walked briskly. We were fortunate that the ground was bone dry now but Samuel warned that we could slip on small stones that could roll under our feet as we stepped on them. Now I was concentrating on stepping only on solid rocks and avoided loose stones. We must have walked around he rocky wall for maybe a half hour when I noticed that we were gradually moving away from it and I could now see that the tree tops on the right were only about fifty feet below us. We now approached a grassy ground strewn with rocks and stones. We were on a considerably level plateau. Soon the huge rock was now behind us on our left. We were ntering a wooded area. We walked for a half hour through this wooded mountain top and when we emerged into the open we could see a few huts some distance away.

"We are there," Samuel told me. After another half hour we got to the first hut on the mountain top where Samuel stopped to talk to a few men. He gave his cargo of chickens to the men he introduced me to as Karen soldiers. As we were talking a man of slight built walked up and the men we were talking to all stood to attention.

"I am Saw Noo," the man said and extended his hand. I took his hand and told him my name and he said, "I know. P'Doh Spurgeon radioed me." P'Doh in Karen is a title one addresses a high official. He then escorted me to his house - and I mean house, not a hut - constructed partly with choice bamboo but largely with teak. It was about half past six and the sun was just beginning to set. Colonel Saw Noo called out to one of his men to prepare the bath room for me to have a bath. The bath room was an enclosure with bamboo walls neck high, with one side of the wall extended and wrapped around again like an entrance to a maze. There was no roof. There was a 50 gallon drum filled with water, an aluminum container to pour water over me, with a towel draped on the bamboo wall and soap in a coconut shell. As I began to undress I felt rubbery balls around my waist. When I took off my belt the leaches, already fully fed with my blood, dropped to the ground. There were leaches also between my toes and on my ankles still sucking away. An orderly brought me a cigar stub and I touched the heads of the leaches with the tobacco to get them to let go as otherwise I'd be taking a part of my skin off if I pulled them off by force. And there were many leaches. I was so tired that after a very delicious dinner of pork and chicken curry I couldn't stay up. I went to bed early. The colonel told me before bed that he would escort me into Thailand early in the morning. It would take us seven or eight hours he told me. Early in the morning I heard the colonel order his orderly to get the horse ready. A horse? The last time I rode a horse was when I was in the seventh standard in Mawlaik. I had never ridden a horse since but I welcomed the prospect of riding a horse again. After breakfast the colonel introduced me to a young soldier who would be my guide across the border into Thailand. His name was Win Maung. Then the orderly brought one horse to where we were standing. The colonel mounted the horse and I looked around for another horse but didn't see any.

"Let's go," the colonel said and galloped away. Win Maung and I followed on foot.

Win Maung was a soldier in his early twenties. He told me that there was no more climbing but that it would be all down hill. That was good news because my legs were still aching from the climb the previous day and my heels were sore. After walking for about five miles Win Maung pointed to a spirit house with a stone marker next to it. He told me that this was the border marking between Burma and Thailand. From now on we were on Thai soil. Excellent, I thought, and we kept descending down the slope. Sometimes the decent was steep and at other times it was gradual but there were almost no vegetation except shrubbery and the ground was dry and firm to walk on. Colonel Saw Noo was now already out of sight. Win Maung explained that he went ahead to contact the Thai Border Police so I wouldn't get into trouble with the Thai authorities. We were now descending and the slopes were getting steep. An hour later my toes began to hurt and my shins were also aching badly. I tried to ignore the pain in my toes, but they were hurting so bad after a while and I my shins were aching so much I thought my shin bones were about to break.

I asked Win Maung to stop for a rest. I sat on a rock and slipped my heel-less shoes off to take a look at my toes. My toe nails were black and blue. They hurt so much I didn't think I could put my shoes back on for the rest of the trip. But Win Maung looked at my heel-less shoes and said, "Why don't you cut the toes off your shoes and put them back on?" I did and now all I had left of my shoes were the soles, the tongue and laces that kept the shoes attached to my feet. While I was resting and tending to my toes Win Maung walked into a nearby wood and shot a couple of large red squirrels. He built a fire and roasted the squirrels. He brought with him some sticky rice and a flask of water. Before we ate Win Maung soaked tobacco in water and got rid of the leaches that still held on to my feet and ankles.

A beautiful panoramic landscape stretched before us as we continued on our trip across a multicolored meadow that extended over acres and acres of rolling hills. The colorful meadow was not all wild flowers as I had thought, but also myriads of butterflies of many sizes and colors, their pretty wings fluttering in the warm breeze under a sunny sky. They would fly away as we walked by them but returned immediately to soak the sunlit meadow again with their beauty. I silently said my farewell to the butterflies as we entered a wooded glen and in less than an hour came out on the other side of it. There was a wooden house standing alone about two hundred feet away. The house was surrounded by a small garden of vegetables and a tiny cornfield. I recognized the horse that was hitched to one of the post of the house. The colonel was there. The ground floor of the house was wide open so that I could see him sipping country whiskey from a tall glass. He got up to greet me and introduced me to a rather dark complexioned woman of about fifty five or sixty years old. She wore a skirt and had a three inch wide web belt around her waist with a holstered forty five pistol on one side and a foot long sheathed dagger on the other side. Her name was Daw Ma Ma Gyi, literally meaning Miss Big Sister. She spoke Burmese in a strong commanding voice with a heavy Tavoyan accent. I took my seat at the table across the colonel.

"You can stay with me for as long as you want," she told me. "Bring your family here and make this your home."

She put down a glass of home made whiskey in front of me. I took a sip. Wow, it had to be a hundred and ten proof liquor because, not expecting it, I choked and coughed and had to ask for some water and had the drink taken away. Later Daw Ma Ma Gyi told me that she was from Tavoy, where we passed through a week ago, and that she came to Thailand several years ago and moon-shined for a living. She had many customers every day, all Thai people, who dropped by in the evening for a few drinks before they went home after working in the mines. She spoke fluent Thai and was well respected and feared by the villagers of Kwai Sod.

"What are you going to do about your wife and sons?" the colonel asked.

"I'm worried. The journey is very rough. What do you suggest?" I asked.

"The best way for them to come is on elephants. They'll have to hire two elephants, one for them and one for their luggage"

"Can you arrange that?"

"No, it is best for your wife to do that herself," he answered. "Write her a letter and I'll see that she gets it."

I wrote a letter on a plain sheet of paper Ma Ma Gyi gave me. I told Nu Nu to hire two elephants and join me as soon as she could. I warned her about the rough journey, to be careful of the low branches as the elephants walked through the forest and warned her about possible vipers and insects that could drop from tree branches. I also warned her to be very careful when the elephants make their way around the rocky cliff. There was no envelope. I folded the letter and handed it to Colonel Saw Noo. That night I had a long chat with God and thanked Him for a safe journey and asked for His blessings upon Nu Nu and the boys and prayed for their safe trip. I thanked the Lord for all the people who were helpful throughout our journey. Saw Noo slept there one night and early the next morning bade me good bye and left.

We left Rangoon at a time when the government froze all private bank accounts with the result that we had very little cash with us when we left home. With what little cash she had left Nu Nu managed to hire two elephants to cross over the range with our two sons to join me in Kwai Sod, at the Thai border. But they were unable to leave immediately because of the flood that followed heavy monsoon rains that left the swift river and treacherous streams to overflow their banks. They waited for twelve days until they could begin their journey. They stayed at the colonel's hut all by themselves and were told that the elephant-man would come by and pick them up to make their trip over the mountain when the flood subsided. The boys were getting bored and restless and Nu Nu had to tell them stories until she ran out of stories to tell. David would say to Nu Nu, "Sing a song." Lester then asked Nu Nu to tell of her experience near the end of the war when the Japanese retreated and the Allies retook Mandalay.

"Alright, you've both got to go to sleep after I finish telling you my story. Promise?" She'd tell them stories of her experiences during the war, her family experience with the communist robbers and the days in Mandalay and Maymyo at the beginning of the Karen insurrection. The kids never got tired listening to those stories.

During those two weeks they had practically nothing to eat except rice, rock salt and hot pepper beans. Colonel Saw Noo's wife went back to wherever she came from. There was no one living with them. They were all by themselves in the middle of the thick jungle. Somehow, Nu Nu told me, she was not afraid. Instead she thought it was so peaceful and she felt secure. At home the boys were fed balanced and nourishing meals with vegetables, eggs and meat but they never ate enough of the food prepared for them. In fact many times they had to be coaxed to finish the food in their plates. But in the jungle at the foot of the mountain range they had unbelievable appetites. After the flood the water in the stream was muddy and no matter how much she washed the rice Nu Nu couldn't get rid of the sands. So naturally the rice was always very sandy. And there was only green pepper and salt to have rice with. In spite of that the boys ate their meals with gusto. Once a man brought them little fishes scarcely larger than minnows which Nu Nu grilled over charcoal for the boys to have and they would eat those with relish.

Finally the elephants came and the mahout, the elephant man, told Nu Nu that they could make the trip. Personal belongings were loaded on one elephant while Nu Nu and the boys mounted the other elephant. There was a howdah, a huge woven cane basket, on the elephant that they had to sit in. The howdah was trapped around the elephant's body. The front of the basket was secured by a thick rope that was strung around the elephant's neck while the back of the basket was secured to the elephant's tail. As they settled into the howdah Nu Nu read my letter again to make sure what she had to watch out for. In my letter I warned her about the sheer drop on one side of the trail on the mountain, about the low branches where I remembered seeing clusters of green vipers and then there were the insects and spiders in many shapes colors that kept falling as we brushed against the branches. In spite of the slippery ground almost immediately after the heavy rains the elephants were sure footed and the amazing thing was, when they did lose their footing they would just sit on all fours and slide down either forward or backwards depending on whether they were climbing or descending. The elephants were also very intelligent. When there were branches that were too low to clear the passengers, they would walk around them, or if the branches were not that thick they would grab the branches with their trunks and push them down and walk over them. If there was anything the elephants were afraid of it was the tiger. On their first day both the elephants stopped all of a sudden in their tracks. The elephant they were riding on trembled, violently shaking the howdah. The mahout whispered, "Tiger. Quiet and he allowed the elephant to remain still. In a few minutes a tiger appeared some fifty feet in front of them. The elephants stood still and continued to tremble. The tiger stared at the elephants for a few seconds and then turned and moved on. It was several minutes before the elephants would move on again. And indeed there were clusters of vipers on some tree branches. As the elephant pushed or pulled the overhanging branches away insects and spiders would drop on the boys and Nu Nu had to keep brushing the insects off the screaming boys. Because of higher ground the streams receded fast after the flood. But there was enough water for the elephants to take a drink when they were tired. They would take in water into their trunks and empty the water into their throats. After they had quenched their thirst they would take in the water with their trunks again and spray it on their bodies drenching the passengers to the delight of the boys.

Eventually they came to the precipice and the elephants had to hug the side of the mountain for a half hour. Nu Nu and the boys never looked down the sheer drop. By now they were almost at the head quarters of Colonel Saw Noo. Nu Nu now was relieved that the top of the mountain was now level and almost without heavy vegetation. They arrived at Saw Noo's head quarters at around three in the afternoon. The elephants made better time than I did. Nu Nu and the boys received a warm welcome from Colonel Saw Noo and the women of the outpost and were treated to a lavish dinner.

That evening Nu Nu witnessed a typical Karen resistance war council in session. Wives of officers, NCOs and other ranks were sitting on the floor with their husbands, some breast feeding their babies. The Karens were planning an ambush. A government patrol was approaching a Karen village. Once they got there and didn't find any rebels they normally could give villagers a hard time interrogating them and demanding food or live stock to kill for food. Occasionally they would search homes and even ransack them and take whatever they wanted without paying for them. If they found any weapon they could torture the villagers and even burn the village down like they had done in other areas to the north.

"How many are in the patrol?" the colonel asked.

"About thirty," someone answered.

"We can easily wipe them out," another suggested.

"No, we won't do that," the colonel told them. "Let them get to the village. If they do not cause the villagers any trouble let them be. Don't attack them. We'll try to get as close to the village as possible so that in case they cause any trouble, we will be there to help the villagers."

"Who knows the village well enough to tell us where outside the village we should wait for the patrol?" asked the colonel.

"You have to wait for them at two places," said a woman. "One, at the deep gully north of the village if you need to ambush them after they get out of the village. And also wait at the bamboo groves behind the village so that you can easily attack them from behind if they harm the villagers."

"How do you know all that?" the colonel asked.

"I had lived there all my life until I got married and came here."

"Naw Dah is right. I know the place well myself," a captain replied.

"You'll be in charge of the two platoons we're sending out, captain," the colonel ordered. The war council was adjourned.

The next morning after breakfast and a grand send off by Saw Noo and the women of the camp Nu Nu and the boys were on their way on their last leg of their journey to join me. On this second leg of the trip there were no thick woods. It was down hill almost all the way and Nu Nu and the boys had to hold on tight to the sides of the howdah to keep them from rolling over and out of it. But it was a trip worth all the dangers and risks because they knew they would soon be reunited with me.

CHAPTER 17

SHORT SOJOURN IN THE JUNGLE OF KWAI SOD

I WAS SIPPING 'JUNGLE GIN' and talking to Ma Ma Gyi, when she stopped talking to listen.

"Quiet," she said, "Listen."

"Listen to what,?" I asked.

"Can't you hear? 'Clang, clang, clang,' "she said.

"Yes. What about it?" I asked.

"Your wife, she's arrived. You'll see the elephants coming out of the woods shortly," she said excitedly, overjoyed as if her own sister was coming home.

The "clang, clang" of the elephant bells sounded louder and in a few short moments we saw the elephants emerge out of the wood. In less than five minutes the elephants unloaded their cargo of tired, weary, passengers right where I was sipping my 'jungle gin'.

"David, you enjoyed the elephant ride?" I asked as I hugged him.

"No, I don't want to ride elephants any more," he quietly answered.

"How about you, Lester?" I asked.

"I think I had enough of elephant ride too," he told me. I introduced Nu Nu to Ma Ma Gyi who then poured hot tea for Nu Nu and then went to the kitchen to prepare the evening meal.

Nu Nu told me how they were alone in the hut with nothing to eat except rice, salt and chilly pepper.

"But the boys ate well," she said, "sand and all. They swallowed everything I gave them."

"What about the sardines and dried fish we brought for emergency?" I asked.

"I gave them away to the colonel's wife. She didn't have anything in the kitchen. I'm glad I gave it to her. She was so happy," she said and continued, "What are your plans?"

"I don't know. I don't have any," I replied. "Now that you have arrived we can plan but I don't know where to start. I don't even know where we are," I told her. Nu Nu laughed.

"I guess you're right. At least we know we're in Thailand. We're in God's given free land, right? I feel so good," she said.

"I feel the same, too," I agreed.

That night after saying prayers with the boys and putting them to bed, we said our prayers again together thanking God for His presence throughout our journey, for providing us with all the help we needed. We prayed for His continued guidance. The next morning Nu Nu asked Ma Ma Gyi how we could get to Bangkok.

"How can you get to Bangkok from here?" she asked Nu Nu. "There is no road from here to Bangkok."

"Then how can we get out of here and make our way to Bangkok? Isn't there any way?" Nu Nu asked.

"If you wait long enough, sometimes a truck might come by to collect tin ores from the mines. That's about once a year or twice, at the most."

"There's no other way?" Nu Nu asked.

"I told you there is no road between this place and Bangkok" she answered.

"Then how did the truck you talked about get here to collect tin ores from the mines?" Nu Nu asked.

"They have to cut their way through the forest, and sometimes they get bogged down and get stuck for days before they can make their way out."

"You said they come once or twice a year. Have they been here yet this year?" Nu Nu asked.

"No. Not that I know, unless they came to areas away from here and I didn't hear about it. You know, you and your family can stay here with me for as long as you need to."

"What are we going to do here? There is no job. How can we survive?" I asked Ma Ma Gyi.

"You can work in the mines, collect the ores from your mine and from the mines of others and sell them when buyers come to collect them," she answered.

"Once a year. How do I feed my family until then?" I asked.

"You can do it," she said, "other people here can do it."

"Then why don't you?" I asked.

"I'm a woman. People don't trust or have respect for women," she said.

"Why did you come to Thailand and settle down here?" I asked her.

"I lived in Tavoy where you came through. My husband died and then Ne Win came to power. I don't like Ne Win, so I came here," she said.

"Why do you moonshine?" I asked.

"That's the only thing I can do. What do you want me to do? Become a prostitute?" she answered angrily.

"No, I wasn't suggesting anything," I laughed, "just curious why you came here all by yourself."

"You see how I keep myself safe from men?" she slapped her forty five and the dagger at her belt.

Nu Nu then proceeded to take her orchids out of the basket and started to hang them on the trees around the house and planted the ground orchids in the soil around Ma Ma Gyi's garden. For the next several days we sat at Ma Ma Gyi's table to sip hot tea or home made whiskey which I called 'jungle gin', and talk politics. The boys had not have nourishing food for several days and we noticed that David was getting very thin and we worried about his health. We needed to get some milk powder, cod liver oil and other dietary supplements for the kids. Ma Ma Gyi said that if we walked a half day we would find a general store where we could get anything we wanted. But we didn't know how to get there.

"I'll take you there in the morning if you want," Ma Ma Gyi volunteered.

So I called Lester and David together and told them that in the morning Nu Nu and I would be going to a place to get things we needed and for them to stay back.

"We'll come along with you," Lester said.

"No, son, it's a long walk. It's a half day's walk. You're too young to make a trip that long," I told him.

"But we want to go along too," Lester insisted.

"No, you'll both stay back and that's it, okay?" I told him.

"What happens when you come back and you don't find us? Suppose we're kidnapped or something. Where will you look for us?" Lester said.

This kid knew how to scare me.

"Listen, both of you," I told them, "you can come along, but I will not carry any of you. It's a long walk. You can rest, but don't ask me to carry you. Will you promise?"

They both nodded eagerly. "Promise?" I asked again and they both said, "Promise."

At six in the morning we left for the place Ma Ma Gyi told us about. Ma Ma Gyi brought along a guide. Fortunately there was no hill to climb but there was a lot of overgrowths and small woods and there appeared to be a regular trail. A barely visible foot path was recognizable over sand and stones. It was sunny and hot. An hour into the trek I asked the boys if they were already tired, and they were not. Matter of fact they were running in circles around us as we were walking until the guide told them not to do that because of the many cobras around the area. They could step on one. Now David stayed close to us, while Lester, the more energetic of the two, kept running ahead of us. We let him run but warned him to watch his steps. Sometimes the trail was a bit rocky and hard to walk over and at times it was just dirt and stones that bore the signs of having been traveled over.

We were about a hundred feet behind Ma Ma Gyi and the guide. Suddenly Nu Nu yelled out, "Stop, Lester, don't move." He was about ten feet in front of us now. It was too late. The snake slithered past between his legs and he didn't even notice that he had just missed stepping on a snake. I held Nu Nu with one hand and David with the other and watched as the snake slithered across the trail and momentarily stopped to turn it's head in our direction and raised it's hood. It was a cobra. We stood absolutely still. Slowly it lowered it's hood, then turned and disappeared behind the rocks. Lester was still hopping up and down on the trail, now thirty feet in front of us. We were walking slower now. Obviously the kids were getting a little tired and so we had to slow down our pace for them. After a couple of hours the guide looked back and said we were just an hour away from our destination. It was ten o'clock. That was great news I thought, but David looked up at me and said, "Daddy I want to tell you something."
"Yes, what is it?" I asked him.
"Don't get angry with me," he said.
"No I won't get angry. What is it you want to tell me?" I asked.
"Promise you won't get angry," he said.
"I promise. What is it?" I asked.
"You promise?" he insisted.
"Yes, David. I promise. Tell me. What is it?" I asked.
Then he burst into tears and sobbed, "I can't walk any more."

Poor David. I never asked him again if he was getting tired. He tried to keep his promise that I didn't have to carry him. I choked as I picked him up and threw him over my shoulder and let his feet dangle in front of my hest. The guide was right. Exactly within the hour we reached the place. I was completely exhausted. It was a huge town with teak and sturdy bamboo buildings. The guide took us straight to the general store which was a very large shed and there we found everything we needed. Nu Nu bought milk powder, Ovaltine, cod liver oil, sardines, corned beef and some preserved fruits, and aspirin. I bought myself a new pair of sneakers. The guide very kindly offered to carry what we had bought and then took us to his friend's house where the hostess cooked lunch for us. We didn't speak Thai language so we had to communicate by signs. While we were having lunch a Burmese college student came over to talk to us. He brought his young Thai wife along. He was very happy to see us. He told us that he escaped from Burma after the July 7, 1962 shooting at Rangoon University. Hundreds of other University students escaped into Thailand traveling separately through the jungle until they got to the Thai border where they regrouped. Many of them were now married to Thai girls and were in trading business or teaching. A few of them came to the house to talk to us while we had lunch. They were happy to see us because we were the first Burmese they saw since their escape into Thailand. We told them that we were there at the Student's Center when the shooting occurred. Then one of them said he recognized Nu Nu because he took his girl friend to her shop to order some dresses for a party.

As we were leaving, this boy took off his slippers, got down on the floor and paid us respect in true Burmese tradition and said he would pray for our long life and well being. We were very touched by his gesture of love and respect for us. It was almost two in the afternoon when we left but we took a more leisurely trek back for the sake of the kids and got back to Kwai Sod around seven thirty as it was getting dark. After dinner we sat and talked for a while and retired early to bed. The kids fell asleep in no time but in spite of the fatigue after the long trek we couldn't get to sleep. Both of us were awake until the small hours of the morning.
We were in Kwai Sod now almost two weeks. The corn in the small garden was now ready to be plucked. There were few other vegetables. Ma Ma Gyi did not raise any chicken. For the next few days all we had to eat was corn with sardine and canned meat we bought at the market. At times we bought chicken from Ma Ma Gyi's customers for curry.

Life was getting monotonous and so I started joining Ma Ma Gyi in the afternoon over a glass of her 'junglr gin' just to while away the time. Every afternoon she would have about ten or a dozen men stopping to have a few drinks and we would sit and talk together. I began to have conversation with Ma Ma Gyi's customers. She was my interpreter. The men worked in pairs in the small mines over an area of a couple of square miles each and brought back their meager find to their homes and sold them to buyers who usually came before the Monsoon set in to collect the ores from them. The ores included tin, and wolfram and sometimes manganese and tungsten. They also had to farm small patches of rice on the hills for their own yearly consumption. Some of them raised chicken and ducks which they took to some other villages to sell. They lived a rather primitive life but seemed quite happy with their hard life.

Ma Ma Gyi woke us up early one morning. "You have a visitor," she called out. We woke up and went downstairs to see who it was that wanted to see us.

"Hey, Hsi Hsi," I greeted the visitor. It was our cousin who went underground years earlier and fought against government forces in many skirmishes but now had left the resistance and became a cattle trader.

"How did you know we were here?" I asked.

"I met Colonel Saw Noo on the way and he told me that he brought you here."

It was a surprised reunion with a cousin. He wanted to make sure that we were doing alright. Ma Ma Gyi invited him to stay at the house for as many days as we needed him. I asked Hsi Hsi about the possibility of getting to Bangkok from there. He answered that he was not familiar with this area and so he had no idea. He said if we could get to Three Pagoda Pass he could arrange for us to get to Bangkok but he wanted to know where in Bangkok we wanted to go. We couldn't tell him because we had never been to Bangkok and we didn't know anyone there.

"You don't want to go into Bangkok with your wife and two children if you don't know anybody. The Police or Immigration authorities could find you out and bring you back to the border. Once they register you at the border as refugees you can never go back to Bangkok."

Hsi Hsi told us that he could only stay with us a few more days as he had to get back to his business of rounding up some cattle and taking them down to Bangkok to sell. A couple of mornings later as we were drinking hot tea, Ma Ma Gyi asked us to be quiet as she strained to listen to something.

"It's a truck," she yelled out excitedly. "This is the truck that picks up tin ores. This is the truck you are looking for. Hsi Hsi, you go and try to catch up with this truck and tell them there are people here who want to get to Bangkok. Go now!" she ordered. Hsi Hsi shot off like a gazelle into the woods.

"You people must get ready because the truck can come any time to pick you up" Ma Ma Gyi told us.

We didn't have much left by now but we packed what we needed to take with us. I asked Nu Nu about her orchids. She said to forget about the orchids. Maybe Ma Ma Gyi could do something with them. We almost had no money left to pay for our fare to Bangkok. While we waited we prayed and asked God to provide whatever our need was. We waited all day but the truck never came. After dinner, Ma Ma Gyi told us that we could go to bed because the truck couldn't travel at night anyway and we had to wait another day and see if it would come at all. We woke up early and had an early breakfast and waited for the truck. At exactly nine the truck rolled up and Ma Ma Gyi shouted, "Your truck is here. Hurry up."

It was an open Dodge truck. Hsi Hsi helped us throw the battered suit case and the cane chest into the truck and then told us that he could not come along with us because of his business and bade us good bye. We thanked Ma Ma Gyi for her hospitality but had no money to pay her for her kindness and I told her so. She said it was alright and that she was not expecting to take any money from us anyway.

CHAPTER 18

BANGKOK BOUND

THE TRUCK LEFT WITHIN A few minutes. Now we were traveling with a company of men we never met before, men who didn't speak Burmese or English while we didn't speak Thai. It was an open truck with a power winch attached to the front bumper. All we did was look at each other, nod our heads and smile. One man tried to talk to us.

"My name, Prasit," he told us.

"My name Spencer," I told him and pointing at Nu Nu I said. "Her name, Nu Nu," then at Lester and David I said, "his name Lester, his name David."

Then we looked at each other, nodded and smiled again. I offered my hand to Prasit. He grasped and shook it vigorously. Prasit was a big man but with a very kindly face. There were three other men. The man at the wheel, dark complexioned and tall, looked like a hired driver, not doing a lot of talking and only taking orders from one of the other two who looked like his boss and who looked very Chinese. The Chinese looking man was short, fair complexioned and smoked opium every once in a while out of a kit he held constantly in his hand. The third man was perhaps a good friend of the Chinaman, talking, arguing and joking with him all the time. Prasit was the only one who tried to talk to us either because he was friendly or he was the only one who knew a few words in English. By sign language he managed to teach us a few common Thai words, as the truck bounced and rocked over the uneven and bumpy terrain, words that he knew in English like 'thank you', 'good', 'bad', 'hot', 'cold', 'come', 'go' etc. The truck suddenly stopped. The driver picked up a machete from the floor of the truck and jumped off. There was a thick vine hanging down right in front of the truck from the top of the tree on the left to the bottom of the tree to the right. With a few quick strokes the driver cut the vine in half and the truck was able to move on leaving the severed vine swinging like a long pendulum. At times the truck moved through tall brushes causing a variety of insects to drop on us. We had to quickly brush off the creepy creatures from our clothes and those of the boys before they could do us any harm. The kids would scream and yell as the insects landed on them. At times the driver recognized an old trail and tried to follow it for a while and then lost it. On a few occasions the truck got bogged down in mud or got stuck in a ditch. On these occasions the driver used the winch to pull the truck back onto solid level ground. There was a time when the right rear wheel of the truck slipped into a ditch. In spite of repeated pull of the winch the truck didn't budge. Then all the men burst out laughing. I wondered why they were laughing. Then I saw the object of their amusement. It was the tree to which the cable was secured. It got uprooted and was pulled by the winch toward the truck. It took all the men a good half hour before they could get the car off the deep rut. An hour later we had another mishap. The driver tried to maneuver a bend at an incline and caused the truck to flip over on it's side throwing all of us out. Fortunately none of us got hurt. It took all of us five men another half an hour to push the truck back on it's four wheels.

We did not have any food to bring with us except the canned food that we bought at the market at the border general store. At the command of the Chinaman the driver stopped the truck under a shady spot on the edge of a clearing. The men had brought with them some food which they were preparing to have. The driver heated the food on a small gas stove. They offered us their food, but we declined and showed them our canned sardine and corned beef. The Chinaman took the cans and had the driver open them and had all of us share the food as we listened to them talk. We didn't understanding a word of what they were saying. Obviously they were discussing us. They must have asked Prasit to ask us what or who we were and why we were in Thailand.
"You Bama?" Prasit asked.
"Yes. But not Bama. I—Karen," I told him.
"Ah, Karian," he echoed and told his friends that we were from Burma but that we were Karen (the Thais called Karen, Karian).
"Karian good. Bama no good. Bama, Ayuthia – " then he gestured with his hands to describe destruction of the old capital of Thailand, Ayutthaya, by the Burmese king.
"I know, long time ago," I responded.
"Bama no good," he repeated.

"I, Burma Navy," I told him and showed him a sign of an anchor, and I placed two fingers on my shoulder to tell him that I was a lieutenant in the service. He understood immediately and told his friends so.

"Bo Mya good man," he told me. General Bo Mya was president of Karen National Union and Chief Commander of the KNLA (Karen National Liberation Army).

"Bo Mya my friend," I lied. (I knew of General Bo Mya but had never met him)

"You big man," he said, and then translated that to his friends. I didn't know what he meant by big man. Perhaps he thought I was a big shot with the Karen rebels. Prasit was a police officer under a previous government which was toppled by the Thai army now in power. So he now had no job and was just a friend accompanying the Chinaman on his trip to collect tin ores from the border areas. When our cousin Hsi Hsi caught up with the truck to tell him that we needed a ride into Bangkok all the men protested and refused to come to pick us up. Prasit pleaded with them, telling them to have pity on us. He told us later when we could understand the language better, that something made him come to help us, he could not explain what. He just had that strange feeling that he had to come and pick us up and to take us to Bangkok. Finally the friends gave in. Nu Nu told him that she was praying very hard to our God to make them come and pick us up and God answered her prayer. Yes, he said, he believed that because he never had that kind of feeling before. He felt strongly that they just had to come and pick us up. Praise God for answering Nu Nu's prayer.

Evening came and we were still in the thick jungle. We ate again before it got dark. After the evening meal out of some more sardine, corned beef and some left over Thai curries, which were heated again, we continued on our trip. The driver hacked away at the brushes and vines as he tried to pick his way out of the thick jungle. There was a light shower as it got dark but only for a short time. We got wet somewhat because the truck had no awning to protect us from the rain but we were so tired that we fell asleep in our wet clothes. We only woke up when the truck stopped and we heard voices of people approaching the truck with flashlights shining into the truck. Prasit told us, "Sleep, sleep" So we kept our eyes closed while lights were shone on our faces. Both boys were fast asleep. There were lengthy conversations in Thai and finally the truck moved on. We opened our eyes and realized that we had just left a military check point. I looked at my watch. It was 9 p.m. We'd been in the truck now for twelve hours. Prasit looked at me and said, "More, more." He meant there were more military security check points still to come. Then I realized that the Vietnam War was on, which accounted for the military security checks. We had at least two or three more check points that we had to go through and every time we approached one Prasit would tell us to sleep. We were exhausted and sound asleep when Prasit woke us up.

"We Bangkok," he told us.

"We are in Bangkok now?" I asked him excitedly.

"Yes," he replied, and asked, "Where you go?"

We never thought of where we were going because we'd never been to Bangkok and so we knew of no place to go to. For the first time I panicked.

"What are we going to do?" I asked Nu Nu. "We have no money and we don't know where to go for help." But the Lord won't fail us. Prasit knew that we knew nobody and the Lord told him to open his house to those poor people in the truck.

"Okay, you come my house," Prasit told us. The truck drove on until we came to a little community on the outskirt of the city and stopped in front of a house.

"My house," Prasit proudly told us. I looked at my time. It was 3 a.m. We had traveled eighteen hours in this truck through a jungle, a journey that would otherwise take five to six hours on a paved road.

We picked up our small suit case and Prasit helped me lug the cane chest. We followed Prasit into his house. There was a hallway in which some children were sleeping under mosquito netting. Prasit woke the kids up and sent them away into a room and made us take over the place where the kids had been sleeping. We gratefully crawled under the mosquito net and onto the mattresses on the floor and soon fell asleep. We woke up early because the kids were getting ready to go to school and were having their breakfast. After the kids left, Prasit introduced us to his wife who 'wai'ed (placing two palms together prayer fashion in front of her chest which is Thai custom for greeting), and we awkwardly returned the gesture. Over breakfast we tried to make conversation the best we could with Ptasit and his wife. After a while she left for work and Prasit also went out. Nu Nu and I went into the sitting room to discuss what we would have to do next. Actually there was nothing to discuss. We did not know any one, and we had no money, so what was there to discuss? Nu Nu suggested that we look for a phone book. We might recognize a name to get started. I looked for a phone book in the house and found one but they were in Thai. The only entries in English in the directory were the phone numbers, 'Coke' and 'Night Club' and 'Wimpy' and such other commercial ads with western names. When Prasit came back I asked him to get me a directory in English. We walked around the house to get familiar with it, for this could be our home for awhile. The rear of the house opened onto a balcony right on top of a *klong* , or canal, a foul smelling waterway with slimy dark stagnant water. The house was very clean with well polished floors and simple furniture.

We were thinking of seeking an asylum because we did not want to be caught being illegal and without any papers. We both left our passports at home because we did not want to be caught by the military authorities with passports in our possession which would be a sure sign that we were escaping. We wondered how we would approach the Thai authorities to ask for asylum. That evening Prasit told us we could sleep in their little spirit room, an equivalent of a little chapel or a prayer room. It was a room of about seven by ten feet, where they had their 'spirit house' on a stand in one corner. We placed our little luggage in the opposite corner from the spirit house and the rest of the space was for our bedding on the floor. On the third night there was a crash that woke all of us up. Then I realized that in my sleep I had kicked a support of the spirit house and brought the whole spirit house down. Prasit and his wife came running into our little bed room. Normally this would be taken as a bad omen or a curse. So I apologized saying, "Sorry, sorry," over and over again. Prasit's wife was obviously upset while Prasit kept telling me, "Mai Pen rai, mai pen rai," meaning, 'never mind, never mind.' The couple put their spirit house back together and told us to go back to sleep.

We did not have much money left to share expenses with Prasit's family and Prasit knew it. That family fed us, hid us from authorities and generally looked after us. On the morning of the fourth day just after breakfast a group of Naval officers headed by a lieutenant commander came marching into the house and asked to see me. Prasit was home and had the officers sit at the dining table. He sat by me across the table from the officers as he introduced me to them. Later he told me that he had his wife call the Thai Navy to tell them about me. We were never warned about the visit and we didn't know what it was all about. My thought was that someone had reported our presence to the authorities and they were here to question us and take us into custody. The lieutenant commander shook my hand and asked me, "May I have your name, please." He spoke good English with a trace of Thai accent.

"Spencer Zan," I replied and gave him the names of my entire family.

"You were in the Burma Navy?" he asked.

"Yes, I was a lieutenant," I told him.

"Why did you come to Thailand?" he wanted to know.

"Well, you know, the army took over from the civilian government, and I don't agree with their policy."

"What is their policy?" he asked.

"It's socialist – extreme socialist."

"Like Communist? That's bad," he said.

"Yes, they nationalize banks and businesses ......"

"I know, I know," he said.

He then asked how I came through, whether I met any Karen rebel leaders, what the Karens were fighting for, and what their strength was etc.

After giving him the general information that he asked for I told him, "I'd like to apply for an asylum for me and my family and I would request you to help me."

"No, I can't help you with that. You'll be alright if you stay with Prasit. You have nothing to worry about," he told me and got up to leave.

"Bangkok is a big city, no one will bother you," he said as he walked away.

Prasit was smiling. "Good man," he told me pointing at the officer who had just interviewed me. Maybe, I thought, but he didn't help me at all. Well, at least he didn't take us into custody.

Prasit dropped a book in front of me. It was a phone directory in English. I grabbed it and said, "Kop Khun Ma, Krup" (thank you very much, sir) and rushed into the spirit room to share it with Nu Nu. We didn't know what to look for. I saw a few companies connected with our timber business in Rangoon but I wouldn't know the people who were operating from Bangkok.

"Let's try the American Embassy," I suggested.

Among the many names we saw O'Brien. We knew an O'Brien in the American Embassy in Rangoon but we didn't know if this was the same O'Brien.

"At least we can find out," I told Nu Nu.

"How about American Baptist Mission?" Nu Nu asked.

"American – American—here's American Baptist Mission on Silom Road, General Secretary, Cecil Carder. Know him? Heard of him?" I asked.

"Never heard of him," she replied, "but he might know your sister, Louise. She's still General Secretary of the Burma Baptist Convention, isn't she?"

"Yes, she is."

I called the number and got Cecil Carder right away.

"Cecil Carder?" I asked.

"Yes. May I know who I am talking to?" he asked.

"My name is Spencer Zan. I recently arrived from Rangoon. Do you know Mrs. Louise Paw, General Secretary of the Burma Baptist Convention?"

"Yes, I do."

"She's my sister. I have arrived with my family at the border and someone brought me into Bangkok. Can I come and see you?" I asked.

"Of course," he answered. He asked for the address and gave us a time the following evening that he would pick us up and hung up.

The next morning we had another unexpected visit. This time it was a colonel from the Immigration department. Colonel Supong interviewed me at length and finally he told me not to worry about my stay and that I would be safe from authorities as long as I stayed out of trouble.

"Bangkok is big place. If you have trouble show this card." He gave me his card after he wrote something on the back. Another good man, but this didn't help us in any way. We were still the guest of Prasit and family, but how long could we stay with them?

"But I need to get a job," I told Colonel Supong. "I can't get a job without having a valid passport to show my identity."

"You go to any school and apply for a job. They need English teachers very very bad. You'll have no problem. They'll give you a job," he told me.

That evening precisely at 5 p.m. Cecil Carder picked us up and took us to his house. His wife, Dorothy, prepared a delicious meal for us and we had a long visit which lasted into the late hours. We spoke about just everything during those long hours because this was the first time since our departure from Burma that we had a chance to talk to someone in a language we fully understood. We came away enriched with essential knowledge of the country and some knowledge of the culture that we were new to. But still Cecil, another good man, could not help me with seeking a job. We were in Thailand illegally, period. Few people would stick their neck out for us and I couldn't blame those who wouldn't help us. I thought of the Y.W.C.A. and wondered if there would be a job for Nu Nu. One day Nu Nu and I went to town to look for Y.W.C.A. Not knowing how to speak the language didn't get us too far. Nu Nu was tired and was sitting on the side walk on the curb massaging her leg when a taxi drew up alongside and asked where we wanted to go. I asked him if he knew where Y.W.C.A. was. He said he did. "Ten Bahts," he told us. We got in. The driver made an immediate U-turn and drew up right in front of the

Y.W.C.A. We didn't notice Y.W.C.A. from where we were sitting across the street, but it couldn't have taken us more than a minute to walk over to the Y just across the street!! We had no luck at the Y. W. C.A.

I wondered who Prasit thought we really were. Perhaps he thought I was a big shot with the Karen resistance. He constantly talked about helping me with getting arms for the Karen but I kept ignoring him. One day a U.S. army truck pulled up in front of Prasit's house with a Thai soldier at the wheel. Prasit had been waiting for this truck all morning. He took me to the truck and told me that he had his connection hijack this truck for me. He lifted the tarp in the back of the truck to show me the weapons meant for Vietnam. He had his friend, the driver, open one case to show me the weapons. We all burst out laughing when we saw bottles of whiskies instead of weapons. I told his friend to take back the truck immediately before the M.P. came looking for it. I believed that Prasit wanted to help me because he hoped to make a few bucks as a broker on the Thai side but it didn't work out for him that time.

When I was in high school and college I had a class mate by the name of Eugene Phoa Lieng Seng, a Chinese from Singapore. Somehow I met someone who mentioned Eugene and gave me his address. We had abosolutely no money left. I wrote to Eugene and asked for some help. He sent me Singapore $250.00. At least now we could contribute a little to pay for our keep at Haw's.

Nu Nu started to write letters to her friends in America. Likewise I wrote to business associates I knew and agents who I came into contact with in the timber industry, those in Europe, England and Hong Kong. Fortunately we brought our address book with us. We were bored as we had nothing to do so we thought we would let friends abroad know that we had escaped from Burma and were now living in Bangkok. We just told them that we were trying to set up a new life in another world. We never as much as asked for or even mentioned about money. But in the following weeks more than thirty letters arrived at our address at Radprao, Bangkok, every single one with a check enclosed in varying amounts. Cecil Carder went with us to the Bank of America where they allowed us to open an account without our having to answer too many questions. The least amount of money received was fifty dollars and there were four checks for two hundred and fifty dollars. The gifts totaled over two thousand and five hundred dollars. When we were a little better off, and when refugees started arriving from Burma, Nu Nu and I calculated the total amount received from friends. We set aside a portion of what we received and used this money to help people coming from Burma who needed help. When we had to help in cash, we always asked the recipients not to pay us back but to use that money to help others after them.

We were now able to rent a house. Prasit managed to get us a house for a very reasonable rent in Raj Pralop, another section of Bangkok not too far from his house. By now I knew how to get around by bus. I applied for and immediately got a job as an English teacher at a high school. I was required to teach three classes each day for high school. It was easy as little preparation was needed. I was there three months and the principal told me he wanted me to teach permanently at their school. "Bring me your passport. I will get you a visa. I want you to teach here permanently," he told me.

I could not let the school know that I had no passport and therefore left the job after receiving my pay check. I tried my luck at another school and taught for about four months when the principal asked me to bring my passport so he could get me a permanent visa. I taught in four different schools during the next several months. Meantime, Nu Nu was visiting American homes to see if they had sewing needs that she could do for them like mending, altering dresses or sewing curtains and drapes. The few jobs that she got did not pay too well since foreigners would only pay more or less according to what they pay local Thais for similar jobs which was much less than what would be paid in Burma at that time. Meantime, with the help of Cecil Carder, Lester and David were able to attend the International School. There was a canal close by the house and the boys could go to school by boat which took them right by the the school. We arranged for a long tail boat to pick them up and drop them back each day.

I had to get some kind of paper so that I could get a job without later getting into trouble with the authorities. I met a young Laotian, William, who was visiting. We got into conversation and he told me that I could buy a Laotian passport for a few hundred dollars and said that I could easily pass for a Lao.
"How can I get it?" I asked him.
"I have a friend who is the son of a Laotian general. He helped other people before."
"How much will it cost?" I asked.
"Maybe a thousand dollars, at most," he replied.

We talked about it for a long time. I was desperate to get a legal status, no matter how illegally, so that I could work. I discussed the full detail with William who said he would go along with me, put me up at a hotel and see to it that the money got to the right officials and he guaranteed that I would get a Laos passport and become a Lao citizen within a month.

Early in December I took out one thousand and five hundred dollars from our account and left with William for Laos. We went by train to Nong Kai and took a ferry across the Mekong River to Vientiane. He put me up at a small French hotel. The first night I was there I heard shells exploding at regular intervals somewhere outside the city. I asked the hotel manager what was going on. He told me that the communists were shelling the army position outside of the city. He said that war was going on not only in Vietnam, but also in Laos. The government was holding the city while the communists were keeping pressure on the capital of Vientiane. I asked the manager why everybody seemed so calm and were going about their business like nothing was happening while the communists were shelling the city. He said, "Life goes on and we just have to continue with our business."

That didn't calm my nerves at all. I couldn't sleep all night until in the small hours of the morning. The next night I felt less nervous. And on the third night I scarcely noticed the shelling which were still going on. Now I was beginning to enjoy the French music played over the intercom. William asked for five hundred dollars for the son of the general who would be issuing passports the following week. He disappeared for several days and came back for two hundred more saying that the passport was being prepared but the junior officer who was handling the job needed some money. I gave him the money hoping that it was the last payment I had to make. I spent my time in the lobby listening to French music interposed by Laotian songs and doing crossword puzzles. William came after Christmas and said the general had to sign the passport but he was busy now with increased communist pressure on the city. There was rumor that the communists would soon be able to make a break through and enter the city. The general was busy and was not seeing anyone. William asked for some more money so that he could get some one to try to see the general on my behalf. He said that was the last payment I would have to make. I gave him the three hundred dollars he asked for. I was skeptic right from the beginning but I was so desperate to get some papers that I just threw caution to the winds and

ery passenger who entered the station had to produce an I.D. of some

tried my luck. Now I realized I was being taken for a ride but I was still willing to just wait and see.

Meantime the communists bombarded the inner city and we had to evacuate the hotel. I had nowhere to go to. William moved me to a Medical College dorm where students were still at school. I was put up in an empty room and a couple of students brought me food from their dining room. While I was at the college I learned that Dr. Russell Andrus was the Ambassador in Laos. I knew Professor Andrus when I was in college in Rangoon before World War II. I went to his house but he was away. I left a note at his door and continued to stay at the dorm. The heavy shelling of inner city continued but since college was outside of the city we were never in any danger. A few days later I had a call from Dr. Andrus via a phone call to the dean. I visited Dr. Andrus and stayed with him a few days. Later he advised me to leave because of the situation that was deteriorating and considering that my family would be anxious for my safety I should return to Bangkok. I asked William to take me to the ferry at the Mekhong River and asked him to rent a boat for me to cross back into Thailand. William told me that the Passport was ready for signature and that he would bring it to me when ready. When I boarded the boat William warned me not to go to the police landing which was directly across because the Thai Immigration would check me and arrest me for not having any paper. He advised that I went upstream to another landing. I disregarded his advice however and asked the boatman to take me straight to the police landing because I figured that if the boat headed for any other landing and the police hailed for the boat to proceed to the police landing, I'd be searched and the situation would be worse for me. I got off at the police landing, and was not stopped by anyone as I walked past the police station and the immigration office. Now I headed straight to the railway station but my heart sank as I entered the station because there were armed soldiers in a surprise check of all passengers. Every passenger who entered the station had to produce an I.D. of some sort. I entered a café and ordered coffee and paid for it, and then bought a ticket for Bangkok. I sat down at a table and sipped my coffee as I pretended to read from the news paper I was carrying. I was hoping that the soldiers would leave the station before the train left but they did not. I was praying hard that I would be able to board the train without the soldiers accosting me. When the conductor blew his whistle I rose and hurried towards the train as it started to move. My heart sank a second time when two soldiers ran towards me. I thought this was it. One got hold of my suitcase and the other took hold of my arm and ran with me and helped me up the train as it started to move. The Good Lord heard me and my prayer was answered.

The conductor came to check my ticket. I gave it to him and said, "Pai Krungthep" (I'm going to Bangkok). I must have mispronounced the word or my accent must have given me away because he said, "This way sir," in perfect English and led me to my seat next to a Buddhist monk. The monk started to speak to me in Thai as soon as I sat down. I had no idea what he was saying. I took out a handkerchief and held it against my face and pretended to have a severe tooth ache. I remained that way all through the night pretending to sleep still holding the hanker chief to my face. When the train arrived at Bangkok station the next morning I took a *samlor* (a three wheel pedi-cab) which was much cheaper than a regular taxi and returned home. I got home with barely a hundred dollars left in my pocket. And I was still without a passport. Of course, the passport never turned up either nor did William. The situation at home was not any better than when I left and our money was beginning to run out. When I asked the kids how they enjoyed their Christmas, David replied, "There is no Santa Claus in Bangkok." A couple of weeks later we had only small change left. I gave Lester all the change I had and told him, "Mom and Dad will be out all day and may not be back in time for dinner. This is for you to buy food from the vender for dinner for you both."

We said a little prayer before Nu Nu left to visit some American homes in the hope of getting some sewing job. I went to visit Prasit from whom I hoped to borrow some money. My luck was out because both Prasit and his wife were not home. Prasit's house was only a mile away from our house. I walked home quite dejected, but I prayed that the Lord would perform a miracle for us as our need was real. I walked around in the market place just to while away time and mentally asked God to provide for our immediate need. Fortunately we had paid our rent for the month and only needed money for food and I believed that it shouldn't be too much for God to take care of. I didn't want to go home empty handed and face Nu Nu but I finally mustered enough courage to go home and meet her. She always tried to get home early in the afternoon to be home for the boys when they got home from school. I wondered how she had fared that day. When I got home, Nu Nu was already back. There were two men talking to her in the sitting room. One of them was Prasit. They must have just got to the house when I arrived. Prasit introduced me to his friend, Su Chai, a business man. Well to do people in Bangkok seemed to be fond of carrying their money loose and showing in their shirt pocket. I could see red notes, which are a hundred bills, sticking out of his pocket. Ptasit seemed to be telling Su Chai that we were refugees and needed money. The next thing I knew, he reached out and grabbed Su Chai's hundred bills and handed them over to Nu Nu. I could see Su Chai's surprised look. But Prasit kept talking to him. Finally Su Chai smiled and nodded. Nu Nu tried to hand back the money to Su Chai, who refused to take it back but only said, "Okay, okay." I tried to tell Prasit to give the money back to Su Chai but he said, "My friend. Very good man. Good heart." That money took care of our needs for the rest of the month. A few days later Su Chai came to visit bringing clothes for the kids and some new pots and pans for our kitchen. We did not want to lose the house for non payment of rent. So every time we made any money, which was not in dollars but in Thai Bhat, we put some aside each week to pay the rent at the end of the month and had just enough left for our food.

A couple of months later we ran out of money again. After we had paid the rent we found that not enough money was left for food for the week. We prayed that God will come to our rescue again. Yet another miracle happened. Nu Nu just started a part time job with an English printing company but she had no idea when she was going to be paid. I came back home late one afternoon and saw the front door open. We always told the boys to lock the door all the time. As I stepped into the house and looked through to the kitchen, I saw an elderly lady spreading vegetables on the kitchen table. I never saw this lady before. She didn't see me and she was humming a hymn softly as she picked up some meat from a shopping basket and placed them on the kitchen table. She looked up when she heard me approach the kitchen.

"Are you Spencer?" she asked. She knew my name. I wondered who she was. I told her yes, I was Spencer.

"I am your parent's friend. I heard that you were here from Cecil Carder so I thought I'd drop by to see you."

"But who are you?" I asked, still puzzled.

"You can call me Aunty Tha Din. I'm the wife of Thra Tha Din, a college mate and friend of your father."

"Where do you live?" I asked her.

"Near Kanchanaburi. Have you ever heard of River Kwai?" she asked. "That's where I live with your uncle."

Thra Tha Din was one of the Karen leaders who took part in the Karen struggle to have a separate state together with Saw Ba U Gyi and others.

Later during our stay in Bangkok, Thra Tha Din and his wife visited us many times. Aunty Tha Din bought a lot of food and she made sure she cooked everything she brought, so that all we had to do was heat the food she had cooked each day because we did not have any refrigerator. Thus the food would last us several days. She had a good visit with us and went back to Kanchanaburi the next afternoon. A few days later Nu Nu drew her first salary from the printing company and we were good for another month with enough money still left for the rent.

Nu Nu was getting frail. She was losing weight and the rings on her fingers were loose. One day after she had prepared dinner and washed her hands, she wrung her hands. As she did her diamond ring flew off. There were gaps of about a half inch between boards on the kitchen floor. The house was about three feet above ground. Nu Nu couldn't find the ring on the floor, so she asked me to look for it on the ground under the house. I went over every inch of the soggy ground for an hour but did not find the ring. Nu Nu was very upset because it was the ring, set with five diamonds, that her mother gave her. We continued to look for the ring each time we were in the kitchen area. Several days passed by and Nu Nu decided to make a last appeal to the Lord. She prayed that if it was the Lord's will, to let her recover the ring as she valued the ring so much because it was a gift from her mother. But if it was not the Lord's will, she'd accept it and she would not let it bother her any more. She was sitting by the low window as she said her prayer. It was a sunny morning. After the prayer, she opened her eyes and just looked out of the window. Something sparkled out there in the mud. The sun was shining directly on the ring resting in the mud, diamonds up. It was indeed a miracle from God.

I got a job with a travel office run by a princess we fondly called Khun Tip, who owned the Princess Hotel. Princess Khun Tip spoke English fluently. A young friend from Burma I cannot name got me that job. This friend had been in Bangkok for sometime. He warned me to watch out for Burma's M.I.S. as they are known to watch everyone from Burma working in Bangkok. If I thought I was being followed by an agent of M.I.S., he told me, "Just cross the street and continue to walk. If he was an agent he would soon cross the street. Then cross back to the other side and if after a while he crossed the street again, take a good look at him. He is your man, an agent of M.I.S. I tried out what my friend had advised when one day I thought I was being shadowed. Indeed after several test I knew that I was being tailed by the M.I.S. He also told me to be aware of a light blue Opel sedan with a white hard top because that car belonged to the M.I.S.

Those days, not many Thais could speak or write English well so I was an asset to the travel agency because I could write letters to travel companies abroad to book tours for Princess Travel Agency. I got them many tour groups. I was never asked about my status as a foreigner. I guess they couldn't care less as long as I could do a good job for them. One day they needed a tour guide to take a group of Spanish tourists the following day on a tour of the Floating Market. Khun Tip asked me to be the lead guide for that day. I protested because I knew nothing about Bangkok.
"You don't need to know about Bangkok, Spencer," she told me, " These are tourists. You can tell them anything and they'll just have to believe you." Wow! I never thought of that. However, I took home a lot of brochures and pamphlets on Bangkok and the Floating Market to study. The tourists were impressed and offered me a twenty dollar tip which I refused to accept.
"Are you the owner?" they asked me, surprised that I did not accept the tip. I just didn't feel comfortable accepting a tip.

At another time we were preparing a tour for a large group to visit the old capital city of Siam, Ayuthiya. It was destroyed the Burmese King, Alaungpaya in 1767, which still remained in ruin to this day and preserved by the Thai government as a historical site. Khun Tip once again asked me to be the lead guide. Uma, one of the tour guides who would accompany me on this tour, and with whom I became very friendly, told me that she hated the Burmese because they destroyed Ayutthaya. She said if she could lay her hand on a Burmese, she would choke the person to death, "with my own hands." So I told her, "Uma, do you know that I am from Burma?"
"Oh! I'm sorry," she apologized profusely. "But you are a very good Burmese," she said.
"Uma, you must forget those incidents that took place a long time ago," I told her. "That was history. Don't let that bother you."
Burmese Premier U Nu was said to have requested a Thai Prime Minister to leave out the account of the Burmese destruction of Ayuthia from Thai school text books. But as far as I'm aware, Thai history books still carry the account of the destruction of Ayuthia by Burmese king Alaungpaya. As a matter of fact the Thais continue to celebrate the defeat of the Burmese army every year by a reenactment of the battle that drove the Burmese out of Siam. The King usually takes part in this celebration

reenacting the battle between the two nations, depicting warriors of both countries replete with their ancient military regalia, riding on horse backs and on elephants, using weapons such as swords, spears, bows and arrows, with Thai soldiers driving Burmese soldiers back into Burma.

CHAPTER 19

HOUSE PARENTS AT BANGKOK STUDENT HOSTEL

Reverend Cecil Carder visited us one day accompanied by another missionary from the Disciple of Christ Church by the name of John Sams to ask whether Nu Nu and I would be willing to be house parents to some thirty to thirty five children of American missionaries, both boys and girls, from fourth grade through high school. These children would be attending the International School in Bangkok but their parents were serving different missions in outlying districts. The children needed a place to stay in Bangkok where they could be taken care of by a responsible couple.

I understood that they had tried to get couples from America but no one responded. The hostel for the kids would be run by us under a board consisting of various Christian denominations. We agreed to serve because we knew the need was there and also we believed that it was God's answer to our prayer to have a permanent job.This time we would be serving God's people in need. Board member, Rev. John Sams, and I visited a few houses looking for a building that would be large enough and suitable for a hostel. We found one that would be unique as a hostel on Soi 11, (or Soi Chaiyote, which was the name for the lane), off Sukumvit Road. Rev. Sams signed a lease for the large imposing mansion which had several bed rooms and a large kitchen, with servant quarters, a laundry room and a two car garage, steel fence and two steel gates. However the two and a half story house with a basement needed to be remodeled to suit our needs. The remodeling was completed in time before school reopened.

Just before the remodeling began I went to check into the large kitchen to see what kind of appliances the house had. I opened the kitchen door and immediately closed it. On all four walls were lizards – the Thais call them *tokay* – dozens of them. They were a good twelve to fourteen inches long. They were fierce looking creatures in gray, purple and white stripes. To make sure they were not ferocious I opened the door slightly and place a cat inside thinking that the playful cat would enjoy chasing the lizards. Within seconds the cat gave out a loud meow and rushed out of the kitchen. I had no idea how the workmen got rid of the lizards. By the time the remodeling was complete the *tokays* were gone.

The boys and the girls each had their two room dorms, with the girls on the second floor and the boys on the first floor. We occupied the third room on the second floor and Lester and David took a small room on the wing of the house on the same floor. The first school year we had thirty eight students, children of missionaries from the American Baptist Mission, the Presbyterian Mission, the Disciples of Christ, and C.M.A. plus a few children from the United States Overseas Mission (U.S.O.M.), and one from Air America. Many parents however had reservations about an Asian couple taking care of their children. I had the advantage of having been a hostel student myself in a private school in my high school days. I knew that discipline came first with so many children living together under one roof. Every child had to be under the same rule and regulation that was set up. Tender loving care should be given to all children. Tardiness should be discouraged. Every child must complete his or her homework on time. We insisted on correct social manners, consideration for others and proper behavior all of which would make a child become responsible and respectable in their later years in their communities. As it turned out some parents thought that we were too strict with their children while some others thought that we were too lenient. But eventually they all accepted us as capable house parents who had the best interests of their children at heart while they were in our care.

In time when the children got to know us better they loved and respected us so much that at the end of the school year some of them refused to return home to their parents. Some insisted on staying with us for a few more weeks and even came along with us on our vacation.

"What have you done to our children?" a mother asked Nu Nu.

"What did we do? What happened?" Nu Nu wanted to know.

"My son would hold my chair for me to sit at the table and the children won't begin to eat until I start to eat."

"You are spoiling our children," another mother complained.

"Now, what have we done?" Nu Nu asked.

"They're not eating the food at home. They said the food at the hostel is much better."

Of course, these were all complements we were happy to hear. Now we had the full support of both the parents and the board. It was such a relief to know that we had been accepted and our work was appreciated. Nu Nu took charge of the seven help that we had, prepared the menu for prope diet and took care of the children's health problem like taking them to the hospital or to dentist or specialists. I looked after the maintenance, the finance, made myself available when the children had problems at school and when there was need to see the teacher or the principal. At one time a girl had a problem with discipline that needed a parent to see the principal. I went along with her to the school and waited to be let into the Principal's office. When finally we were called in and I walked into the office with the girl, the Principal ignored me and told the girl,
"I told you I need to see your father."
"This *is* my father," the girl replied.

The children affectionately called us Uncle Zee and Aunt Nu Nu. Like any teenagers anywhere else, they could also be playful and mischievous like raiding the refrigerator at night or locking the dining room door so we could not get in. At one time they even came into our bedroom while we were away and shorted our sheets. In October on Halloween night, they wanted me to tell them ghost stories. Nu Nu and I organized a haunted basement for them which they thoroughly enjoyed. Every once in a while we showed movie out doors and passed pop corn or cookies around. We also took them out on trips to the shore on some weekends where the older ones were allowed to rent Honda motor bikes. We rented tire tubes for the younger ones so they could frolic in the water. We had to be alert and watchful all the time to make sure they didn't get hurt, or get into any trouble. We never had any serious problem and we were very proud of them. We just wanted them to enjoy themselves. They loved and enjoyed the trips we organized for them. The children always looked forward to such outings. All these activities were rewards for their general over all good behavior and each time we had such extra activities we let them know that they deserved it as a way of encouraging them.

One day I had a call from an American friend from the Embassy in Rangoon whom we knew was now in Bangkok. Bill O'Brien, whose name we saw in the phone directory when we first arrived in Bangkok used to live on Dubern Road right across a small stretch of Inya Lake from our house. He somehow found out that I was in Bangkok and called up to say that he had a couple of kids from Burma who needed help and asked me to try to help them. They came across the border like we did. Somehow word got around that I was available to help any *'Maung'* or *'Ma'* (John or Jane) coming through the border. Refugees, one after another over the following months and years were sent to our house by the American Embassy, the Catholic Mission or even by the Thai Immigration Department. We usually invited these new 'escapees' to our house for a meal and try to find out about their background and what their needs were. We also needed to know what their plans were. Most of them had visas pending for various countries, mostly the U.S.A., the United Kingdom and Australia, and a few for India. They needed a place to stay while they waited for the issuance of their visas or for their plane tickets to be sent to them by relatives. They also needed temporary jobs to sustain themselves while they waited for their papers to arrive. Nu Nu and I managed to raise funds enough to rent a small house for a few of them. We told those who received financial help from us that they need not repay us. Instead we asked them to use that money for those who came after them who needed help.

In spite of our busy schedules we managed to help them with getting their visas and even jobs. Later when they had received their flight tickets from friends or relatives abroad, we surrendered them to the immigration authorities and had them deported to the country they were going to. The first complaint about Burma from these 'escapees' was that the rice that was rationed back in Burma was the kind they used to feed their dogs. I remember a young man who sat down at a meal at our house. He ate nothing but the rice. When I asked him why he didn't have the curries, he replied, "This rice is so good and tasty. It is so different from the rice we now get in Burma."

At about this time a team of observers from America led by Ambassador Cabot Lodge was visiting on a fact finding mission in connection with the war in Vietnam. Many of them were staying at the Erawan Hotel on Rajdamri Road. I met two of them, Thechter and Checkter, (the spellings may not be correct) from Time and Newsweek magazines. I asked them if they would write about Burma, since they were in the area, to inform the world about the true situation in the country. To my dismay, both of them told me that their magazines could only write about news that will interest their reading public and that the world at that moment had no interest at all in what was happening in Burma. Any story on

Burma would just be a waste of space and would earn no revenue for their magazines.

Later an American official from U.S.O.M. (United States Overseas Mission) dropped by to see me one day. His name was Eugene W. He asked me a lot of questions about Burma, and about the Karen. He wanted to know who their leaders were, their combat strength etc. I told him I couldn't give him any information because I knew very little myself and even if I did I couldn't give him information he asked without first consulting the K.N.U. authorities. He was obviously from the CIA. He appreciated my position and never pushed me to give him answers. He became our good friend, visiting us and inviting us to his home for dinner. There were also other Americans visiting me from time to time. Some were from the army because they came in army uniform while others were with USOM. I knew they were all CIA agents. They all wanted to know more about the army regime and the Karen insurrection. To all of them I said flatly that I was not a K.N.U. representative which was the truth. I told them that I would rather like to see that all the resistance forces and politicians get together and form a united front so that they have the support of the entire population, that they should then make an overture to the military government for a meaningful dialogue to take place for the sake of the country. That was what my father asked me to tell Bo Let Ya when Bo Let Ya asked Dad to join him. Not that Dad believed that such approach would be successful but he told me that should be the first step to take before any other action is considered. I believed that it was the right thing to do. Gene was very impressed with that line of thought.

A shady looking slightly built American visited one day and told me he wanted to take me to dinner so that we could have a talk about the situation in Burma. It sounded good to me, especially the dinner, because I assumed most Americans knew the best restaurants in town. I hopped into his Ford Galaxie and we headed to the city. It was getting dark. He parked his car and took me to a back alley. As we walked through the dirty alley, dodging garbage and stray dogs and a couple of transvestites, I asked him where we were going.
"We have to be careful," he told me. "We don't want to be seen together."
He knocked on a back door and when the door opened he led me up a darkened staircase into a small dimly lit hallway. There were a few chairs and a small table on which sat a telephone. Extremely loud music was

coming from the floor downstairs and each time the bass boomed the floor vibrated in rhythm with the sound.

"What's this place?" I asked him. "I thought you're taking me to a restaurant."

"We have to be careful," was all he said. Then he picked up the phone and ordered beer. He saw me still standing so he asked me to take a seat as he took a chair next to the table.

He began to ask me questions, much the same questions asked by previous Americans. After I answered just a few questions I said, "Why don't you identify yourself? I don't even know who you are."

"Call me Joe," he said.

A Thai girl in a very tight mini skirt brought two glasses of *Kathein Htong, Thai bee..*

I picked up my glass of beer and took a sip.

"Joe, what do you want to know? I've given answers to all the guys before you and you guys come back and asked me the same questions. And Joe, honestly I don't like this place. I'm sorry."

Actually I was getting scared but I didn't tell him that. I didn't know what Joe was up to. I couldn't help thinking that he might hand me over to a Burmese agent. I reached my hand out to him to shake but he didn't take it. I turned away and walked down the stairs and instead of taking the back door, I walked through the dancing couples in the noisy and smoke filled hall and out of the front door of the night club. I hailed a taxi and went home, looking back all the time to make sure no one was following me. I was really scared. I didn't mention that incident to Eugene.

By about this time the Mahadevi, had managed to find us. She somehow knew that we had left Burma. She escaped with three of her children, two of whom we met, Eugene and Ying Sita. The Mahadevi suspected that we would be getting out of Burma too, but she never thought we would have to walk out through the jungles as she did. She became our regular visitor and later became very close to us. At that time, the son of a politician came to see me. I did not know him but he heard of us and wanted to meet us. His father, Bo Set Kya, at that time was in Paris and he told us that his father would soon be coming to Bangkok. Bo Set Kya was one of the famous Thirty Comrades who returned to Burma with the invading Imperial Japanese army in 1942. Bo Set Kya became another regular visitor to our house. Meantime we had news that Bo Yan Naing, another member of the Thirty Comrades, had gone underground and was passing through the Karen rebel area on his way to Bangkok. He finally turned up in Bangkok with his brother in law Zali Maw, and a large entourage. Next came Brigadier Saw Kya Doe, my old boss at Let Ya and Company. All of them made a bee line to our house. A short time later the ailing Bo Let Ya, my old boss at Let Ya and Company, turned up.

Now we have a great gathering of top notch Burmese political big wigs all of whom wanted to topple the military regime. They started meeting almost daily at our house while the children were at school, and the meetings would end before the children returned home in the afternoon from school. There were also a Mon leader, who was a Buddhist monk, whose name I do not recall. Then General Zaw Seng, Commander of the Kachin Independent Army and General Bo Mya, president of the K.N.U. (Karen National Union) and Commander in Chief of K.N.L.A. (Karen National Liberation Army) arrived and joined this group of politicians in the meetings. Here was a formidable political group, and I thought they would make a powerful representation of the peoples of Burma who wanted the army ousted. They were preparing to publish a manifesto which as far as I knew, was never published. I thought of Dad's advice to Bo Let Ya which I strongly believed in now, and mentioned to Bo Yan Naing and Bo Set Kya about it. Dad was not a politician and certainly not known among politicians but his advice to Bo Let Ya to consolidate political opposition sounded like he was a pro in politics. But the replies I received from Bo Yan Naing and Bo Set Kya were an identical "We'll fight the son of a bitch to death." Later when Bo Let Ya arrived I reminded him of what Dad had asked me to tell him and his reply was the same, that he would 'fight the son of a bitch to death'. Zaw Seng declined to go along with my suggestion. He said Ne Win killed too many of his people so it would be impossible to have any dialogue with him. The Mahadevi also said she could not agree to a dialogue with Ne Win because he killed her son at the outset of the coup.

The Burman political leaders were all "fighting the son of a bitch to death", but what were they going to fight with? How many soldiers did they have? This was a great opportunity for a show of political solidarity, not military strength, telling the world that the Burmese political leaders from all political camps were united. Whether Ne Win agreed to a dialogue or not was not important. A show of solidarity was what we needed the most now. I was not a politician then nor am I one today. I was only hosting daily meetings of my countrymen who, I acknowledge, were great leaders. I had hoped that together they would come up with some workable and powerful plan that will convince the military government under Ne Win to agree to a dialogue. I had also hoped that they would try to reach all ethnic groups who were fighting the military regime, give them leadership and come up with some strategy for a concerted operation against the military. In spite of all the political and military leadership present, it was a great opportunity missed. Only two leaders present believed that my suggestion was worth trying. They were General Bo Mya of the KNU and Brigadier Saw Kya Doe. Gene was very impressed with this line of thought and encouraged me to persuade the political leaders to adopt it. I tried but I failed to convince them.

One day I had a visit from Major Gladstone of the KNLA. After he introduced himself he came to the point.
"I've come to buy arms ," he told me, "and I was asked to come and see you for advice."
"What makes you think that I can help you?" I asked him.
I told him that I had no connections and I am not about to be involved.
"I heard that you know some senior Thai officers. Maybe they can help," he suggested.
Those days Thai officials were in sympathy with the Karen struggle and so perhaps Gladstone thought that I could help him grease a few palms. I invited him to have lunch with us and while we were having lunch Prasit turned up. I introduced Prasit to Gladstone. Prasit sat at the table but did not join us. When I mentioined to Prasit that Gladstone wanted to buy arms, his face lit up. After lunch the two of them left together. Afterward when Gladstone came to Bangkok to buy arms, he went straight to Prasit and only visited us a few times.

Gene paid me a visit one day to tell me that he was returning to the U.S. He told me that a colleague of his will call on me soon so that we could continue to keep in touch. Bob S. was a wounded Korean war veteran. Like Gene, he was a perfect gentleman and we became very good friends. Bob visited regularly every month and although I couldn't give him any information, he brought me up to date with situations relating to the Karen issues.

Now a blue Opel sedan with a white top was parked on the road across our house almost everyday from morning till night. What kind of military intelligence was it that would openly park it's car right in front of the house they were watching? Or were they just trying to scare or intimidate me? Certainly they were watching who all were coming to the house. I'm sure they were surprised when they saw their own Ambassador's car driving into our driveway several times. The Ambassador's uncle, U Thaung Tin and his wife were very good friends of Nu Nu and they were one of our frequent visitors. When school was closed and the children were away, we would often ask our friends from Burma to get together at our house. Many people who were opposed to the army rule had left Burma in disgust and some of them were now in Bangkok. Since our house was a hostel, we had many servants to do the cooking and the clean up. We also caught up with Tommy Smith, who was Commander and Chief of Staff of Burma Air Force whose daughter Carol, became very friendly with Nu Nu and often visited with her boy friend, whom she married while we were still in Bangkok. Tommy Smith was a close friend of Thai Air Marshall Dawee, and he stayed clear of politics. Bo Yan Naing meantime rented a house for his group. Now that they held meetings at that house I thought that the blue Opel Sedan would now be withdrawn and deployed to watch Bo Yan Naing's house. I was mistaken. The car was still there in front of our house four or five days a week from morning till night.

I received a letter from my sister Louise which was mailed from India informing us that Mom had passed away. The letter arrived thirty days after Mom's death. In the same envelope was also a short note from Nu Nu's father. Mother died quietly in the arms of Louise who was with her at the time. Ever since Dad died Mom would pine for Dad and there was nothing we could say that would bring her comfort. "I miss Dad. I want to die to be with Dad," she kept saying. Mom and Dad were truly in love. Mom was not ill and must have died of a broken heart. In his short note Nu Nu's father wrote that after Mom died a group of soldiers searched Dad's house and when he asked them what they were looking for, one officer replied, "We're looking for a person." However, they did not question any member of the family. This was confirmed by one of Burma's footballers who a few months later visited Bangkok with the Burmese football team. The Burmese team was one of the top teams contending for the Asian Cup playing against the Thai team at that time. This young footballer, a friend of the family, told us that at Mom's funeral there were plain clothed secret police moving among the crowd of mourners scrutinizing every male. This friend thought they were looking for me. Probably, but why?

Escapees continued coming into Thailand. While some came legally, there were others who came across the border like we did. The U.S. Embassy or the Catholic church continued to send them to us. We had occasions when some of them were detained by the Immigration Department and thrown in jail. Invariably I had to bail some of them out and guarantee that they would leave Bangkok within a required period of time. Although some of them came illegally they already had in their possession visas and air tickets to countries they were going to, countries where they had relatives. In such cases I had to book them the flight to wherever they were going and request the immigration to escort them, as deportees, to the plane since they had no legal papers for Thailand. The immigration officers soon recognized me but never questioned my legal status.

My good friend Prasit, one day took me to a general Somsak, (not his real name) who wanted to see me. I wondered why the general wanted to see me. I wondered if he found out that we came through the border and were now living illegally in Thailand? Prasit introduced me to the general who asked his wife to join us. It turned out that he heard about me working for Princess Travel Agency at one time. His wife wanted to start a Travel Agency and wanted t know if I would like to be her business partner. It would have been a wonderful opportunity for business. But I realized I had my obligation with the Mission Board of the Bangkok Student Hostel. I couldn't possibly be involved now that I'm fully occupied with running the hostel. I also had an obligation to help those refugees from Burma who depended on me for help. I had too much on my hand. I told the general's wife that I would try to help by writing correspondences and answering mails for them. After lunch the general gave me his business card after writing a short note in Thai in the back of the card.

"Keep this card with you," he told me, "and if you have problem with the authorities any time, show this card."

Prasit must have told him that we had no legal papers.

We were told by missionaries not long after we arrived in Bangkok from the border that my oldest sister Nita, Saw Ba U Gyi's wife, had now remarried. Her husband was Benny Gyaw, another cousin of Ba Thet Gyi, Nita's first husband. She was now a hostel parent with her husband in Maeseriang in north western Thailand taking care of Karen village children from the surrounding hills who were attending school there. I knew Benny when he was a customs officer with Ba Thet Gyi in Rangoon before the war. He was a very jolly man and I was happy for Nita that she was married to him. Nita now used her Karen name, Naw Lah Say. She was also affectionately called Mo Nita (mother Nita) by many who knew her earlier and now the children and their parents called her Thramu Lah Say. Nu Nu and I visited them after school closed for the summer holidays in the second year of our job at the hostel. We took our driver and our house keeper with us for the long trip. I never thought that we were going to be checked by the Thai military on the way. But the Vietnam war was on and the Thai government was very nervous about possible communist infiltration in the north. However, we didn't have any problem until we were about half way through our trip. We were stopped at an army check point. An officer approached our van and asked for our passports. Our driver showed his license. The officer then asked for my passport which I did not have. The driver tried to tell him something in Thai but the officer insisted that I showed him my passsport. Nu Nu remembered the business card General Somsak gave me and asked me to give it to the officer. I pulled out my wallet, took out the card and gave it to the officer who took a look at the card and read the note written on the back of the card. He returned the card to me, stood to attention and gave me a proper military salute and let our van through. We had to go through two more check points and at each check point the N.C.O.s who checked the card stood to attention and gave me a salute. Both the driver and Wina, the house keeper, were curious and asked to see the card.

Our house keeper read the back of the card.

"O, madam, you are big people," Wina said.

"What does the card say?" Nu Nu asked her.

"You are guest of King and Queen. Must help you in trouble," she replied. General Somsak wrote in effect that we were guest of the Royal Family and all courtesy and assistance be accorded to us. Then Nu Nu asked me to take out the other card given by the immigration colonel and showed it to Wina. She read it and said, "You are guest of Thai government. Must give you no problem." Actually these cards were more valuable than any identity paper I could think of.

We had to drive up the mountain to reach Maeseriang. The road was not paved those days but fortunately it had not rained, as otherwise there could be landslides which frequently caused accidents and deaths. Nita and Benny were overjoyed to see us. The last time I saw Nita was some twenty years ago when I joined the navy after Nita lost her first husband. She and Benny had some forty Karen children from villages in the hills near the Burma border. They were boys as well as girls from ages around six or seven attending elementary school to age fifteen or sixteen attending high school. The hostel, run by the American Baptist

Mission, was a plain large teak building with a section of the dorm for girls and a separate section for boys all sleeping on the well polished floor. The hostel was kept very clean. The children helped maintain the upkeep, while Nita and Benny supervised. My sister had adopted a little girl she named Ruthie whose parents were animists. Ruthie was retarded but she was adorable and adored and loved dearly by my sister and her husband. We spent two delightful weeks with Nita and Benny and met some wonderful American Baptist missionaries and their families working among the Karen people in the hills surrounding Maeseriang. We invited Nita and Benny to come and visit us in Bangkok the following Summer

The International School reopened after the Summer holidays and the children were back when we received a surprise letter from Louisa, wife of the late Brigadier Lin Htin of the famous 5th brigade of the K.N.L.A. Louisa was commanding her husband's Brigade in the jungle in the Karen territory after her husband was ambushed and killed by the Burma army. She would be coming down to Bangkok shortly to meet a friend, she wrote. She was expecting an American friend whom she had met while she was attending school in Boston several years ago. Glenn Craig was coming to visit her and she wanted us to meet him. We went to meet Louisa at the air port. As she was getting out of the passenger area a man approached her and handed her a note written in Burmese. It read, "Ama Gyi (Big sister), please come with us. We'd like to have a talk with you." The MIS recognized her but why would they want to talk to her? I'm sure they planned to kidnap her. They must have received information from their source that Louisa had left the airport at Chiangmai for Bangkok and they were waiting at the airport to nab her. She ignored the note and we rushed her into our waiting van and came back to the hostel where she would be staying with us. Glenn had not arrived yet, but Louisa told us that Glenn wanted to marry her and she wanted our advice on what she should do. She had her brigade that depended on her for leadership and morale, at the same time Glenn would soon arrive to ask her to return with him to the U.S. She loved Glenn but she also loved her men and felt that she would be letting them down if she married Glenn. Nu Nu and I both agreed that in as much as she was needed by her brigade, it would be a lot better for our people that she married the man she loved and went to the U.S. where she would be able to promote the cause of the Karen people. As a well educated Karen woman she would be invaluable as an ambassador for the Karen people. As woman to woman, Nu Nu talked to her about our feeling about her attachment to her brigade, that we agreed with her that her men needed her and it would break her heart to leave them. Nu Nu told her that Glenn was coming all the way to Thailand to take her back as a bride to the U.S. and it would equally break her heart and his too, to let him return to the U.S. without her. By coming out of the jungle and going to the U.S. she would be able to help her people, and let the world know of the plight of not only the Karen people, but all the peoples of Burma.

That night I was alerted by our maid that there was a man trying to climb up the iron gate which was closed at night. I looked though the blind and saw a rather slim man by the gate. I got my thirty eight that wass given me by Prasit and ran down the stairs and rushed to the gate where the man was still standing unable to climb over the iron gate. When he saw me he immediately sat down and pretended to look for something on the ground.

I asked him in Thai, "Who are you? What are you doing?"

The man stood up and ran, then jumped into the waiting blue Opel sedan which made a quick U-turn and sped off into the night. The next day Prasit came to visit and I introduce him to Louisa. Nu Nu planned to take Louisa shopping that day so we asked Prasit to come along with us. Prasit sat in front by the driver and he turned round occasionally to talk to me. While he was looking back to talk to me he suddenly looked shocked and turned to the driver and gave him instruction to speed up. Then he told the driver to turn left into a street, and right into another street. The driver asked what he was doing that for.

"Mai penrai. (never mind). Kap rod reo noi.(just drive fast)" Prasit told him. After many more turns he relaxed and heaved a sigh of relief, placed his hand on his forehead and told me in Thai that a car belonging to the Burmese embassy was following. They were now gone. He volunteered to stay with us all day that day.

When the children came back to the hostel after school Nu Nu introduced Louisa to the girls. They were thrilled to have a Miss Burma and an actress, staying in the hostel with them and they were excited about her up coming wedding. When we told them that it was not a sure thing because Louisa was still undecided, they were disappointed. Glenn arrived the next day and came to the hostel to visit. The children were still away at school. When they returned from school and saw Glenn, some of the girls screamed. One girl said aloud, "If Louisa won't marry him, I will. O, he's so handsome." Louisa and Glenn went off to the shore for a few days to talk things over. Nu Nu reminded her of what we had told her regarding our feelings about her situation. A few days later they returned and Louisa told us that she had decided to marry Glenn. So now we had to arrange for the wedding. We attended the International Church on Soi 19 (Soi Watana), several blocks from the hostel and decided that we would ask the pastor to conduct the ceremony. It was to be just a private wedding, but Louisa invited the children at the hostel as their only guests. I gave Louisa away. Glenn and Louisa had a wonderful wedding with thirty five American teenagers as their only guests. Before the wedding Louisa hurried back to the jungle to bid farewell to her brigade. It must have been a heart rending parting because her men loved her and depended on her so much.

Before she left, Louisa told us that her father was already in the U.S.A. He went ahead to prepare for his wife to follow at a later date but now the government was not allowing anyone to leave Burma legally. Several months later, Mrs. Benson, turned up in Bangkok and came for my help. It would be very difficult for me to help because she did not bring her passport with her. Having a passport would make it a lot easier for me to help, but there were other things involved. For instance getting the Thai immigration to help would certainly involve money and some influence. I conveyed that to Saw Benson, who said he would send enough money to me to take care of all the expenses. But we needed someone in Bangkok who would be able to take care of everything to enable her to leave legally on an outbound flight to the U.S.A. She had to have a valid passport, the passport had to have an endorsement of her arrival in Thailand and she had to have a visa to the U.S.A. Her husband wrote that her visa was already approved. Now all I had to do was get her a passport and the necessary endorsements. I told an immigration officer with whom I became friendly about my problem to help a dear friend. I told him everything and asked if he had any suggestion. He gave me the name of a broker, who had connection high up in the immigration but the cost would be exorbitant. He would take care of everything from getting her a passport, getting all the endorsement necessary, to seeing her off at the airport. But we had to supply the money and the visa for the U.S.A. Saw Benson had already obtained the visa for his wife and the money was no problem with him. He was a rich man. In a little more than three months Mrs. Benson was able to fly out of Bangkok to join her husband in the U.S.A. I was fortunate to have been introduced to Mr. Pratit because later I needed his services for my family and he was able to help me out. I had wondered why people had to come to me for help? There were so many other Burmese who have settled down in Bangkok to whom they could go. Of course, once they came to me, I just couldn't refuse to help them. Once I had two Anglo Burman brothers who were stuck at our servant quarters for several months until they could get their papers straightened out and their plane fare paid for before they could join their relatives in Australia.

The phone rang incessantly one night. I looked at the time. It was two in the morning. I went down to the office and picked up the phone.

"Phi Zan?" (big brother Zan) It was Prasit.

"Where are you?" I asked him in Thai.

"I'm in jail," he replied. He gave me a phone number. It was Generaal Som Sak's house number.

"Please call the general in the morning," he told me, "and tell him to arrange for my release. I called but no one answered the phone." He told me to go and see the general on his hehalf. He also said that a letter was in the mail for the general and me.

Two days later the letter arrived. It was a copy of letter he addressed to the general. I had to ask the house keeper to translate the letter for me. It transpired that Prasit, or his contact, hijacked two U.S.army trucks and were taking them up north to the border. Someone must have tipped off the authorities. As they neared the border near Maeseriang, the U.S. and Thai military Police were waiting for them. Prasit had contacts and in less than three months he was released from prison.

Bob S. my CIA contact visited one day to tell me that he would be returning to the USA. He introduced me to Bill, a rather tall and handsome man who looked like an actor. I'm sure Bill wasn't his real name but here was a character who wanted to impress me with the importance of his role in the organization as well as it's glamour. He was another gentleman who treated me with respect. One day he took me to his home. As we entered the house I could hear girls talking in Thai and laughing in another room. Bill opened the door to the room. Five pretty Thai girls were in the room, some sitting on the sofa and others on the bed. They stopped talking when Bill walked in.

"Scram!" Bill yelled.

They all sped out of the room like scared kittens. At once I could picture 007 in my mind.

"Close the door behind you," Bill yelled after them.

A girl ran back and pulled the door shut.

Bill pulled up a chair for me.

"Have a seat, Spencer," he said as he sat down in another chair.

"Do you know Mahn Ba Zan? Are you related to him?"

"No, I don't know Mahn Ba Zan," I told him, "and I am not related to him. Same last name does not necessary mean we are related."

"I need to find out more about him," Bill said.

"Bill, I know of Mahn Ba Zan but have never met him. I don't know anything about him."

"I want you to find out for me," he said, "if he is a communist sympathizer or is he leaning toward communism."

"How can I do that?" I asked Bill "The only way to find out is to go into Kawthoolay and talk to him and hope he tells the truth."

"Can you do that for me?" Bill asked.

"It's two more weeks before school closes for summer and the hostel kids go home," I replied.

"That will give you enough time to arrange for a meeting with him," he told me.

"How would I know if he will want to meet me?" I said. "He doesn't even know me."

"Ask your brother in law to arrange for the meeting," Bill suggested.

"You mean Benny?" I asked.

"Yes. Mahn Ba Zan is attending a meeting in Mae Hong Son and Benny can easily contact him there," Bill suggested.

Bill continued, "You can fly to Maeseriang and either travel to Mae Hong Son to meet Mahn Ba Zan or you can invite him to come to Maeseriang to meet with you. Your expenses will be paid in full."

I agreed to go to Maeseriang because I can now go and visit my sister, all expense paid for by the CIA. I wrote to Benny to try to contact Mahn Ba Zan and invite him to Maeseriang for a meeting with me. Or in the event he couldn't make it to send someone to come and see me in Maeseriang. The children had now left the hostel for the holidays I flew to Chiangmai and took a taxi to Maeseriang.

Mahn Ba Zan did not come to Maseriang but sent a representative instead. I believe it was his secretary. I asked the secretary pointed blank whether his boss was a communist sympathizer. The secretary apologized that Mahn Ba Zan could not come to meet me because of the on going meeting at Mae Hong Son. The secretary assured me that his boss certainly was not a communist sympathizer. I spent two more days with my sister and returned to Chiangmai to fly back to Bangkok. I reported the result of my mission to Bill and told him that I was convinced that Mahn Ba Zan was no communist and neither was he a communist sympathizer.

Lester was thirteen now and joined a Karate class offered at school while David at ten, joined a Judo class. Some of the children in the hostel joined the Karate class with Lester. One day Lester and another boy, Al Yonkin, were practicing their high kicks on the front lawn, as I was taking pictures with my Cannon 38mm camera. A very tall and handsome man walked into the compound and stood by to watch the boys do their routine. He then picked up a board used for kicking and held it up high for the boys to kick. I quickly ran into the house and announced that Ron Ely, Tarzan, was with Lester and Al. Ron Ely did not stay long and the girls were disappointed. In my excitement I forgot to take pictures of Ron Ely and the boys. The girls later asked me to invite Ron Ely to dinner, so I wrote a nice letter inviting Ron Ely to dinner and took the invitation to his hotel. He never turned up. We read later in the papers that he was making a 'Tarzan' movie at that time and probably was on his way back to the United States when he dropped by.

David liked to practice his Judo with Nu Nu who had had Judo lessons back in Rangoon. Some kids didn't believe that Nu Nu knew Judo when David boasted that his mother 'can flip anyone of you over.' They challenged Nu Nu to demonstrate on the lawn so everybody could see. One after another the boys would try to approach Nu Nu and she astonished them by throwing over every one of them. And they were all bigger than Nu Nu who later told me that if she had not been practicing with David, she probably couldn't have flipped any of those big kids.

One day a young lady by the name of Veronica came to us for help. She was Chinese from Burma but was now living in Hong Kong. She had a boy friend who had escaped from Burma with a group of other college students after the July 7, 1962 shooting at the Student Union in Rangoon University. He had not turned up anywhere and she was worried about his safety. I knew that many students tried to cross into Thailand and some of them were fired upon by the army. On one occasion we heard that the soldiers fired on a group that was crossing the Salween River and many were killed. I asked Veronica about her boy friend and she told me his name was Noel. I knew of a Noel and to be sure, I mentioned the name of Noel's father. She was surprised that I knew the family. I told her that Noel's father was my father's best friend and that when the K.N.D.O.s in Insein were waiting for reinforcement for possible attack on Rangoon, my father asked Saw Ba U Gyi to deploy a special platoon to protect the Robert Maung Tin family at their house on York Road from looting or from trigger happy Karen soldiers. I promised Veronica that I would do everything possible to try to find Noel. I told her that if he had arrived safely in the Karen controlled area, he would be perfectly safe and it would be easy for me to find him and that I'll have him escorted to Bangkok to join her. I paid a man and sent him to all areas occupied by the Karen and even sent letters to some area commanders to look for a Burman student by the name of Noel Tin stressing that he was my friend and if found to give him all assistance and to escort him to Bangkok to my place. We waited for almost three months for news about Noel when the man I sent came back to say that he met a lot of students from the University and met one who said Noel was with his group. After they crossed the river and got to the Thai side they waited to regroup and to account for everyone. Noel was one of those who didn't make it and they thought he could have been shot while he was crossing the river and drowned or carried further down stream and landed in another area. I had to tell Veronica that I had tried to do my best but could not find Noel.

In the Summer of 1965 I had a call from Cecil Carder that missionaries in Burma had been expelled and many would be coming through Bangkok on their way home to the U.S.A. One mission family after another came to see us as they passed through Bangkok. We knew most of the missionaries back home and it was heart breaking to hear their stories, of the work they had to leave behind, and of the heart breaking farewells to friends they had embraced as their own families for many years.

In the summer of 1967 my sister and her husband visited us and spent two wonderful weeks with us. We were able to take them around for sight seeing and visiting friends because school was closed and all the children had gone home to their parents. I felt sorry for my sister because she and Benny were housed in a somewhat shabby housing, sharing the same building as the kids. She was doing a great job taking care of the children and was considered a gold mine by the missionaries. But I thought she should have been given better living condition and paid a decent salary. After all she had a double degree, a Bachelor of Arts and Bachelor of Education. It pained me that after being called a gold mine by the American Baptist Mission she and her husband were poorly paid. After all she had had a life of plenty and luxury, had lived in big houses with servants at her beck and call. I felt that she deserved much more than what she was receiving for being a gold mine. I mentioned to her that if she wanted, I would apply for her a Preference Visa to go to the United States where she could teach, or get a decent job in America and earn a decent salary and enjoy a higher standard of living. However, she put me to shame when she answered that she was doing God's work and she would not change it for any thing else. She had had a good life and it was her turn now to help the Karen children of the jungle and prepare them for better lives ahead of them. That was the mandate that God had given her and she would continue to care for these children and look forward to seeing them do well in life. Many of them do.

On our visit to Thailand thirty five years after we had left that country, Nu Nu and I met a few old students of my sister's whom they affectionately called Thramu (Teacher) Lah Say. Some still called her Mo Nita (Monita). One girl who was now a high school teacher, changed her name to Lah Say because she felt indebted to my sister for having constantly guided her, coaxed and encouraged her, and she believed, made her become the person she was today. My sister had since died. When this girl was introduced to me she hugged me and cried over my shoulders. That night she and her husband took us out to a dinner theater. There were other students who Nu Nu and I met, who had graduated from college and were now holding responsible government jobs or working with the community. I went to visit my sister's grave in Maeseriang. She, Benny and Ruthie were laid side by side within an enclosed fence. I choked, but I realized that she had had a good life, rich and rewarding, the last twenty years of it. And now she was at home with her heavenly Father.

I remember the story they told us. It was about a Karen attack on Maesod, a Thai border town. The Karen torched the town during the attack. The Thai authorities were furious and were determined to punish the Karen responsible for this attack. Benny and Nita were both arrested in Maeseriang by the Thai police charging them for involvement in the attack on Maesod. They were held in custody for several months but were later released when no evidence was found to connect them to the incident. What actually happened was this. The Karen had been buying ammunition from the black market through their Thai contacts. But on one occasion they were introduced to another group of gun smugglers from whom they bought 303 rifle ammunition. Later when the Karens were defending their position during an engagement with government troops, their weapons misfired and many Karen soldiers were killed. The commander was furious that the Thais had cheated them and sold them dud ammunition. They raided Maesod where the deal to purchase the ammunition was made and torched the town. Of course that was not the right thing to do. Later the KNU Head quarters apologized to the Thai authorities for the incident.

Their lives together were a blessing to those who needed them, especially the Karen children from the surrounding hills. Benny was featured in an article in the National Geographic Magazine, describing the work he had done among the hill people of Thailand. He organized Rice Banks, where villagers brought their surplus rice to store in granaries across the region in the jungles so that when there was famine, there was enough rice to distribute to those who needed them. Nita and Benny had lived in Maeseriang all these years with no legal papers, but because of their great work among the peoples in the hills, the King himself, when he was visiting Maseriang, recognized their work and presented them with Thai citizenship. When Nu Nu and I visited them before we left for the U.S.A. in 1969 Ben proudly showed us the woven cane chair the king had sat on when he visited, which he hung up on a wall in the sitting room. He would not let anyone touch that chair.

While I was at the American Embassy in Bangkok helping a young escapee from Burma get his papers in order, the Vice Counsel told me, "Spencer, you have been helping people go to the United States and elsewhere, and now" she continued, "I think you better think about your own future. Things are not going to get any better in Burma. You better apply for a visa to the U.S. Do it while I'm still here."

"My intention is to return to Burma as soon as the situation gets better," I told her, "and I hope things will get better soon."

"Don't you believe it," she replied. "Things will not get better in Burma. Think of your children's welfare. Think of their education, their future."

She made me think of myself and the future of my family and I was glad that she did. I had never given a thought to go to the United States of America until then.

CHAPTER 20

OUR FINAL JOURNEY TO FREEDOM

I WROTE TO MY SISTER Louise in Rangoon asking her to go to Dad's home and look for our passports and have them sent to us. Because mails were censored in Rangoon I sent the letter by hand through someone visiting a relative in Burma. Meantime I applied for Preference Three U.S. Immigrant Visa for my family as advised by the Vice Consul. At the same time I wrote to a cousin who was already living in California that we were planning to come to the U.S. and might come to California.

Then, at a prayer meeting at the home of one of the Baptist missionaries we met a new missionary by the name of Carol Jochen, who had just arrived in Thailand to work with young people in Bangkok. To prepare her for a cultural shock, she told us, the American Baptist Mission sent her to live several months in a slum area in Philadelphia with scanty amenities so that she would get used to the kind of life she was expected to live in Thailand. However, she said, the cultural shock she was prepared for worked in the reverse for her. The beautiful apartment she was living in belonged to a princess. It was tastefully furnished, and had brand new appliances and other modern facilities, unlike the shabby apartment she was made to live in Philadelphia to get used to the life she was told she would be having in Thailand. She also had a servant who took care of practically everything and she didn't have to lift a finger. It was a cultural shock alright, she said. She landed in luxury instead of in a squalid tenement.

As we were introduced to her she was told that we were planning to go to the United States as immigrants. She wanted to know where in the States we planned to go. I told her that we had a cousin in California and that was where we planned to go.

"Oh no," she protested, "you're not going to California. You're going to Pennsylvania."

"My cousin already had planned for our arrival and is in the process of looking for an apartment for us," I told her.

"Never mind that. You are going to North Wales in Pennsylvania," she insisted.

"Next Sunday we are having a tele-mission," she said. "At the Sunday evening service at our church we will be connected by radio to North Wales Baptist Church during their morning church service. I will be talking to the Pastor. I will tell him to sponsor your family and you will go to North Wales."

"Where in Pennsylvania is North Wales?" I asked her.

"Do you have a map so I can show the Zans where North Wales is?" she asked the host who found a map and gave it to her.

She looked for North Wales but didn't find it on that map.

"O, it's here somewhere," she circled a spot on the map.

Of course it meant nothing to us because we didn't even know anything about Pennsylvania except that the American Declaration of Independence was signed in Philadelphia. But it bothered me because if North Wales could not be found on the map, could it be much of a city or town to live in?

Nu Nu and I attended the church service the following week. It took a little while for radio connection to be made with North Wales before the service could start. It was a wonderful experience attending a service with two churches participating at the same time, one in the United States in the morning and the other in Thailand in the evening, a half way round the world from each other. It was the usual order of service with hymn singing where two congregations blended their voices together, and prayers that could be heard by both congregations. Then the Pastor of North Wales Baptist Church, Reverend Sydney Kane, called on Carol Jochen to take the mike. Carol started to talk about her trip to Thailand, and about meeting new people and new workers and how excited she was with her assignment, working among young Thais. She also mentioned about the reverse cultural shock she experienced and before ending her talk, she told the pastor, "There is a family here who are planning to go to the United States. Can our church possibly sponsor them so they can migrate to the United States and settle down in North Wales?"

"Do they speak English? Can we talk to them?" Rev. Kane asked.

"Here he is," she told the pastor. Then she handed me the mike.

"Hello," I spoke into the mike.

"Hello," Rev. Kane said. "What's your name and can you tell us about yourself?" he asked.

I gave him my name, and told him I had a wife and two sons, aged thirteen and ten. I briefly told him of the circumstances leading to our having to escape from Burma, and what we were now doing in Bangkok and that we had applied for Immigrant Visa to the U.S.A. which we hoped would be issued shortly. He didn't ask a lot of questions. Then he addressed his congregation.

"You just heard Mr. Zan tell us about himself and his family. Would our church be willing to sponsor this family?"

We could hear a resounding "Yes" over the speakers.

"There you have it, Mr. Zan. Our church will sponsor your family," said Rev. Kane. There was a thunderous applause in the church in Bangkok that could be heard in the Church in North Wales. I couldn't help being emotional. With a lump in my throat I managed to say "Thank you very much."

The next day I wrote to my cousin in California that we would not be going to California after all but to Pennsylvania instead.

It took a while for our passports to arrive, because Louise sent it through a friend who went to India instead of sending it to Thailand. There was more likelihood of someone going to Thailand to be searched by security staff. Our passports were mailed to us from a missionary in Bombay, India. Now all we needed was for our passports to be endorsed for our arrival into Bangkok Airport but there was no way we could do that by ourselves. I called Pratit, the man who helped Mrs. Benson with her papers to join her husband in America, to find out if he could help us out of our predicament. Of course he was willing to help us, but for a very stiff fee.

"Remember, there are four of you." he told me. "So that will be four times you had paid for Mrs. Benson. But you pay a little less because you have passports."

He named a price we could not afford. I tried to beat his fee down to a reasonable figure.

"I will have to pay too many people," he told me. "If I bring the price down there will be nothing left for me."

Nu Nu told me that she would take care of the extra money we needed. "Time Magazine Bureau Chief is looking for a secretary cum office manager," Nu Nu told me. "It is part time, from nine in the morning to two in the afternoon. The kids go to school at eight in the morning and they're not back till three in the afternoon. I'll be gone from the hostel after they leave for school and be back before they get back from school."

We made ardent prayers to the Lord about this matter and believed that the Lord will help us with our intended journey to the U.S.A. The next day Nu Nu drove to Time office in downtown Bangkok and met Terrence Smith, Time magazine's Bureau Chief, who hired her on the spot. Now I felt comfortable to make an advance payment to Pratit so he could start working on our papers right away. He told me that it would take a while because there was a lot involved and that I'd have to be patient. I told him it was all right. Our visas had not been issued yet and Pratit could take as long as he needed to get the work done. As a matter of fact if he had been able to get us the required endorsements right then we would not have enough cash to pay him. Only Nu Nu's salary from Time Magazine over the next several months would make up for the difference we needed to pay Pratit.

Since working for Time Magazine, Nu Nu was always able to get Press Pass for any national and international events covered by the media. I was even able to accompany Nu Nu on all of her trips. I had a Super Eight millimeter movie camera and could pass as a press photographer. I wore the official 'PRESS" arm band as I accompanied Nu Nu to a few events she attended. She was not representing Time Magazine on any of these trips. She was just taking advantage of her press pass to enjoy herself, taking me along as her photographer. The highlight of these excursions was the very picturesque Annual Royal Regatta at Pattaya where the King competed with others in this prestigious yearly yachting event. We took many pictures of the King and his ministers in the Royal tent. It was one of the most beautiful events we had ever seen. There was also the coverage of President Johnson's visit to Bangkok, and the ceremony heralding the farming season attended by the King. There were other events where both the King and the Queen attended and covered by the press and we were there to take pictures. Fortunately all these were during the Summer seasons when the children had left the hostel to return to their parents and it did not interfere with our work. Meantime we had to keep calling Pratit to make sure he was working on our papers and he assured us that everything was working out well but it would need a little more time. One day soon after, Pratit came and told us that his plan was complete to have our passports legally endorsed for entry into Thailand at the Bangkok Air Port.

"But we are already in Bangkok," I told him.

"Yes. So you must enter Thailand again legally from Malaysia," he told us.

"What do you mean, from Malaysia?" I asked.

"You must travel to Penang and then apply for a visa to Thailand."

"But how can we travel to Penang without an endorsement of our arrival in Bangkok?" I asked, "and without a visa to Malaysia?"

"That is my problem," he answered. "Your visa is guaranteed. You will have to return from Penang by plane to Bangkok Air port and your passports will be endorsed for entry into Thailand."

"But how can we get into Malaysia without any visa?" I asked him.

"I already arranged for that," he told me.

"I am confused. Tell me clearly and slowly everything we need to do," I told him.

"You must take a train to Malaysia. You won't have any problem because I will be traveling with you and I will get you through the Malaysian immigration without problem. Then you take a taxi to Penang. While you are in Penang, you apply for a visa for Thailand. I arranged for your visa to be issued without delay. I will return to Bangkok and see to it that your visa is granted. Then you take a plane back to Bangkok. I will meet you at the air port to make sure everything is all right. Your passports will be endorsed for entry into the Kingdom of Thailand and then you are legal residents in Thailand. But you must apply for Foreigners Registration. You see, that is why it is so costly. I'll do everything for you till you leave for the United States of America."

"But if something goes wrong and I am arrested will you be able to help me?" I asked.

"You know General Somsak?" he asked.

"Yes, very well."

"How about Colonel Chainalom of the immigration?" he asked.

"Yes."

"So you are all right. There will be no problem," he assured me.

"Pratit, we have a problem. I have a pass port. Nu Nu has a pass port. But how about the boys?"

"Easy. Show me Nu Nu's pass port." I gave him Nu Nu's Passport.

"Okay," he said, "see this space here? You just write 'accompanied by' and put your childrens's name and their dates of birth. Easy."

In anticipation of our leaving for the U.S. we had submitted our resignation, and of course we were still allowed to remain at the hostel while a new couple was being sought to replace us, but we later moved to the Bangkok Christian Guest House. From there we made the trip to Malaysia by train. As promised, Pratit accompanied us. He gave us our train tickets as we took our seats on the train. Then he started to tell passengers in the coach that we were refugees from Burma and that he was trying to help us. But knowing that the Thais generally have no love for the Burmese, we were worried that the Thai passengers might react negatively upon learning that we were from Burma. Our concern however was soon removed when a Buddhist monk presented David with a Buddha pendant, and other passengers offered food to the boys. They even came around and spoke to us and tried to make friends with us. Meantime Pratit was lavishing himself with Thai whiskey all night and walked up and down the aisle to talk about us, bragging that he was helping us get legal papers so that we could go to the U.S.

The train arrived early in the morning at it's terminal town right across the border from Malaysia. There was a fence separating the two small towns but there was a gate that people would get through after immigration and customs inspections. However, after asking for our passports Pratit lead us through the gate without bothering with the routine procedures. Instead, after we passed the gate, he entered the Malaysian immigration office and took us in and shook a few hands. We sat waiting in the waiting area as he talked and joked with the officials. A half hour later he came out smiling and handed our passports back to us and led us to a taxi stand. He hired a taxi and took us to Penang. When we arrived in Penang he took us to a hotel and told us that he was leaving to take care of the rest of the business. He handed me a few papers. They were our visa applications for Thailand and told me to sign and mail them the same day. He also handed us Thai air reservation vouchers for our flight back to Bangkok. As soon as we got settled in our hotel room, we thank the Lord for His blessings that everything had worked out for us. The children naturally wanted to go on a sight seeing tour but we had very limited cash in our hands and wanted to keep the money for other needs. However, we did go to the market to do some window shopping. At a shop we asked for a phone book to see if we knew anybody in Penang that we could drop by to say hello to. I came across a name, Sonny Pillay, and suddenly remembered someone in college who was my brother Saunder's best friend by the name of Sonny Pillay. Sonny and Saunders used to play trio with with another student by the name of Ikie Isaac at a night club while they were in college. They plyed strictly jazz. I asked the manager of the store if he knew Sonny Pillay and whether he knew if Sonny Pillay went to college in Burma.

"I don't know about his going to college in Burma," he told me. "But this Sonny Pillay is a big shot. He is the Governor's Aide. I don't think you know him."

"Can I use your phone?" I asked the manager.

"Sure," he said and gave me the phone.

I dialed the number of Sonny Pillay's residence.

"Hello," a voice answered.

"Mr. Sonny Pillay?" I asked.

"Yes," the voice answered.

"Were you Saunder's best friend in Judson College in Rangoon?" I asked.

"Yes, I am. But who is this?" the voice wanted to know.

"Sonny, this is Spencer, Saunder's younger brother."

I told Sonny about how we left Burma and up dated him about our family back home. He wanted to know about my brother Saunders. I told him that Saunders got drowned in the Irrawaddy river while on holiday with the family near Myitkyina. He also asked me to tell him about some old friends he used to hang out with. Then he told me not to go anywhere because he would send his chauffer to pick us up for dinner. He asked me to give the phone over to the manager so he could talk to him to get direction to the place. Now the manager had an improved attitude and became very friendly, taking us into his private room while we waited for the car to pick us up. He had his secretary to bring us coffee and soft drinks and snacks for the boys.

The first thing I noticed when I walked into Sonny's beautiful mansion was his red Gibson Guitar lying on a couch in the sitting room. Sonny came out to meet us and I introduced Nu Nu and the boys to him. He didn't look much older than when I remembered him although it was a good twenty eight years ago since I last saw him. Coffee was served, with Ovaltine and cookies for the boys. We had such a lot to catch up on but he was a gentleman and never neglected to ask a question or talk to Nu Nu. So the evening was most pleasant and enjoyable. We continued to talk over a few glasses of wine before dinner. He reminisced about Saunders, Ikie Isaac and him playing trio together. Then he asked about a lot of his friends, most of whom I knew. Then he asked me, "How are you for cash? You escaped from Burma but could you bring any money out?"

"Right at the time we were getting away, the government froze all banking accounts and we came away with only the cash we had at home which we spent even before we got to Bangkok," I told him. I told him that we were house parents in Bangkok to American children for four years and managed to save some money which we had to spend on our papers. He then asked me to tell him in detail how Saunders got drowned. They were very close friends. Then he asked me again about his old friends some of whom have passed away. It was like he was reliving his good old days in Rangoon.

Dinner was strictly Malaysian cuisine served by a uniformed butler on a mahogany table with elegant setting of silverwares and delicate China. Sonny couldn't stop asking me questions about his friends, about World War II in Burma and the politics of independent Burma. Conversation continued well into the late hours and when we were preparing to leave, Sonny pressed into my hand an envelope containing five hundred Malaysian dollars. God does take care of His own when they are in need. I never asked Sonny if he was married but there was no evidence of a woman being in the house though the house looked spick and span and was tastefully furnished.

Now we were able to take the boys sight seeing and we did. After mailing our application for visa for Thailand, we took the boys downtown and tried to visit as many sights as we could on our first day. On the second day we did some more sight seeing and did a lot of walking, shopping for the boys. We returned to the hotel on foot instead of taking a taxi although it was several blocks away. We wanted to save money for more important things. David was walking ahead of us carrying the key to our hotel room. When we arrived at the hotel David was already in the room massaging his feet. He didn't see us coming in as he was massaging his feet.
"My poor feet, my poor feet," he kept saying.

So we decided to take a break on the third day and stayed at the hotel as we waited for the mail. It didn't come. But the next morning after breakfast, when I walked over to front desk, the desk clerk gave me the mail we were waiting for. Our visas had been granted. So I walked over to the Malaysia Airline office and presented our airline reservation vouchers and booked a flight to Bangkok for the next day and sent a telegram to Pratit that we were arriving on the Malaysia Airline the following day. When we arrived at Bangkok airport the next day Pratit was there to make sure that everything was all right. After we were cleared by customs and immigration he took our passports to register us as foreign residents at the Immigration Office. On arrival at the Guest House we saw that there was a mail was waiting for us. Our visas to the United States had been granted and we were to collect it at the office of the U.S. Counsel. At that time the host and hostess of the Guest House were having their children visit from the U.S. and wanted to go on a month vacation so they could take their children around the country. Since we were staying at the Guest House, the Governing Board wanted to know if we were willing to run the Guest House for the duration of their vacation. We agreed to do so and almost regret it later. One day in the second week the sewer backed up in the entire building in the middle of the night. So we had to call for professional septic tank maintenance company to have the system cleaned out. The crew worked throughout the night into the early hours of the morning. However, we were lucky that there were only few complaints from the guests. We also had an electrical outage in the entire area of Silom road that lasted several hours and fortunately it was during daylight hours when most of the guests were out on business or out sight seeing. Having had experience with travel and tourism I was able to book a few tours for the Guest House and finalized some of the tour that had been booked. We were happy that we were able to help out the host and hostess during the time that they needed to be with their children and we thank the Lord for the opportunity to let them spend many wonderful days with their children.

Now was the time for us to go on our last vacation in Thailand. We left Bangkok to visit my sister Nita in Maeseriang. We took a train to Chiangmai where we borrowed a land Rover from one of the missionaries to continue on our trip to Maeseriang. There had been heavy rain in the area and we were warned of slippery road on the mountain. What we did not expect was a landslide which we came across as we neared Maeseriang. I had to skirt around the debris and mud deposited by the landslide leaving me very little room to maneuver the car, perhaps only about two to three feet to spare before a drop of a couple of hundred feet. There were no safety guard rail and the road was still very slippery after heavy rains a few days ago. After I maneuvered the Land Rover past the debris and mud we came right onto a wooden bridge which was resting on the edge on the other end by just two feet or so because that part of the road had been washed away by heavy rain. I hesitated but the front wheel of the vehicle was already on the bridge when Nu Nu yelled out, "If you go, go quick or back up.The bridge is moving."
I realized that the bridge was shifting as the front wheel landed on it. I was using four-wheel drive and slowly eased the Land Rover forward and got the front wheels safely onto the other end but could feel the rear wheels drop. I revved so the wheels could clear the bridge. I did not

look back because there was a turn on the road ahead and it was very slippery.

"Look back at the bridge," I told Nu Nu, "I felt the bridge dropping a bit."

"Oh. My God. The bridge has dropped further," she cried out. I couldn't stop to see as I had a curve in front to steer the car around. We were still climbing and the road was slippery. If it wasn't a Land Rover I was driving, and if I hadn't used four wheel drive, we would never have come out of the trip alive. The road soon leveled off and we arrived at Maeseriang safely. As soon as we arrived I reported to the authorities the condition of the road and the possibility that the bridge was out or not there any more. The road was immediately closed as army engineers cleared the landslide and rebuilt the bridge which took them ten days before they could declare the road open. We meant to stay with my sister for just a week but because of the closed road we spent twelve wonderful days with her and her husband. Now we were just a month or so away from departing for the United States. We had a rather sad farewell with my sister and her husband and drove back to Chiangmai and took the train back to Bangkok.

The day after we arrived back to the Guest House I had an attack of Dengue Fever. I had an appointment with the U.S. Counsel the day I had the fever so I had to postpone the appointment to receive our U.S. visas to the following week. When I went to see the Counsel I was still very weak. I also found that the previous Counsel had returned to the U.S. and a new Counsel was there in her place.

"You were supposed to be here a week ago," she told me.

"I'm sorry. Didn't your secretary tell you? I was sick with dengue fever."

"Let's have your passports," she told me.

I gave her our passports. She took a look at Nu Nu's passpsort first and checked every endorsement and returned it to me.

"Good," she said.

She checked my passport. After a while she frowned and said, "This passport is not good."

"Why is that?" I asked. It is valid.

"Your passport is valid only up to December 20th, 1969."

"But we'll arrive in the United States long before that date, end of October or early November," I told her.

"I can't let you go to the United 'States with a passport that is only valid for one month after your arrival. You have to extend your passport by at least a year."

"But how can I do that?" I asked her.

"Take your passport to your Embassy and have it extended," she advised.

"But I can't do that. I can't go to my Embassy because I escaped from Burma and they will never help me," I told her.

"It's your Embassy. It is their duty to help you," she replied.

"But I left my country illegally," I told her.

"You don't understand. Your Embassy has a duty to help it's citizens. All you do is go to the Embassy and request that your passport be extended."

I was feeling very weak from my illness and I almost felt that I would pass out any moment.

"But why would you want my passport to be valid so long after my arrival in the United States when I am entering the country as an immigrant and don't even need to show my passport to the immigration officers?"

She didn't say that it was regulation or anything like that. She said, "After your arrival, if we find out that you are a persona-non-grata, then your passport has to be valid so that we can deport you."

"Yes, Maa'm," I said and left.

I got back into my rented car and before I started the engine I prayed to God to get me out of this predicament. The Counsel refused to hand over our visas to me because I needed to have the validity of my passport extended. I knew she was doing her job. I couldn't go to the Burmese Embassy for help. As I drove back I continued to pray. I stopped for a red light. As I looked ahead I saw a sign which said, "Rubber Stamps, Seals." I crossed the street when the green light came back on and parked at the nearest parking spot I could find. I walked back to the printing shop.

"You make rubber stamps?" I asked the man at the counter.

"Yes. What kind?" he asked me.

I thought of a Burmese name and wrote it down on a piece of paper. Then I showed him my passport and showed him how I wanted the name printed with a line over it for signature, and under the name I asked him to print 'First Secretary'.

"Oh, easy," he told me.

"How long?" I asked him.

"Come back tomorrow this time," he told me.

"How much?" I asked.

"Ten dollars," he said.

When I got the stamp back I practiced signing the Burmese name along the line above the name and entered the date on a piece of paper. It looked good to me. I opened my passport and turned to endorsement page, and wrote neatly, "This passport is validated for a further period of twelve months." I stamped, signed a Burmese name and dated the passport. I waited till I felt stronger and went back to the Counsel and showed her my passport.

"Didn't I tell you that your Embassy will help you?" she said.

"Yes, Maa'm," I replied as she reached for the file that contained our papers.

She explained to me all I needed to know about the documents.

"Congratulations. I wish you good luck." She smiled for the first time as she handed the visas to me.

Then she asked, "When are you leaving for the United States?"

"I have to get my departure papers at the Thai Immigration and then make reservation for our flight. I'll come and see you before I leave," I told her.

"Good, you do that," she said and smiled again.

I breathed a sigh of relief. At last we've cleared all obstacles.

The following day Nu Nu and I went to the Thai Immigration Office, to obtain our departure papers. We were there when the office opened but by lunch time the officer who handled our case hadn't worked on to our papers yet. As he was preparing to leave for lunch I accosted him and asked him when he would be able to start working on our papers. He told me that immediately after lunch he would start working on our papers. So with that assurance Nu Nu and I left the building to walk back to the Guest House for lunch. When we returned to the Immigration Office after lunch the officer handling our case was already back at his desk. When he saw us he asked for our passports. I told him that he already had them. He started to look for the passports on his table and inside his drawers but couldn't find them. Then he asked if we were sure we had given it to him. I reminded him that he took them from me and even looked over them to see if endorsements were in order in the passports and then placed them right beside the telephone. He looked at me and said a cuss word in obvious anger, not at me, as he rose from his seat. Then he marched straight across the office to the opposite end of the office and stopped at the desk of another officer. That officer had a news paper lying on his table and was reading another paper. The officer who was working on our paper asked him in Thai if he had a couple of Burmese passports with him. The other officer shook his head, but the officer who was working on our papers angrily pulled the news paper that was lying on the desk revealing our passports underneath. There were some angry words exchanged when our immigration officer picked up the passports. Our officer went back to his table fuming. He muttered under breath, something like, 'that Burmese Thai half cast dog,' which suddenly took me back to the time almost six years earlier when I first arrived in Thailand. Prasit, my Thai friend, took me to visit an elderly Burmese gentleman who had lived in Thailand long before World War II. This gentleman told me that the famous Thirty Comrades gathered at his house before the war and performed a swearing ceremony during which they vowed to drive the British out of Burma with the help of the Japanese Imperial Army. The old gentleman showed me the silver bowl into which the comrades poured blood from their wrists as they made their vows and drank their mixed blood out of it. This gentleman and his Thai wife had a son and he told me at that time that his son was an immigration officer. Then obviously this was the 'Burmese Thai half cast dog' who tried to steal our passports with an intent to report about our departure to the Burmese Embassy, which was right next door to the Immigration Office. At that time the Burmese intelligence paid informers to pass on any information on activities of suspicious nature by citizens of Burma. Our son Lester who was now fourteen years old was furious. He had just sat for his Black Belt in Karate and was dying to beat up the man. Both Nu Nu and I had a hard time convincing him that this was not the time to do anything rash because we didn't want any more obstacles to spoil our plan to go to the United States. As it was, we had had quite a few already and overcame them all. We shouldn't push our luck. Also it was not the right thing to do. I made a quick trip to the U.S Council to make a courtesy call on the Vice Consul to say my farewell but she was away and I did not get to see her.

Brigadier Kya Doe became very attached to our family, especially to Nu Nu whom he said he loved like a daughter. Brig. Kya Doe and his wife never had any children and we were like his kids. He was overjoyed when he found us in Bangkok and became a part of our family. All the servants loved him.. Sometime in 1966 Brig. Kya Doe had an attack of cerebral malaria and was hospitalized in the Seventh Day Adventist Hospital. In spite of her heavy work at the hostel Nu Nu managed to see him at least every other day. At one point the resident doctor, Dr. Nelson, had given him only a fifty fifty chance of survival. However he rallied around and soon was convalescing and after a few more weeks fully recovered. He was grateful to Nu Nu for the care and for the nourishing food that she brought him at the hospital and for her many visits. Whenever he visited at the hostel our servants would pamper him and attend to him hand

and foot. They just loved him. So when we were preparing to leave for the United States he told us that he would see us off at the air port. But we told him not to because we knew the Burmese intelligence would be there and we didn't want him to be unnecessarily exposed to them. He told us that he knew they would be there but he didn't care and he would be at the air port to see us off.

When we arrived at the air port, a young couple, very good friends of ours who had helped us many times and took care of many of our needs when we first arrived, were there waiting to send us off. This young couple had been very helpful to us since our first arrival into Thailand. While we were having conversation together with them over coffee the husband whispered to me that the M.I.S. was watching us. The men were standing in a group at a discrete distance, and a few of them held cameras in their hands. After we had had our coffee the young couple discretely disappeared and didn't return. At about that time Brig. Kya Doe walked in. We sat down and talked in the lobby. A man holding a camera walked by and as he passed us there was a flash as his camera clicked. After a little while another man walked by and took another picture of us. Brig. Kya Doe got up from his seat and walked over to the group of young Burmese looking men standing at a discrete distance and shouted angrily at them, "You son of a bitches, if you want to take my picture you don't have to sneak up to me to do it. Here, I'm standing in front of you. Now, come and take my picture." They all walked away in a hurry and never returned. Finally we had to board the plane. We said farewell to Brig. Kya Doe and walked onto the tarmac to our plane.

What were we feeling at that time? For me it was a feeling of anger, anger that we were all made to leave against our will, the country of our birth, the country we love, not knowing if we would ever return to see our parents and loved ones, to return and help rebuild the country destroyed by the ruling dictator. Then there was a feeling of frustration and disappointment, a disappointment that after having all those political big shots together with a lot of facilities and opportunities to do something for the country without thinking of self interest or personal glory, nothing developed in spite of rhetoric's like, "We'll fight the son of a bitch to death." Then there were a lot more different feelings, conflicting ones like whether we had done the right thing. Then there was a feeling of apprehension. Would I be able to find a job compatible with my experience and qualifications? As I walked up to the plane I was preoccupied by these conflicting feelings. Nu Nu and I held hands and quietly said our prayers after we settled down in our seats, thanking God for blessing us with a safe trip into Thailand, for His blessings during all the years we had spent in Bangkok, and now for the great opportunity we have to build a new life in a new country we had chosen to adopt as our new home. I never realized that I carried a heavy load all these years. Now it hanged heavy. It bothered me that in spite of our prayers after we settled into our seats, I continued to have feelings of excitement, anger, anxiety, disappointment, uncertainty and apprehension coupled with home sickness. I was even on the brink of tears. I closed my eyes as the plane revved up for the take off. I silently continued to pray to God to get rid of whatever was still bothering me. Yet I couldn't shake off that terrible feeling that seemed to bore into my very being. Finally the plane shook and vibrated as it made a run for the take off. I looked down to see the scene quickly passing by as the plane sped past the terminal. After a few more seconds the plane was air borne. Like a miracle, the heavy load I felt earlier disappeared. It just vanished. What a sense of great relief to know now that we were safe and free. Once again silently I thanked God as I reached out to Nu Nu and held her hand to ask, "How do you feel?"

"O God, what a relief. I can't believe it. We are free now. Thank you Lord," she said softly.

WE ARRIVED AT THE PHILADELPHIA airport at ten in the morning on October 30, 1969. There was no one to meet us although we were told that some representative from North Wales Baptist Church would be there. So we telephoned Reverend Kane, whose telephone number was given to us by missionary Carol Jochen. Rev. Kane told us that he would come down soon to pick us up. It was a long wait and the kids were getting restless so I invented a game.

"Let's see who will be the first to spot Reverend Kane," I told the kids.

We sat on our battered luggage and started our guessing game. One after another they walked towards us, fat ones, thin ones, the tall and the short. We made our guesses but they all walked past us never even giving us a glance. Then after an hour or so just when we got tired and gave up on our guessing game, a tall man stood over us and asked, "Zans? I'm Reverend Kane."

We shook hands. Reverend Kane apologized that no one turned up because it was Friday, a week day, and everyone was working. He got us a porter and we walked out of the terminal where his little Volkswagen was parked. There were four of us besides Reverend Kane, plus there were four suit cases beside our carry on bags.

"Where do you want me to put the suit cases?" the porter asked.

"I guess we'll have to put them on the roof," Reverend Kane told him.

"But how?" the porter asked. "You ain't got no roof rack."

Reverend Kane looked around, then opened the hood of the Volkswagen and after a short while pulled out a very long thin rope. Fortunately it was long enough and strong enough to tie down all the suit cases on the roof.

As the Reverend drove off I looked back to see the porter standing there watching us leave, hands on hip, shaking his head. Forty five minutes later we arrived at a small two bedroom house in North Wales, a house already rented for us by the North Wales Baptist Church. Reverend Kane opened the door and let us in. Then he said, "Welcome to the United States of America. And welcome to North Wales."

This is not just a story of the life of my family or of events that took place during the period of our lifetime from good old days under British rule, and the prosperous days we were enjoying after independence to the days after the coup when Burma took a plunge from riches to rags. This book is a testimony of God's presence in our lives. We prayed to God for our every need and He was always there for us, providing for us and introducing us to total strangers who became our loyal friends. God also provided us with opportunities to help others along the way.

He shall give His angels charge concerning thee: and in their hands they shall bear thee up, lest at any time thou dash thy foot against a stone. Matthew 4:6

Born in 1923 in Paan, Karen State, Burma, SPENCER ZAN grew up during the days under British rule where his father U Zan was a judge under the British administration. He was attending Judson College in 1941 and was half way through college when war came to Burma and his education was interrupted. When war ended in 1945 he joined the Royal Navy Volunteer Reserve as a cadet, changed his service to Burma Navy after independence and rose to the rank of Lieutenant. At the outset of the Karen uprising in 1949 he was interned in prison and later detained in a detention camp for three and a half years. Upon his release from detention, he started a new life and later led a life of intrigue, and cloak and dagger which is the subject of his memoir, *Life's Journey in Faith.*

"This exciting and inspiring memoir is a tale of family and faith, war and revolution. Spence Zan portrays Burma's joys and sorrow with great clarity and the wisdom born of experience. A must-read for those who follow the Karen struggle and Asian history." – Edith Mirante, author of "Burmese Looking Glass" and "Down the Rat Hole"

"A fascinating insight into life in Burma – a life of war, bombings and bullets, a life of endurance, escape and exile, a life of fighting and faith. Spencer Zan recounts in remarkable detail his memories of colonial

Burma, the Japanese occupation, Burma's independence and the military coup. At times humorous, at other times horrifying, this book is a remarkable read." –
Benedict Rogers, author of "A Land Without Evil: Stopping the Genocide of Burma's Karen People.

"A powerful testament of devotion and resilience. Life's Journey in Faith is a gripping and unforgettable historical account. With a profound sense of purpose and wisdom, Spencer Zan takes the reader on an inspiring journey to Burma during war and political turmoil. This book is an important piece of work that will surely contribute to a much needed awareness of Burma's continuing struggle." – Jennifer Scheel Bushman, author of Hard Sleeper.

LIFE'S JOURNEY IN FAITH, is a true story of the Zan family, spanning a period from the British colonial rule, through World War II when Burma was under Japanese occupation, to the chaotic period after independence and the coup by General Ne Win, which changed the entire history of modern Burma. Zan recounts the good old days that he remembers so well during the British rule. He describes the trials the nation went through after independence and the struggles to keep democracy alive, only to llose it to military dictatorship when General Ne Win staged a coup and toppled a democratic government.

LaVergne, TN USA
24 September 2009
158832LV00003B/23/A